SANTAYANA ON AMERICA

Essays, Notes, and Letters on
American Life, Literature, and Philosophy

❧ EDITED, AND WITH AN

INTRODUCTION, BY *Richard Colton Lyon*

AN ORIGINAL HARBINGER BOOK

SANTAYANA
ON
AMERICA

{ornament}

Essays, Notes, and Letters on
American Life, Literature, and Philosophy

HARCOURT, BRACE & WORLD, INC.   *New York*

First edition

Library of Congress Catalog Card Number: 68-25370

Printed in the United States of America

Acknowledgments:

The editor wishes to thank the following for their permission to reproduce
material in this book:

Mr. Daniel Cory, George Santayana's literary executor.

George Allen & Unwin, Ltd.: The essay, "A Brief History of My Opin-
ions," by George Santayana, reprinted from *Contemporary American
Philosophy: Personal Statements,* Volume II (1930), edited by George
Plimpton Adams and William Pepperell Montague.

J. M. Dent & Sons, Ltd.: The essay, "The Genteel Tradition in American
Philosophy," reprinted from *Winds of Doctrine: Studies in Contemporary
Opinion* (1913), by George Santayana.

Constable & Company, Ltd.: Chapters I, III, IV, and VII of *Character and
Opinion in the United States* (1920), by George Santayana.

Charles Scribner's Sons: Selections from "Restricted Democracy," "The
American 'Melting-Pot'," and "The United States as Leader": chapters
from "Book Third" of *Dominations and Powers.* Reprinted with the permission of Charles Scribner's Sons from *Dominations and Powers* by
George Santayana. Copyright 1950, 1951, Charles Scribner's Sons.

ᛞ Preface

These essays, notes, and letters were written by Santayana over a period of sixty years. The earliest, "Walt Whitman: A Dialogue," was written in 1890 by a young philosophy instructor—"a young prig," Santayana would say—just beginning to teach at Harvard. The latest appeared in 1951, a part of the book *Dominations and Powers*, the mature reflections on politics and history of a man who was then one of a handful of venerated patricians in philosophy, a wise man of the West. Between those dates Santayana wrote copiously about the United States; even in the later years, after long residence in Europe, the Spaniard's thoughts came back and back to the country where he had spent half his life as student and teacher. Many of his judgments—his indictments of "the genteel tradition," his essays on Emerson and Whitman, Royce and William James—have become indispensable, not so much for our knowledge of America as for our thinking about America, then and now.

These major essays, appearing at different times in different books, are for the first time gathered together here.

I have, in addition, included a number of Santayana's shorter essays on America and Americans, written as addresses or for journals here and abroad. These essays, never collected by Santayana for book publication, deserve to be known, for they manifest again his difficult virtues: his scope, his detachment, the unrelenting energy of his conceiving. Especially is this true of the essay titled "Americanism," discovered among his papers after his death and published posthumously by his literary executor. In it Santayana attempts once more (and for the last time on so ambitious a scale) to catch the quality and direction of life under the aegis of the great god Acceleration, reversing his earlier sanguine view of this country's commercial and industrial enterprise in a warning of the tyrannies latent and actual in a mechanized democracy. And even the less ambitious occasional pieces included here extend and complicate the judgments of Santayana's better-known essays—though in the last analysis I think they will serve to clarify a general view that is remarkably coherent.

When asked in the late 1930's to name the philosopher of his time most likely to be read in the future, Alfred North Whitehead replied, "Santayana." Perhaps the essays collected here will lead the reader to share his view.

For permission to reprint much of the material in this book and for his encouragement of the project I am especially grateful to Mr. Daniel Cory, George Santayana's literary executor. I wish also to thank the several librarians and their assistants who gave me help in consulting the Santayana papers under their care: Miss C. E. Jakeman of the Houghton Library at Harvard, Mrs. Mary M. Hirth of the Academic Center Library of the University of Texas, and Mr. Kenneth A. Lohf of the Department of Special Collections of the Columbia University Libraries. These libraries have granted me permission to quote certain portions of the unpublished writings of Santayana in their collections.

For research grants I am indebted to the Faculty Research Council of the University of North Carolina at Chapel Hill, and to the Cooperative Humanities Program of Duke University and the University of North Carolina.

R. C. L.

Hampshire College
Amherst, Massachusetts
April 1968

Contents

IV. *The American Imagination*

Introduction: George Santayana (1863-1952)

American literature and philosophy fell on a dry season in the years after the Civil War. A poetry "sunny and sweet and wholesome clean to the core," exemplified in Longfellow or James Whitcomb Riley, provided for the public a steady dispensation of homely pieties, and the local-color writers and early Realists lapsed into stock sentiment as effortlessly as the poets. The period's dominant figure, Mark Twain, relied for a good deal of his wit on his caustic sense of the banality and hypocrisy in such moralizing utterances, and of the banality and hypocrisy in the lives of those who responded to them, yet he could suggest no clear, available alternatives to what he condemned, and ended his days writing tracts which served only to prove how easily a sentimental optimism could generate by reaction a sentimental pessimism. The other humorists were not very humorous. And in high culture, too, the American mind of the post-war years tended to run thin, devoting its energies to problems thought to be problems because Europeans said they were. Hegelian idealism, for example, arrived at St. Louis from Germany, and by the century's end had been carried by powerful exponents to nearly every major American college and university. It was challenged there by the American advocates of Darwin and Herbert Spencer, but they were advocates who (more often than not) found in their masters not a defense of a tentative empirical science but a final proof of the beneficence of Providence, the inexorability of Progress, or the sanctity of laissez-faire capitalism.

Yet in the midst of the imaginative and intellectual poverty
of these years down to (say) 1912, an extraordinary effort of
mind was in fact under way late in the century among certain
discursive prose-writers and thinkers, men with the desire and the
capacity to explore the implications of their preferences and baf-
flements. Of course Henry James was developing (aside from his
novels) his powerful critical canon, as Walt Whitman before him
had enunciated in prose (along with his poetry) a program for
literature quite outside the bounds of the dominant conventions.
But in addition to these acknowledged masters, a number of other
writers, adopting prose exposition as their essential medium, were
joining intellect, sense, and feeling in new and hard-won orderings of experience: Henry Adams, William James, C. S. Peirce,
Justice Holmes, Josiah Royce, Thorstein Veblen, John Dewey.
These writers of the period have pre-eminently, we now see, the
power to deliver the modern reader to awareness, to wake him
to new perception in his own present.

Among these men was a young Spaniard who knew most of
them and was in part shaped by them, and who began late in the
1880's to add his voice to the general running commentary on
each other's ideas which so often entered their conversation
and letters and occasionally their essays and reviews. George Santayana may in time seem the most circumspect of all these original
minds; it is certain that his voice is indispensable to their colloquy,
complicating and illuminating it through perspectives radically
his own and radically other than those of his time and place.

We cannot, for example, speak of American letters of the late
nineteenth century without relying in some measure on his phrase
—subsequently adopted by a hundred critics—"the genteel tradition." In defining that tradition Santayana points to the curious,
fatal irrelevance of American intellectual life—the discourse of
preacher, professor, and man of letters—to the general life of the
nation in its commercial and technological preoccupations. The
American intellect, he writes, is stale because derivative, drawing
what little sap it can from the American or European past; the
American will is bent to the tasks of aggressive enterprise, ignorant of all high culture and needing none. Meantime the man of
imagination, wedded to his impassioned intuitions and little inter-

ested either in conclusions or in practical action, finds himself in America an unnecessary *tertium quid.*

Intellect, will, imagination: these terms designate loosely powers which Santayana found exercised by Americans in strange isolation one from another. They serve to mark disparate phases of a fragmented experience, and in light of them certain inconsistencies and disharmonies in our life and letters can be understood. That the three might be made to run in harness together was his hope; that they do not constitutes his indictment of America.

I. A Spanish Materialist at Harvard

Santayana would not have agreed with William James that philosophy is the biography of philosophers, yet his criticism draws much of its power from his ability to dramatize ideas in the context of character. And his interest in a work of mind extends not only to the man who produced it but to the beliefs and practices of the culture which informed both man and work. This lively historical sense is apparent in the first essay, "A Brief History of My Opinions," and makes it especially valuable, for Santayana describes here the genesis of his own ideas in the context of his life, his place and time.

"How came a child born in Spain of Spanish parents to be educated in Boston and to write in the English language?" His opening question is revealing. The quiet insistence on his Spanish origins—too often, he thought, overlooked—and his sense of anomaly in the circumstances of his life, of irony in his having spent half his days in America respected as a master of a language he had had to acquire: these testify to his alienation. Santayana thought of himself always as the inveterate stranger here, as standing apart in feeling—"detachable"—from the men and ideas among which he moved.

The Spanish boy in Boston was an unhappy stranger at first. He had grown up in Spain under the care of his father (for reasons his essay explains) and at the age of eight found himself transplanted to America. Circumstances here seemed to require that he make the acquaintance (never much more than that) of the woman pointed out as his mother, and of his half-brother and two half-sisters. Though he mastered quickly the language and manners of the new world, and though he was soon popular as a student at the Boston Latin School, Santayana remained in spirit a solitary even in his own family, where life seemed to him (he wrote later) like life in a boardinghouse. "The wretched poverty-stricken real world in which I was condemned to live" was light-years away from the congenial visions of his imagination. For the boy had his sure refuge, his worlds within. One of these was Spain, in recollection, and the walled city of Ávila where he had grown up. In his "Brief History" he tells of another, a world summoned before his fancy whenever his father or mother recalled their early years in the Far East, a world of "interminable ocean spaces, coconut islands, blameless Malays, and immense continents swarming with Chinamen, polished and industrious, obscene and philosophical." And to these perspectives on times and places so emphatically not-Boston others were soon added as he began to read omnivorously in books of religion and architecture and fiction. Boston might seem stranger still, in the presence of Don Quixote, Alexander the Great, or Byron's Don Juan.

In his autobiography, *Persons and Places,* Santayana recalls these early years and his double life, his submission to the routines of school and family belying the vagrancies of his intense imagination. That that dream life was all a dramatic self-indulgence, a playing of parts, seemed certain to the autobiographer, as in his "making plans of vast palaces and imaginary islands, where I should one day be monarch like Sancho Panza." And it was clearly a means of consolation. The boy was unhappy. But as Santayana began to move with ease and success at the Latin School and then Harvard College, actively engaged as lieutenant-colonel of his school regiment or as *Lampoon* cartoonist or editor of the Harvard *Monthly* (which he helped to found) or as Harvard instructor, he saw no reason to abandon those dramatic visions, as if only the here and now could honorably dominate a man's mind and engage his energies. His studies carried him more and more into the past, especially to ancient Greece, and his first-hand acquaintance begun in 1887 with the life of aristocratic England made New England seem all the more barren, as barren as it had seemed to Henry James a few years before. Like James, Santayana found his natural affinities far from the Harvard Yard.

A few days before his bachelor's diploma was officially conferred by Harvard in 1886, Santayana left America to take up a two-year traveling fellowship, given to the sporadically brilliant undergraduate for study in Germany. Though the chairman of the fellowship committee, William James, found it necessary a year later to send his pupil an urgent request for hard evidence of solid research, the truant was in fact busy enough. Like a score of New England scions sent to Germany he was romancing with history, a wandering scholar, indolent and intense, seeing again "with my own eyes old towns, cathedrals, castles, and palaces . . ." and finding in Europe the sharp contrast and definition in society and nature which he found absent in America, where everything seemed to him "half formed and groping after its essence." Until 1912, when he resigned as professor of philosophy at Harvard and took up permanent residence in Europe, Santayana spent every summer (and two sabbaticals) abroad. These yearly infusions of Europe gave definiteness and substance to his imagination, not merely a refuge now but a resource; discovery of the men and societies which could win his allegiance gave him the means of self-definition. In that process the American foreground diminished, yet was seen all the more sharply for being seen in the context of the past and of Europe. Santayana set out, first in his *Interpretations of Poetry and Religion* (1900) and then in his five-volume *Life of Reason* (1905-1906), "to say plausibly in English as many un-English things as possible."

He said them without ill will. He laughs when he speaks of that critical stratagem. Santayana's alienation did not bring rebellion but a stance of ironic detachment (in itself, perhaps, an un-American attitude), nor was his a medically suspect failure to adjust happily to his environment (a very American suspicion). Perhaps it is right to say that Santayana's admirations of remote traditions served him as guarantees of his apartness from all that he found offensive in America, permitting and sanctioning a disassociation that was after all a little proud, a little spiteful. But we would then have said with some malice what we would like to say of every man: that he has found his difference, and can name his aversions because he knows what he loves.

The habits of mind which Santayana found barren or constricting in American life and letters—and what he found vital and enlarging—will be made clear enough in these pages. But two very general criticisms follow from what I have noticed here. A rebuke to all present-minded provinciality is implicit in the sweeping historical review of diverse orderings of societies, religions, and the arts undertaken by this "inquisitor of structures" in his early books. And he found American criticism in politics and philosophy unsure of its allegiances, therefore weak in the power to affirm. Though powerful in attack, Mark Twain and Sinclair Lewis and the liberals of the '20's, for example, seemed to Santayana halting, inconsistent, or vague in suggesting alternatives to the evils they condemned. "What is a good life? Had William James, had the people about him, had modern philosophers anywhere, any notion of that? I cannot think so." These strictures, justified or not, indicate one of Santayana's strengths: his sense of the past yielded ideas of order which made definite his sense of the possible. In this direction he serves us as do those two other spiritually deracinated Americans, Henry James and Henry Adams. By the fineness of their sympathy with the alien and the remote all three enlarge our sense of the possibilities open to mind and even, perhaps, to society. But that is a proposition which Santayana, as we shall see, would sharply qualify.

In a letter to his old friend Daniel Cory, Santayana speaks of the destructive element in the fiction of Henry James, "the alienation of the intellect from the milieu." But he goes on to remark that alienation may be of two kinds: political, or mystical and moral. Of the latter he observes that a man "might feel such alienation in any country at any epoch, the convention destroyed by reflection being morality or life itself, not a special form of society." To a well-traveled imagination certain habits of mind and feeling in America might seem local and arbitrary, but to the eye of wonder so are all merely human conventions, so is morality itself, so is the whole queer frame of nature. It is emphatically true of Santayana that he felt himself not only a stranger in America but a stranger in the world. And we need to take account of this more radical view, since it leads at once to certain fundamental premises of his philosophy, the philosophy which in the last analysis underpins and gives point to his particular criticisms of America.

The definitive statement of his philosophy would finally occupy five volumes, *Scepticism and Animal Faith* (1923) and the four volumes of *The Realms of Being* (1927-1940). But the seed of that prodigious growth may have been planted (so we may conjecture) when the young Spaniard was first set down in Boston. Put the case: the boulder-strewn moors and ancient wall of Ávila are suddenly, unaccountably supplanted by the high narrow houses of Beacon Street with their back views of wooden sheds and wooden fences. Nothing in the boy's experience could have prepared him for this. The cold blear landscape must be an apparition, a stage set perhaps, summoned by magic to displace his familiar Spain. The shock of that dislocation was perhaps the beginning of philosophy, for the sense of the *contingency* of existence never left Santayana—the sense of how arbitrary, how deeply unintelligible is the fatality which imposes on the watching self this precise irrevocable world and no other. An apprehension of the world as an irrational given, intensely present yet present for no reason, lies near the center of his philosophy. The Romantics gave the name "wonder" to this sense of strangeness in the midst of familiar things, and from their perception that the solid world was after all only an apparition, an appearance, "a dream and a shade," they went on to suggest that nature was ideal, continuous with mind. Santayana developed the insight to support a very different conclusion, yet it led him to share with the Romantics their celebrations of the power of imagination.

The lesson is an old one but needs to be underscored. As an imposed fact, the necessary scene of our action, the world is marvelous—and in two senses: as a vivid self-declaring presence, and as an absurd shutting down of possibility. This door or this fence or this wheelbarrow appears to the innocent eye in the fullness of its strange particularity, and the given datum (Boston, for the Spanish boy) just because it is emphatically *this*, implies the infinity of things not this thing. That the whole of nature or any single fact within it should take this form rather than another is a perfect marvel of exclusion. Because it is by its very nature addressed to all being, the imagination has, intrinsically and on its own ontological plane, an absolute dominion. So far is it from being intimidated by the substantial world, it wonders at that world's helplessness, for nature seems bound (for no sufficient reason) to endless repetitions of an ancient circle of forms. Such perpetual insistence on the same arbitrary tropes—the seasons, for example—is clearly the mark of an old dame whose inspiration has given out.

What I have been calling the imagination was for Santayana the principle of mind itself. When he says of the world that it is absurd, he testifies to the mind's ability to outrun in its conceiving what merely happens to exist, its ability to distance local place and present time and range through the indefinitely extensible region of possibles which he called the realm of essence. But essences are the counters of all consciousness, the fundamental terms of awareness, the identities through which we figure this world to ourselves, or any world. Essences are what the common man calls ideas, but ideas critically viewed and seen to be what intrinsically they are and can only be: fictions or figments, the stuff of which dreams are made.

I underscore this aspect of Santayana's philosophy (one aspect only of his theory of essence) partly for the reason that it makes clear the ground of his affinity with the transcendentalists. The two essays on Emerson (Section IV) make plain how easily and sympathetically he could take up the view of the man who made the land and the sea "revolve around the axis of his primary thought," who could resolve Nature without remainder into the congenial visions of immediate intuition. So, too, his considerable sympathy (extraordinary in the 1890's) with the all-seeing "I" of Whitman. And Santayana's view of experience as a succession of momentary pictures-in-the-head allies him to William James, whom he thought of as an heir of the New England transcendentalists. To his Harvard mentor he owed a great debt, even greater perhaps than he acknowledges in his "Brief History." From James he acquired that "sense for the immediate: for the unadulterated, unexplained, instant fact of experience" which entailed for both men an equally vivid sense for "the fact of contingency, or the contingency of fact."

But Santayana disagreed finally with James, and he was not a transcendentalist. On the contrary, as Professor John Herman

Randall, Jr., has noted, he was the key figure in transforming nineteenth-century materialism into twentieth-century naturalism—"the very term and the christening are his." Santayana carefully marks a distinction between romantic naturalism, "like Goethe's, for instance, or that of Bergson," and his own "hard, non-humanistic naturalism." To avoid the risk of that confusion he often gives the name materialism to his views, thus accepting the further risk of the imputation that he would ignore or deny consciousness (as in early behaviorist theory) or the urgency of moral questions. But for Santayana materialism means simply that matter and not thought or consciousness is genetically prior, the doer of all that is done; that ideas are products of material energies at work in the body and in the world; that a man is a mode of nature, an integrated system of physical energies, and may therefore leave his mark in passing, though the cosmos which produced him will move on with a massive indifference to his claims; and that final causes asserted to be operative in nature are, accordingly, willful deceptions. The implications of these principles, understood as Santayana understood them, profoundly inform all that he had to say in criticism of the American intellect and its subservience to the genteel tradition.

II. The American Intellect

Paganism, Platonic love, Catholicism: these are among the traditions of the West for which Santayana would be spokesman, traditions which should be propagated, he sometimes seems to say, in the new world. He has frequently been portrayed as the nostalgic traditionalist who would turn away—and who would have us turn away—from the barren present in order to relive the European past. But that is a caricature, and suggests Santayana less than his own portrait of the sweetly sad Professor Norton, reminding his Harvard classes with a sigh that the Greeks did not play football, and that in America there were no Venetian paintings, no French cathedrals, nor even gentlemen. No: Santayana knew and everywhere argues that vital philosophies and religions and works of art are concomitant expressions of an ongoing surrounding life, and because they draw their vitality from the culture of a time and place they cannot be injected by transfusion into an alien culture in the hope that it might live after all.

It is this conviction which underlies his definition and indictment of the American genteel tradition in a now famous address in 1911 to the Philosophical Union of the University of California, "The Genteel Tradition in American Philosophy." It is a tradition he found dominant in our high culture—not only in philosophy but in literature, religion, and the arts as well. His indictment rests on the assertion that the habits of thought and expression which that tradition sustained lacked roots in the practices and problems and instincts of modern America in its characteristic daily life. However lively the genteel tradition might be in the affairs of intellect, it was moribund with reference to American experience in the American present. The argument of Whitman's *Democratic Vistas* reappears in Santayana's declaration that valid expression must be informed by living purposes and fresh observation; his appeal is in one sense as old as the oldest appeal for an indigenous, original American expression, responsive to the special circumstances of a new nation's experience.

What was vital and spontaneous in contemporary American experience was to be found, Santayana thought, in invention, science, and industry, in politics and social organization—in the achievements of the American Will, symbolized by the skyscraper. And in "Tradition and Practice" he looks hopefully to a time when these native traditions of practical mastery will be made to yield equally native traditions in literature, philosophy, and the arts—traditions derivative from practice, exacting from it tributes to the mind. But for the present, he argued, intellect in America stood apart from the common life, borrowed its categories and its language from traditions appropriate perhaps in the American past or in Europe but without organic ties to the homely realities of every day. Those who pursued the life of the mind tended to believe, as F. O. Matthiessen puts it, "that the essence of beauty must lie in what James Russell Lowell read about in Keats rather than in what Walt Whitman saw in the streets of Brooklyn."

When the intellect is in this way wedded to inherited sanctities, or spins out its subtleties in isolation from life beyond the study, it serves a merely verbal, an ornamental "culture" which is bound to prove oppressive to those taught by it to look away from their own experience to that of other men in other times. The past, to be sure, continues to have its indispensable uses for the student able to appropriate it imaginatively and turn it to the service of his own clearness and integrity. But for the American intelligentsia, Santayana thought, the study of the past did not serve a demand for synthetic views and a total sensibility but had become, rather, a conscientious inspection of venerable relics kept under glass and comprehended by their labels. In 1928, in a letter to the American art critic, Thomas Munro, he protests the modern habit of regarding works of art as objects which "had been made to be placed and studied in a museum":

There is another quality in discussion now . . . which has fallen upon the world since the days of my youth. You must remember that we were not very much later than Ruskin, Pater, Swinburne, and Matthew Arnold: our atmosphere was that of poets and persons touched with religious enthusiasm or religious sadness. Beauty (which mustn't be mentioned now) was then a living presence, or an aching absence, day and night: history was always singing in our ears: and not even psychology or the analysis of works of art could take away from art its human implications. It was the great memorial to us, the great revelation, of what the soul had lived on, and had lived with, in her better days. But now analysis and psychology seem to stand alone: there is no spiritual interest, no spiritual need. The mind, in this direction, has been *dessicated:* art has become an abstract object in itself, to be studied scientifically as a *caput mortuum:* and the living side of the subject—the tabulation of people's feelings and comments—is no less dead.[1]

This same protest against art for art criticism's sake informs his final judgment of his old friend Bernard Berenson. A long walk in Venice with Berenson led Santayana subsequently to report his amazement at his friend's disinterest in the extraordinary effects of light in the evening's sky, the art critic preferring instead to discourse on light as treated in the paintings of Veronese:

[1] Letter to Thomas Munro, Rome, December 13, 1928; in *The Letters of George Santayana*, ed. Daniel Cory (New York: Charles Scribner's Sons, 1955), pp. 238-239.

Berenson surprised me by talking with juvenile enthusiasm about "art". . . . It is impossible for me now to regard "art," any more than traditional religion, as a supreme interest in itself. It is an illustration to history, and a positive joy when it really reveals something beautiful in the material or in the spiritual world. But the social world, the world of convention, to which the criticism of art belongs, has come to seem to me rather a screen that keeps the material and spiritual worlds out of sight. . . . It is lucky for B. B., in one sense, that he keeps the old flame alive; but I can't help feeling that it was lighted and is kept going by forced draft, by social and intellectual ambition, and by professional pedantry. If he were a real poet, would he turn away from the evening sky to see, by electric light, how Veronese painted it? [2]

The protest against a spurious, dissociated intellectuality recurs in his letters again and again. He writes to a former pupil that Spinoza is that rarest of men, a genuine philosopher, for the reason that in and through his scholastic categories his actual experience of a quotidian world takes shape and is wholly realized; the conceiving mind and reality meet and are one in the elaborate fictions of his system. But philosophy in America is quoits and backgammon: "speculation [he writes to another student] is seldom a genuine expression of life, but rather a parasitic tradition expressing what is effete in the contemporary world." As he saw knowledge becoming an industry, and the criticism of criticism proliferate, he warned a young correspondent at Columbia against the "habit of drinking life in its fifth dilution only":

Read the originals instead, and be satisfied with the impression they make upon you. You know Plato's contempt for the image of an image: but as a man's view of things is an image in the first place, and his work is an image of that, and the critic's feelings are an image of that work, and his writings an image of his feelings, and your idea of what the critic means only an image of his writings,—please consider that you are steeping your poor original tea-leaves in their fifth wash of hot water,

[2] Letter to Mrs. C. H. Toy, Venice, October 10, 1939; in *ibid.*, pp. 341-42.

and are drinking slops. . . . What you need is not more criticism of current authors, but more *philosophy:* more courage and sincerity in facing nature directly, and in criticizing books or institutions only with a view to choosing among them whatever is most harmonious with the life you want to lead.[3]

The kind of thinking which Santayana termed genteel is a special case and an especially flagrant case of thinking dissociated from experience. Yet its irrelevance is a secondary question: Santayana's predominant concern is to define—and condemn—a particular transmitted characteristic of the genteel tradition which he thought to be its essence. When he expresses his hope that the yoke of alien tradition might be lifted, he is not speaking, as so many had before him, as a patriot, nor as a democrat inveighing against the decadent past, nor as a transcendentalist declaring the mind's power to make the world new. He speaks for his own subtle kind of naturalism, opposing it to a habit of mind he found everywhere in American letters. That habit he called egotism or the anthropocentric conceit: the reduction of the cosmos to the categories of the mind that thinks it (idealism) and the enlisting of the cosmos on the side of some partial good (moral absolutism).

That we are here at the crux of Santayana's objections to the genteel tradition is plain if we consider the kind of double judgment he tends to pass on American writers. When the conception of the genteel mind as the secondary mind comes uppermost in his consideration, his list of America's original minds—those whose honest speech belies the conventional and derivative—grows remarkably long. It includes Emerson and Whitman, Poe and Hawthorne, orators and humorists, the James brothers. And yet most of these, even John Dewey, come under his guns when he conceives them, by a subtle shift of emphasis, as carriers of certain anthropocentric attitudes and beliefs which he found pervasive in all our wisdom. These attitudes and beliefs, the positive content of the genteel tradition, are the irritants which produced his many-sided attack. In sum—though in a hundred guises—they constitute an American orthodoxy bent to the task of humanizing or domesticating the universe, an orthodoxy concerned

[3] Letter to George Lawton, Rome, March 29, 1922; in *ibid.*, pp. 195-96.

above all to assure us that we live in a universe somehow coex-
tensive with our human interests or our human powers. "There
was still an orthodoxy among American high-brows at the end
of the nineteenth century, dissent from which was felt to be
scandalous; it consisted in holding that the universe exists and is
governed for the sake of man or of the human spirit." Yet what
was true of the 1890's was no less true of the 1940's, when Santayana observed that "the latent and permanent principle of
almost all the hostility" he had encountered in his American
critics was "belief in an absolute reason or duty determining
right judgment and conduct" or a belief in "the actual dominance
of reason or goodness over the universe at large."

Santayana found everywhere in American thought the tendency
to impose the categories of human logic and value on nature, then
to feign that they have been discovered there as revelations of its
essence. He found it in the transcendentalists when they attempted
to systematize their intuitions, and in the American (as well as
the German) Hegelians, his special target in 1911; his Harvard
colleague Josiah Royce was simply the most ingenious of those
dialecticians in quest of a solution to the cosmic riddle, a logical
system or dramatic unity "which all experience exists to illustrate."
He found it in the disciples of Herbert Spencer: they, too, had
"the notion that nature dances to the tune of some comprehensive
formula or some magic rhyme." And in American pragmatism and
instrumentalism, in William James and John Dewey, as well as in
the presumably hard-headed positivists who were the heirs of British idealism, Santayana found the same tendency to dislodge nature to put experience in her place, to turn psychology into metaphysics. In all of these diverse philosophies the Spanish naturalist
found a common refusal to acknowledge man's place in nature, his
finitude, the relativity of his knowledge and morality, and their
superficiality in the context of an omnificent, relentless, indifferent nature which brings him into being and sustains him.

Santayana's view that a man's world is an air-castle in his
imagination, his view of experience as a succession of momentary
perspectives radiating meanings from the present, his view that
reality for us is constituted of dramatic and pictorial terms (essences) in themselves insubstantial and visionary, does not lead
him as it leads the idealist to reduce the universe to a human

locus, the thinking mind. If essences are the fundamental terms of our awareness they are not for the naturalist the ultimate forms of *existence*. They are the forms of our merely local, human apprehension of a world which indefinitely outruns all presence to thought or dream. No matter how diverse or internally complex a man's ideas may be, and no matter how accurately they prefigure further experience and so become the terms of valid knowledge, they remain fictions with respect to the generative order of nature, the dynamic hidden powers of matter which sustain the world and all ideas of it in human heads. Our words and images are the signs or symbols of a surrounding physical world which provokes them, the human transcripts of the natural world which forces itself upon our consciousness and refuses finally to be managed or mastered. Essences indicate outlying things, bodies, and other minds; they cannot define them. Essences mediate for us a reality not ourselves which scorns to be known in its internal essence. We cannot meet nature face to face.

In "The Moral Background" Santayana puts this view in sharp contrast with genteel egotism:

> As the senses open to us only partial perspectives, taken from one point of view, and report the facts in symbols which, far from being adequate to the full nature of what surrounds us, resemble the coloured signals of danger or of free way which a railway engine-driver peers at in the night, so our speculation, which is a sort of panoramic sense, approaches things peripherally and expresses them humanly. But how doubly dyed in this subjectivity must our thought be when an orthodoxy dominant for ages has twisted the universe into the service of moral interests, and when even the heretics are entangled in a scepticism so partial and arbitrary that it substitutes psychology, the most derivative and dubious of sciences, for the direct intelligent reading of experience! [4]

To dwell on the inscrutability and inhumanity of nature will seem perverse to those schooled by the genteel tradition to believe in the soul's supernatural destiny, the autonomy of the will, or

[4] *Character and Opinion in the United States* (New York: Charles Scribner's Sons, 1920), p. 32.

the mind's power to create its world by thinking it. It will seem perverse to propose as axioms "that life is a dream, that men are animated automata"—for if life is a dream the things we think important must be unimportant, and if we think ourselves machines then the springs of motive, choice, and action are broken. In the man who held these views there must be an unmanly passivity, perhaps a secret bitterness, or a desire to mock men of good faith. Perhaps all three. Thus the anxiety of those mothers who warned their Harvard sons away from the dark Spaniard's lectures.

Now those who found despair and ethical irresponsibility lurking in Santayana's propositions had warrant for their suspicions in view of the general temper of naturalist opinion in America at the turn of the century. The conclusions that life is a dream and men automata were precisely the axioms Mark Twain, for example, was maintaining all through his later years, the years of Santayana's career at Harvard—and in Twain they were indeed the axioms of misanthropy, sometimes naughty, sometimes bitter. The American literary Naturalists, when they were not celebrating impulse and will, were delivered by their mechanistic determinism to a sense of helplessness, and even to terror by their vision of an uncaring Nature. If we are not our own masters but only dream that we are, would it not be better to collapse at once, consent merely to vegetate, or do as Edwin Arlington Robinson suggested, plunge "To the dark tideless floods of Nothingness / Where all who know may drown"?

But Robinson and Mark Twain and the literary Naturalists were themselves children of the genteel tradition; they had been to the great abyss of Nothingness and had returned, and must now either close their eyes to it in order to win their way back to the faith of the genteel fathers or lapse into despair. Yet despair was itself a function of a remembered orthodoxy: one hears in it the cry, as Malcolm Cowley has observed, "God *ought* to be good; God *ought* to be kind." Such desperate oscillation between the poles of faith and bitter disillusion is tragic testimony to the absence in America of traditions other than those of gentility to which men might have recourse. Even William James, who was no true believer but an agnostic, felt that he must believe "in the right of believing that you might be right if you believed." The young, wry Brooks Adams quietly noted that the philosophers of the country seem to be "hired by the comfortable class to prove that everything is all right."

Now Santayana knew the anguish of confronting a universe which inspires our ideals but will not sanction them—his dialogue "Normal Madness" is testimony to it—but he refused the impulse to hurl defiant bricks at the temple; he seems to have been resolved from the beginning to build his philosophy on an acquiescent recognition that there are no bricks and no temples. Spinoza was Santayana's great master here, as he was also for Justice Oliver Wendell Holmes, the one American of Santayana's time who seems also to have rejected the petulance and bathos which predictably followed their countrymen's discovery that man (in Holmes's phrase) is merely "a ganglion of the irrational Cosmos." From Spinoza both men learned acquiescence; both found a true measure of the sanctity of human life in the understanding that man is a finite mode of nature and not a fallen angel. The dignity of man can be proved, but as Spinoza (or Sophocles) might prove it, by showing that it is open to man to acknowledge his finitude with the more than good grace of an acceptant piety.

Perhaps in a less genteel contemporary America Santayana's assertions of the animal status of mind and the transcendent power of matter will not seem perverse but simply unnecessary. The relativity of knowledge and the relativity of moral judgments— principles which, he once said, summarized his philosophy—may now be conceded. But to dwell on them, to insist on our irremediable human limitations, may seem idle. Our problems are not less acute when we are told they are merely human problems; the business of man is man. If the grammar of the intellect is local and all morality provincial, what of that? They are, *ex hypothesi*, limitations we are helpless to overcome.

Santayana would agree. "Those who perceive the relativity of human goods [and of human knowledge] are tempted to scorn them—which is itself unreasonable—and to sacrifice them all to the single passion of worship or of despair." Yet he would ask still for the *Lebensraum* beyond life which a steady awareness of the natural ground of experience makes possible. The anxious, characteristically American quest for the Absolute can be checked by the understanding that our keenest insights cannot penetrate to nature's last secrets—for even science, the most trustworthy of our symbolisms, knows only the contingent ways of matter, not matter, and knows them by refraction, through the medium of essences. Our even greater readiness to convert our moral preferences into dogma can be checked (and charity can begin) through the understanding that only the given human nature of each man, a nature variable from man to man, can provide the criterion by which his life can be judged.

In another direction Santayana's insistence on our finitude is an urging of distracted men back to the thought of ultimate things. He asks those preoccupied by human affairs to summon and hold in mind an image of the actual terraqueous (mainly aqueous) globe on which their affairs are spun out, and to understand how precarious our hold on the planet is. At times his reflections sound a note one finds in Jonathan Edwards' meditations on the littleness of man and the greatness of God—near the end of his life, in his *Apologia pro Mente Sua*, Santayana did indeed acknowledge his affinity with that side of the Puritan-Protestant tradition. This is the key to his discussion of Dewey, in whose philosophy, he thought, "the dominance of the foreground," an exclusive devotion to "the distinctly modern and American subject matter of social experience" shuts down the sky. In a posthumous essay published in 1957, "The Idler and His Works," Santayana proposes that we repent of our pride by grounding politics and psychology in nature:

All this needs to be grounded in physical facts and at the same time shown to be purely relative to special phases of human life and to special predicaments. The surface of human experience must not be taken for its ground or for its own motive power. It is all an effect of sub-human or super-human forces. The liberal, empirical, psychological philosophy into which I was plunged was miserably artificial, like a modern town laid out in squares. There was nothing subterranean acknowledged in it, no ultimate catastrophe, no jungle, no desert, and no laughter of the Gods. Mankind lived lost in the fog of self-consciousness, persuaded that it was creating itself and the whole universe. They had forgotten their religion; and their philosophy, when they had one, was a glorification of their vanity and of their furious impulse to make money, to make machines, and to make war.[5]

III. *The American Will*

Santayana said of his father that he had a profound respect for material greatness, "yet not unmixed with a secret irony or even repulsion." It is clear in retrospect that the son shared his father's ambivalence. The life of commerce, industry, and technology pursued by "that amiable monster, American Big Business" is one of Santayana's recurrent subjects, and the monster does not always seem to him amiable; it often appears, especially in the later writings, diabolic. No other subject put his sentiments and convictions so much at war among themselves. Aggressive enterprise in the perfection of material arts—what he called simply modernism, "purer in America than elsewhere because less impeded and qualified by survivals of the past"—could elicit from him spirited praise, warning prophecies, scorn. And in the attempt to accommodate such irresolution he often ends in ambiguity: the "Why be dissatisfied?" of *The Genteel Tradition at Bay* or the playful irony of his letter to Logan Pearsall Smith.

The deepest motive in Santayana's praise of American commercial and industrial enterprise is made clear in his Oberlin address, "Tradition and Practice," and again, on the eve of his departure from America, in "The Genteel Tradition in American Philosophy." His fundamental distinction between the theorizing Intellect of the country and its working Will clearly declares a preference for the Will. In the present-minded American's engagement with practical affairs Santayana finds an intensity and spontaneity, an easy competence and satisfaction which testify that in these occupations the country's native genius finds outlet; a certain "harmony subsists between the task and the spirit, between the mind's vitality and the forms which, in America, political and industrial tradition has taken on." [6] Thus when Stephen Spender

[5] *The Idler and His Works and Other Essays,* ed. Daniel Cory (New York: George Braziller, Inc., 1957), pp. 7-8.

[6] In this direction as in others Santayana is an ally of those empiricists—Holmes, Veblen, Dewey, Beard—who mounted early in the century what Morton White has discussed as their revolt against an *a priori* formalism. James or Dewey might also have said to the young philosophers of Califor-

accused the young T. S. Eliot of locating "tradition" in books,
Santayana, in the margins, seconded the charge and extended it:
"This fallacy infects American minds. It stinks at Harvard." Of
course Santayana thought that a particular tradition, the genteel,
could all too easily be located in American books. His complaint
is elliptical, and records again his judgment that if we mean to
locate the traditions which inform our common practices and
characteristic values we must look past those books which fail
precisely because they offer themselves to our understanding (as
the New Critics proposed that they should) as autonomous entities, lacking a close, direct relation to the lives of their authors
and the life of their times. And this means that we must look past
the nation's traditional literature and traditional religion.

Only the third great stream of American tradition, the scientific and economic, "has grown up in our race under conditions
such as those we still live in." That it *is* a tradition may be overlooked, for the practical genius of America proves its vitality
almost in the measure that men are unaware that it is traditional
at all. Yet medical science, machine technology, the insurance
industry are legacies of a long experience and of a knowledge
slowly accumulated; these works of "Will" are made possible by
the works of a transmitted intelligence. In this light it is clear that
Santayana's doubts about the American "Intellect" are directed
only to some (and by no means all) of its manifestations. His
scepticism is mainly a response to American high reflection, with
its moralistic and psychologistic preoccupations, and to American
intellectuality, with its self-conscious pursuit of Cultivation. As
he says in a letter to Van Wyck Brooks, "It is veneer, rouge,
aestheticism, art museums, new theatres, etc. that make America
impotent." [7] Yet "*all* learning and all 'mind' in America," he
writes to Logan Pearsall Smith, "is not of this ineffectual sophomoric sort. There is your doctor at Baltimore who is a great
expert, and *really knows how to do things. . . .*" [8]

Santayana's sympathy for the spirit and achievements of the

---

nia, "It is the daily discipline of contact with things, so different from the
verbal discipline of the schools, that will, I trust, inspire the philosophy of
your children."

[7] *Letters of George Santayana*, p. 226.

[8] *Ibid.*, p. 193.

liberal industrial society appears again (though crossed now with irony) in the early '30's, in his criticism of the New Humanists led by Irving Babbitt and Paul Elmer More. In *The Genteel Tradition at Bay*, in the course of criticizing their program for the instauration of right feeling and right thinking, Santayana pits against that program not only his own naturalism and moral relativism but the spirit of American Big Business. The latter— amiable, inarticulate, tolerant of all opinions which do not jeopardize the gospel of work—Santayana finds admirable, and admirable especially in contrast with the absolutistic spirit and the articulated principles of salvation advanced by the New Humanists. Not only does technocracy, in his view, breed its special kinds of intelligence, favoring "the most startling triumphs of mind in abstract science and mechanical art," it also provides the perpetual romantic lure of the yet-to-be-discovered, and immediate satisfactions in material improvements and rewards to competitive ambition. The vision of the good life said by the Humanists to characterize America and condemned by them—i.e. to make money, spend it freely, be friendly, move fast, and die with your boots on—Santayana thought a plausible ideal (a "sturdy" ideal, to use his own ambiguous adjective) exacting its own kinds of virtue: fidelity to duty, club spirit, good humor. "Why be dissatisfied?" he asks the Humanists, and goes on to suggest that their protest against the spiritual anarchy of the industrial state, a protest made in the name of an inner voice of reason or conscience supposed uniform in all men, is the work of censorious minds "designed by nature to be the pillars of some priestly orthodoxy." They are not "humanists" in the old sense of the word but are Calvinists in disguise, hoping to ground all judgment in express principles themselves grounded in some revealed absolute standard.

The fact that American enterprise is a blind adventure, carried on without philosophic commitments regarding its ultimate truth or value, is in Santayana's view a positive recommendation. Or at least it is so when he contemplates the programmatic reforms proposed by the New Humanists, who would stop the American giant in the midst of his cheerful unquestioning labors and show him that if he really wishes to be happy he must change his ways and acquire a philosophy. But the very absence of an articulate ideology serves as a sign of America's health, a warrant that its "spirit of free co-operation" is alive—this is the argument of Santayana's "English Liberty." As acclimatized in the United States, English liberty has bred kindliness and self-reliance, and above all an empirical temper which aims at an accommodation of interests and refuses to prejudge issues. "The general instinct is to run and help, to assume direction, to pull through somehow by mutual adaptation, and by seizing on the readiest practical measures and working compromises. Each man joins in and gives a helping hand, without a preconceived plan or a prior motive." [9] This absence of policy and determinate aims makes possible the plasticity and openness which he thinks to be America's strength —and its virtue. For it is the dogmatic *a priori* mind, character- istic of the Puritan Fathers and of most contemporary societies, which "smells of fustiness as well as of faggots."

"English Liberty" reveals more clearly than any of his other writings, and with the fewest qualifications, Santayana's admira- tion for the "hearty unity and universal hum" of American Big Business. For the qualities of American idealism which he de- scribes here he sees—in a way very similar to Henry Adams's earlier view of "American Ideals"—as a function of American materialism. Free cooperation would fail at once were there not a fundamental unanimity of interest in society at large, a tacit common agreement that "to exploit business opportunities and organize public services useful to all" constitute the essential tasks of the good citizen. Thus his belief, first expressed in the 1890's, that the country's two political parties are in fact one, and draw their platforms from a common text of Benthamite political economy. "The national faith and morality are vague in idea, but inexorable in spirit"—and there will be woe for the man who will not be strapped to the wheel of the national orthodoxy. For the business society is a kind of tyranny, permitting absolute freedom in indifferent matters (such as religion) but exacting an absolute allegiance to its main articles of faith, "the gospel of work and the belief in progress." Even those who escape the national routine of nine to five at office or factory "are none the less prevented by it from doing anything else with success or with a

---

[9] *Character and Opinion in the United States*, p. 196.

good conscience." In America there is only one way of salvation: to work and to rise by that work, adhering to a regimen not less strict than that of the old monasteries, for the sake of an ill-defined but somehow better future.

Why, then, does Santayana admire a system which in his own view is characterized by such "overpowering compulsions," a system which he once described as "the union of severity with worldliness, of exaction with emptiness"? "Of all words in the modern lexicon," he wrote in one of his drafts, "to me the most odious was Progress." It seems clear that his admiration could be sustained only by holding in abeyance his deepest, most visceral reactions to American life. What led him to defend America and to criticize its critics was the testimony provided by his own observation: astonishing yet undeniable was the fact that most Americans freely consented to be atoms in the constantly accelerating mass, and seemed to find happiness in the sense of its momentum. Progress may be a hard master, but theirs was a willing service. He writes to Henry Ward Abbot in 1924, "The [Americans] I see are so full of health, good-will, pleasantness, and money that I can't believe things can be seriously wrong there —I mean, granting the American postulates—work, progress, democracy, and whoop-her-up." [10] If Americans ardently pursued goods which Santayana thought trivial and a waste of spirit, he would not, in behalf of his own preferences, condemn the generality. As moral relativist, he reminded L. P. Smith that all the tribes of men need not sacrifice at his altar, and on this ground he condemned the too narrow dogmatism of the New Humanists.

It is on somewhat different ground, the ground of the Burkean conservative, that he condemns "America's Young Radicals." [11] The Burkean is no reactionary, as Arnold reminded us, but makes his judgments with reference to the Zeitgeist, and the "Young Radicals" were Santayana's Jacobins, theorizing rebels whose com-

[10] *The Letters of George Santayana*, p. 209.
[11] The "radicals" were the contributors to *Civilization in the United States, an Inquiry by Thirty Americans* (New York: Harcourt, Brace & World, Inc., 1922), edited by Harold Stearns. Among them were Van Wyck Brooks, Robert Morss Lovett, H. L. Mencken, Lewis Mumford, Ring Lardner, J. E. Spingarn. Santayana's review-essay appeared in England; his "Marginal Notes," written in response to the same book, appeared in the United States a month later.

plaints ignored tradition and the general life. "Those who rebel against America," he wrote to Abbot, "are doomed to fail even in what America is busy about."

Yet at some time in the mid-1930's Santayana gave full audience to his doubts, and in a statement as rebellious as any by the Radicals or Humanists, and with few of the old ambiguities, he questioned sharply the temper and direction of America's mechanized democracy. His essay on "Americanism" protests the plight of the Babbitts (he had read Sinclair Lewis's novel in 1931), whose willing service he now sees as a pathetic servitude. Not that the public faith in prosperity through industry is not kept up. On the contrary, he thought the spirit of "unity in work" for the sake of property and the machine more pervasive than ever, and in *Dominations and Powers* (1951) sees it imposed by its missionaries even on Asia. But he is now convinced that the gospel of material well-being does not really inspire the lives of even those who profess it, and brings no real fulfillment. The marginal freedoms which nineteenth-century liberalism had always allowed so long as they did not undercut the essential work of material progress—those freedoms have brought license and a growing moral chaos. Such free play as is permitted has become trivial or mean, and not really satisfying; for the mechanized man "in his leisure, any sort of sensual or emotional pabulum will do. . . ."

The essay's indictment is long and many-sided but makes its central point unrelentingly: the American faith in commerce and industry—and in abstract science and technology, which Santayana thought to be "other forms of Big Business and congruous parts of it"—is driving steadily toward "the manufacture of Homunculus, or the mechanical man." The Greeks, Santayana's touchstone of sanity, acknowledged the gods but felt no desire to pry into their inscrutable ways; and whatever they felt of fear or of worship towards the unseen did not lead them to forgo the cultivation of their specifically human powers. For them it was "the part of man to cultivate his arts and purify his spirit." But the Greeks, with their modest "thinking on the human scale," have been supplanted in America's world by Dr. Faustus. Hypnotized by the discovery and exploitation of his powers to penetrate the secrets of matter and control it, and encouraged in his arro-

gant impersonal ambition by the philosophers of romantic transcendentalism and pragmatism, he has forgotten the human purposes which matter should be made to serve. Moral autonomy
and the free exercise of mind are no longer the purpose and end
of man's labors; intellect in the modern world has been enlisted
for the wars, and must justify itself as a means to other ends.
Santayana is witness here to the twentieth-century man's flagrant
abdication of what should be in human affairs the directing role of
the moral imagination.

IV. The American Imagination

Santayana's philosophy from first to last speaks for the imagination and celebrates its powers. In his "Brief History" he testifies
to his conviction even as a boy that the works of imagination alone
are good, "and the rest—the whole real world—is ashes in the
mouth." And his preference for the visionary mind is determining
for his sense of America, where he found that the rigidities of the
genteel Intellect and the enthusiasms of men pledged to optimism,
hustle, and duty left no room for the idler poet. He expressed in
1905 in a letter to William James his irritation—"greater than I
let it seem"—with those whose worship of the facts or of the
Absolute led them "to cancel the passing ideal," "that vision of
perfection that we just catch, or for a moment embody in some
work of art, or in some idealised reality: . . . the concomitant
inspiration of life, always various, always beautiful, hardly ever
expressible in its fullness." [12] For Santayana the imagination is
mind functioning freely, realizing in act its innate but often
suppressed powers. The mind is empowered only when free of
the incubus of fact and pressing circumstance, free of the need of
certitude and doctrine, and free of domination by the conceptual
and linguistic conventions which serve our merely practical needs.
Only then is the mind enabled to discover its essentially imaginative nature, and its capacity to transcend the world by reason of
its infinite ideal scope. Conceiving becomes both a pure good in
itself and the source of those ideas of worth and of order in terms
of which the otherwise blind miscellany of experience may be
judged.

[12] *The Letters of George Santayana*, p. 83.

Santayana is a member of that beleaguered band of artists who fought a rear-guard action throughout the nineteenth century. Their opponents were everywhere: philosophers who measured the world by rule and line, utilitarians who thought pushpin good enough, political prophets who declared the millennium, theologians who insisted on the Fact. Pre-eminent among the literalminded were the men who carried the day for commerce and industry, and who were content to indulge art, poetry, and fiction as harmless make-believe for the idle hours of ladies. It is not surprising that in one of the earliest essays to be published by the young Santayana he should identify the enemy as the prosaic acquisitive Philistine, scoring him on three counts as the type of the anti-poetic. "What Is a Philistine?" he asks, and his reply suggests that he is hardly distinguishable from modern man. How shall he be distinguished? By his having forfeited a simple life lived in the senses and the affections, by his incapacity to conceive and hold an ideal of the good or true to which all his acts are responsive, and by his consequent indifference to the arts. It amounts to a betrayal of consciousness, and a denial of the demands of our full human nature; a dedication to the making and doing of things proceeds on the tacit, insane assumption that the ends of living somehow lie beyond man himself.

Over forty years later, in the essay on "Americanism," the judgment of 1892 had not changed. It is true that between those dates Santayana frequently and roundly defended the American consensus—when he thought the strictures of those who opposed the work of material progress were irritable or effete, absolutistic in spirit, or, above all, when he found absent from their criticism a clear vision of the good life which might supplant so much servility to mechanism. For his own part he was always sure of what ought to supplant it: a life made free by a recovery of the capacity to *have* a vision of the good life. Santayana's well-known definition of the fanatic, the man who redoubles his efforts because he has forgotten his aims, might serve to define also his sense of America. "What irony there would be in having learned to control matter, if we thereby forgot the purposes of the soul in controlling it, and disowned the natural furniture of the mind, our senses, fancy, and pictorial knowledge!"

The substitution of "blind work for free imagination" is a chief characteristic of Santayana's 1892 Philistine, the man who has forgotten "the primitive source of all value in the senses and affections." But the full implications of this charge were not made plain until 1900, in the final chapter of his *Interpretations of Poetry and Religion*. "The Elements and Function of Poetry" has become a major document in the history of American aesthetics.[13] In its assertion of the primacy of sensation and emotion in our apprehension of the world, it argues for a view of the poet as realist, for it is the poet, by reason of his fidelity to immediate experience, who is able to break up "the trite conceptions designated by current words into the sensuous qualities out of which those conceptions were originally put together." In thus recovering the world for the innocent eye he is carried to a closer engagement with reality than the somnolent utilitarian can know. The practical man, as also the scientist and the philosopher, moves among abstractions, while the sensuous impractical poet, absorbed by his images, declares his preference for the concrete. It is Santayana's recognition of this need and this capacity in the poet which explains his admiration for Whitman, the master of all poets in his ability "to seize the elementary aspects of things" and, by the wealth of his imagery, to convey a sense both of the multitudinousness of the world and "of the individuality and the universality of what he describes—it is a drop in itself, yet a drop in the ocean."

Yet if Santayana admired Whitman for a more direct grasp of the world than is given to the practical intellect, he condemns Whitman's "barbarism" for reasons which have also their most adequate statement in "The Elements and Function of Poetry," in

[13] At a time when Symbolism had only begun to have advocates in England, and had scarcely been heard of in America beyond New York and the Harvard Yard, Santayana's essay advanced a theory of poetry which still stands as a powerful rationale of Symbolist aspiration and method. The essay is crucial, too, by reason of its influence. T. S. Eliot—who said so little of Santayana, in R. P. Blackmur's judgment, because he "incorporated so much of him"—drew from it, or perhaps from the lectures at Harvard on which it was based, his theory of the "objective correlative," though his professor's theory of "correlative objects" does better justice to the psychology of expression; and Santayana's theory of the poet's "idealization" of experience is a Platonist's argument for the necessity of artistic impersonality. The essay was a primary source for Wallace Stevens, whose theory of "the supreme fiction" will hardly be understood without reference to this essay by the man he called "Master."

Santayana's conception of the tasks of imaginative synthesis and construction which must follow the poet's disintegration of conventional experience. The poet's retreat to the primitive level of sense, instinct, and passion, while it brings a saving recovery of vitality, may nonetheless end in a denial of the claims of the understanding or of the need of discriminating judgment, a disavowal of patient reason's work in comprehending experience within a synthetic view of the total drift and meaning of his existence. Sympathetic intuition in both Whitman and Emerson had led to mysticism; both, by reason of their sympathy with all men and all modes of being, declared the annihilation of good and evil through their absorption in the All; both were pantheists, with the impassioned conviction that "all eggs are good because the hen has laid them." Emerson's definition of evil as merely privative the Spaniard found intelligible as inspiration, but the ahistorical innocence it implied he found inadmissible in this ancient world. Santayana, especially in his later days, often gave himself to a disinterested transmoral contemplation of Being, very like Emerson's, yet he continued to regard that stance of mind as one of many to be accommodated within reason's economy. He continued to believe of Emerson, as the McStout of his "Dialogue" says of Whitman, "It is immoral to treat life as a masquerade, as a magic pantomime in which acts have no consequences and happiness and misery don't exist." Intense imagination is not enough; it must be the historical, the reasonable, the moral imagination.

In 1936 Santayana astonished his followers in America by producing a novel, *The Last Puritan*, a novel that for a time supplanted Sinclair Lewis on the best-seller lists. It was in fact his own version of Lewis's earlier *Babbitt*, though his protagonist is not a booster but an Emerson (or a Jonathan Edwards) come down into the America of industrial democracy and stifled by its exactions and its emptiness. Oliver Alden is a young man with the spiritual vocation of a poet or a priest—and yet, "though ready for every sacrifice," he "had nothing to pin his allegiance to." Santayana saw Oliver's plight as the plight of a whole string of Harvard poets at the turn of the century, young men who could not accept the roles their society urged upon them nor any imposed faith, even the Christian. They, and not the sad young men of the 1920's, were America's first Lost Generation, grown up to find all gods dead, all wars fought, all faiths in man broken. All of them died when still young, and Santayana—who knew them all—thought they were "visibly killed by the lack of air to breathe." The deepest tragedy in their lot, he writes in the letter to Mrs. Sturgis, is that "they lived in a spiritual vacuum. American breeding can be perfect in form, but it is woefully thin in substance; so that if a man is born a poet or a mystic in America he simply starves, because what social life offers and presses upon him is offensive to him, and there is nothing else." [14] Had the Oliver Aldens of America been more robust they might still have dominated their experience by giving it imaginative form; the career of Robert Frost or Wallace Stevens or George Santayana stand as proof of that. But the odds were against them. Perhaps the odds —Santayana's version of the American tragedy—were on Stevens's mind when, imagining the convent-hospital cell in Rome where Santayana died, he wrote of "the pity that is the memorial of this room."

R. C. L.

[14] *The Letters of George Santayana*, p. 302.

I

A Spanish Materialist at Harvard

✑ A Brief History of My Opinions*

How came a child born in Spain of Spanish parents to be educated in Boston and to write in the English language? The case of my family was unusual. We were not emigrants; none of us ever changed his country, his class, or his religion. But special circumstances had given us hereditary points of attachment in opposite quarters, moral and geographical; and now that we are almost extinct—I mean those of us who had these mixed associations—I may say that we proved remarkably staunch in our complex allegiances, combining them as well as logic allowed, without at heart ever disowning anything. My philosophy in particular may be regarded as a synthesis of these various traditions, or as an attempt to view them from a level from which their several deliverances may be justly understood. I do not assert that such was actually the origin of my system: in any case its truth would be another question. I propose simply to describe as best I can the influences under which I have lived, and leave it for the reader, if he cares, to consider how far my philosophy may be an expression of them.

In the first place, we must go much farther afield than Boston or Spain, into the tropics, almost to the antipodes. Both my father and my mother's father were officials in the Spanish civil serv-

* From *Contemporary American Philosophy: Personal Statements*, ed. by George Plimpton Adams and William Pepperell Montague (New York: The Macmillan Company, 1930).

ice in the Philippine Islands. This was in the 1840's and 1850's,
long before my birth; for my parents were not married until
later in life, in Spain, when my mother was a widow. But the
tradition of the many years which each of them separately had
spent in the East was always alive in our household. Those had
been, for both, their more romantic and prosperous days. My
father had studied the country and the natives, and had written
a little book about the Island of Mindanao; he had been three times
round the world in the sailing-ships of the period, and had incidentally visited England and the United States, and been immensely
impressed by the energy and order prevalent in those nations.
His respect for material greatness was profound, yet not unmixed with a secret irony or even repulsion. He had a seasoned
and incredulous mind, trained to see other sorts of excellence
also: in his boyhood he had worked in the studio of a professional painter of the school of Goya, and had translated the tragedies of Seneca into Spanish verse. His transmarine experiences,
therefore, did not rattle, as so often happens, in an empty head.
The sea itself, in those days, was still vast and blue, and the lands
beyond it full of lessons and wonders. From childhood I have
lived in the imaginative presence of interminable ocean spaces,
cocoanut islands, blameless Malays, and immense continents
swarming with Chinamen, polished and industrious, obscene
and philosophical. It was habitual with me to think of scenes and
customs pleasanter than those about me. My own travels have
never carried me far from the frontiers of Christendom or of
respectability, and chiefly back and forth across the North Atlantic—thirty-eight fussy voyages; but in mind I have always seen
these things on an ironical background enormously empty, or
breaking out in spots, like Polynesia, into nests of innocent parti-
coloured humanity.

My mother's figure belonged to the same broad and somewhat
exotic landscape; she had spent her youth in the same places;
but the moral note resounding in her was somewhat different.
Her father, José Borrás, of Reus in Catalonia, had been a disciple
of Rousseau, an enthusiast and a wanderer: he taught her to re-
vere pure reason and republican virtue and to abhor the vices
of a corrupt world. But her own temper was cool and stoical,
rather than ardent, and her disdain of corruption had in it a touch

of elegance. At Manila, during the time of her first marriage, she had been rather the grand lady, in a style half Creole, half early Victorian. Virtue, beside those tropical seas, might stoop to be indolent. She had given a silver dollar every morning to her native major-domo, with which to provide for the family and the twelve servants, and keep the change for his wages. Meantime she bathed, arranged the flowers, received visits, and did embroidery. It had been a spacious life; and in our narrower circumstances in later years the sense of it never forsook her.

Her first husband, an American merchant established in Manila, had been the sixth son of Nathaniel Russell Sturgis, of Boston (1779-1856). In Boston, accordingly, her three Sturgis children had numerous relations and a little property, and there she had promised their father to bring them up in case of his death. When this occurred, in 1857, she therefore established herself in Boston; and this fact, by a sort of prenatal or pre-established destiny, was the cause of my connection with the Sturgis family, with Boston and with America.

It was in Madrid in 1862, where my mother had gone on a visit intended to be temporary, that my father and she were married. He had been an old friend of hers and of her first husband's, and was well aware of her settled plan to educate her children in America, and recognised the propriety of that arrangement. Various projects and combinations were mooted: but the matter eventually ended in a separation, friendly, if not altogether pleasant to either party. My mother returned with her Sturgis children to live in the United States and my father and I remained in Spain. Soon, however, this compromise proved unsatisfactory. The education and prospects which my father, in his modest retirement, could offer me in Spain were far from brilliant; and in 1872 he decided to take me to Boston, where, after remaining for one cold winter, he left me in my mother's care and went back to Spain.

I was then in my ninth year, having been born on December 16, 1863, and I did not know one word of English. Nor was I likely to learn the language at home, where the family always continued to speak a Spanish more or less pure. But by a happy thought I was sent during my first winter in Boston to a Kindergarten, among much younger children, where there were no books, so that I picked up English by ear before knowing how it was written: a circumstance to which I probably owe speaking the language without a marked foreign accent. The Brimmer School, the Boston Latin School, and Harvard College then followed in order: but apart from the taste for English poetry which I first imbibed from our excellent English master, Mr. Byron Groce, the most decisive influences over my mind in boyhood continued to come from my family, where, with my grown-up brother and sisters, I was the only child. I played no games, but sat at home all the afternoon and evening reading or drawing; especially devouring anything I could find that regarded religion, architecture, or geography.

In the summer of 1883, after my Freshman year, I returned for the first time to Spain to see my father. Then, and during many subsequent holidays which I spent in his company, we naturally discussed the various careers that might be open to me. We should both of us have liked the Spanish army or diplomatic service: but for the first I was already too old, and our means and our social relations hardly sufficed for the second. Moreover, by that time I felt like a foreigner in Spain, more acutely so than in America, although for more trivial reasons: my Yankee manners seemed outlandish there, and I could not do myself justice in the language. Nor was I inclined to overcome this handicap, as perhaps I might have done with a little effort: nothing in Spanish life or literature at that time particularly attracted me. English had become my only possible instrument, and I deliberately put away everything that might confuse me in that medium. English, and the whole Anglo-Saxon tradition in literature and philosophy, have always been a medium to me rather than a source. My natural affinities were elsewhere. Moreover, scholarship and learning of any sort seemed to me a means, not an end. I always hated to be a professor. Latin and Greek, French, Italian, and German, although I can read them, were languages which I never learned well. It seemed an accident to me if the matters which interested me came clothed in the rhetoric of one or another of these nations: I was not without a certain temperamental rhetoric of my own in which to recast what I adopted. Thus in renouncing everything else for the sake of English letters I might be said to have been guilty, quite unintentionally, of a little stratagem, as if I had set out to say plausibly in English as many un-English things as possible.

This brings me to religion, which is the head and front of everything. Like my parents, I have always set myself down officially as a Catholic: but this is a matter of sympathy and traditional allegiance, not of philosophy. In my adolescence, religion on its doctrinal and emotional side occupied me much more than it does now. I was more unhappy and unsettled; but I have never had any unquestioning faith in any dogma, and have never been what is called a practising Catholic. Indeed, it would hardly have been possible. My mother, like her father before her, was a Deist: she was sure there was a God, for who else could have made the world? But God was too great to take special thought for man: sacrifices, prayers, churches, and tales of immortality were invented by rascally priests in order to dominate the foolish. My father, except for the Deism, was emphatically of the same opinion. Thus, although I learned my prayers and catechism by rote, as was then inevitable in Spain, I knew that my parents regarded all religion as a work of human imagination: and I agreed, and still agree, with them there. But this carried an implication in their minds against which every instinct in me rebelled, namely that the works of human imagination are bad. No, said I to myself even as a boy: they are good, they alone are good; and the rest—the whole real world—is ashes in the mouth. My sympathies were entirely with those other members of my family who were devout believers. I loved the Christian epic, and all those doctrines and observances which bring it down into daily life: I thought how glorious it would have been to be a Dominican friar, preaching that epic eloquently, and solving afresh all the knottiest and sublimest mysteries of theology. I was delighted with anything, like Mallock's *Is Life Worth Living?*, which seemed to rebuke the fatuity of that age. For my own part, I was quite sure that life was not worth living; for if religion was false everything was worthless, and almost everything, if religion was true. In this youthful pessimism I was hardly more foolish than so many amateur mediævalists and religious æsthetes of my generation. I saw the same alternative between Catholicism and complete disillusion: but I was never afraid of disillusion, and I have chosen it.

Since those early years my feelings on this subject have become less strident. Does not modern philosophy teach that our idea of the so-called real world is also a work of imagination? A religion—for there are other religions than the Christian—simply offers a system of faith different from the vulgar one, or extending beyond it. The question is which imaginative system you will trust. My matured conclusion has been that no system is to be trusted, not even that of science in any literal or pictorial sense; but all systems may be used and, up to a certain point, trusted as symbols. Science expresses in human terms our dynamic relation to surrounding reality. Philosophies and religions, where they do not misrepresent these same dynamic relations and do not contradict science, express destiny in moral dimensions, in obviously mythical and poetical images: but how else should these moral truths be expressed at all in a traditional or popular fashion? Religions are the great fairy-tales of the conscience.

When I began the formal study of philosophy as an undergraduate at Harvard, I was already alive to the fundamental questions, and even had a certain dialectical nimbleness, due to familiarity with the fine points of theology: the arguments for and against free will and the proofs of the existence of God were warm and clear in my mind. I accordingly heard James and Royce with more wonder than serious agreement: my scholastic logic would have wished to reduce James at once to a materialist and Royce to a solipsist, and it seemed strangely irrational in them to resist such simplification. I had heard many Unitarian sermons (being taken to hear them lest I should become too Catholic), and had been interested in them so far as they were rationalistic and informative, or even amusingly irreligious, as I often thought them to be: but neither in those discourses nor in Harvard philosophy was it easy for me to understand the Protestant combination of earnestness with waywardness. I was used to see water flowing from fountains, architectural and above ground: it puzzled me to see it drawn painfully in bucketfuls from the subjective well, muddied, and half spilt over.

There was one lesson, however, which I was readier to learn, not only at Harvard from Professor Palmer and afterwards at Berlin from Paulsen, but from the general temper of that age well represented for me by the *Revue des Deux Mondes* (which I habitually read from cover to cover) and by the works of Taine and of Matthew Arnold—I refer to the historical spirit of the nineteenth century, and to that splendid panorama of nations and religions, literatures and arts, which it unrolled before the imagination. These picturesque vistas into the past came to fill in circumstantially that geographical and moral vastness to which my imagination was already accustomed. Professor Palmer was especially skilful in bending the mind to a suave and sympathetic participation in the views of all philosophers in turn: were they not all great men, and must not the aspects of things which seemed persuasive to them be really persuasive? Yet even this form of romanticism, amiable as it is, could not altogether put to sleep my scholastic dogmatism. The historian of philosophy may be as sympathetic and as self-effacing as he likes: the philosopher in him must still ask whether any of those successive views were true, or whether the later ones were necessarily truer than the earlier: he cannot, unless he is a shameless sophist, rest content with a truth *pro tem*. In reality the sympathetic reconstruction of history is a literary art, and it depends for its plausibility as well as for its materials on a conventional belief in the natural world. Without this belief no history and no science would be anything but a poetic fiction, like a classification of the angelic choirs. The necessity of naturalism as a foundation for all further serious opinions was clear to me from the beginning. Naturalism might indeed be criticised—and I was myself intellectually and emotionally predisposed to criticise it, and to oscillate between supernaturalism and solipsism—but if naturalism was condemned, supernaturalism itself could have no point of application in the world of fact; and the whole edifice of human knowledge would crumble, since no perception would then be a report and no judgment would have a transcendent object. Hence historical reconstruction seemed to me more honestly and solidly practised by Taine, who was a professed naturalist, than by Hegel and his school, whose naturalism, though presupposed at every stage, was disguised and distorted by a dialectic imposed on it by the historian and useful at best only in simplifying his dramatic perspectives and lending them a false absoluteness and moralistic veneer.

The influence of Royce over me, though less important in

the end than that of James, was at first much more active. Royce was the better dialectician, and traversed subjects in which I was naturally more interested. The point that particularly exercised me was Royce's Theodicy or justification for the existence of evil. It would be hard to exaggerate the ire which his arguments on this subject aroused in my youthful breast. Why that emotion? Romantic sentiment that could find happiness only in tears and virtue only in heroic agonies was something familiar to me and not unsympathetic: a poetic play of mine, called *Lucifer*, conceived in those days, is a clear proof of it. I knew Leopardi and Musset largely by heart; Schopenhauer was soon to become, for a brief period, one of my favourite authors. I carried Lucretius in my pocket: and although the spirit of the poet in that case was not romantic, the picture of human existence which he drew glorified the same vanity. Spinoza, too, whom I was reading under Royce himself, filled me with joy and enthusiasm: I gathered at once from him a doctrine which has remained axiomatic with me ever since, namely that good and evil are relative to the natures of animals, irreversible in that relation, but indifferent to the march of cosmic events, since the force of the universe infinitely exceeds the force of any one of its parts. Had I found, then, in Royce only a romantic view of life, or only pessimism, or only stoical courage and pantheistic piety, I should have taken no offence, but readily recognised the poetic truth or the moral legitimacy of those positions. Conformity with fate, as I afterwards came to see, belongs to post-rational morality, which is a normal though optional development of human sentiment: Spinoza's "intellectual love of God" was a shining instance of it.

But in Royce these attitudes, in themselves so honest and noble, seemed to be somehow embroiled and rendered sophistical: nor was he alone in this, for the same moral equivocation seemed to pervade Hegel, Browning, and Nietzsche. That which repelled me in all these men was the survival of a sort of forced optimism and pulpit unction, by which a cruel and nasty world, painted by them in the most lurid colours, was nevertheless set up as the model and standard of what ought to be. The duty of an honest moralist would have been rather to distinguish, in this bad or mixed reality, the part, however small, that could be loved and chosen from the remainder, however large, which was to be rejected and renounced. Certainly the universe was in flux and dynamically single: but this fatal flux could very well take care of itself; and it was not so fluid that no islands of a relative permanence and beauty might not be formed in it. Ascetic conformity was itself one of these islands: a scarcely inhabitable peak from which almost all human passions and activities were excluded. And the Greeks, whose deliberate ethics was rational, never denied the vague early Gods and the environing chaos, which perhaps would return in the end: but meantime they built their cities bravely on the hill-tops, as we all carry on pleasantly our temporal affairs, although we know that to-morrow we die. Life itself exists only by a modicum of organisation, achieved and transmitted through a world of change: the momentum of such organisation first creates a difference between good and evil, or gives them a meaning at all. Thus the core of life is always hereditary, steadfast, and classical; the margin of barbarism and blind adventure round it may be as wide as you will, and in some wild hearts the love of this fluid margin may be keen, as might be any other loose passion. But to *preach* barbarism as the only good, in ignorance or hatred of the possible perfection of every natural thing, was a scandal: a belated Calvinism that remained fanatical after ceasing to be Christian. And there was a further circumstance which made this attitude particularly odious to me. This romantic love of evil was not thoroughgoing: wilfulness and disorder were to reign only in spiritual matters; in government and industry, even in natural science, all was to be order and mechanical progress. Thus the absence of a positive religion and of a legislation, like that of the ancients, intended to be rational and final, was very far from liberating the spirit for higher flights: on the contrary, it opened the door to the pervasive tyranny of the world over the soul. And no wonder: a soul rebellious to its moral heritage is too weak to reach any firm definition of its inner life. It will feel lost and empty unless it summons the random labours of the contemporary world to fill and to enslave it. It must let mechanical and civic achievements reconcile it to its own moral confusion and triviality.

It was in this state of mind that I went to Germany to continue the study of philosophy—interested in all religious or metaphysical systems, but sceptical about them and scornful of any romantic worship or idealisation of the real world. The life of a wandering student, like those of the Middle Ages, had an immense natural attraction for me—so great, that I have never willingly led any other. When I had to choose a profession, the prospect of a quiet academic existence seemed the least of evils. I was fond of reading and observation, and I liked young men; but I have never been a diligent student either of science or art, nor at all ambitious to be learned. I have been willing to let cosmological problems and technical questions solve themselves as they would or as the authorities agreed for the moment that they should be solved. My pleasure was rather in expression, in reflection, in irony: my spirit was content to intervene, in whatever world it might seem to find itself, in order to disentangle the intimate moral and intellectual echoes audible to it in that world. My naturalism or materialism is no academic opinion: it is not a survival of the alleged materialism of the nineteenth century, when all the professors of philosophy were idealists: it is an everyday conviction which came to me, as it came to my father, from experience and observation of the world at large, and especially of my own feelings and passions. It seems to me that those who are not materialists cannot be good observers of themselves: they may hear themselves thinking, but they cannot have watched themselves acting and feeling; for feeling and action are evidently accidents of matter. If a Democritus or Lucretius or Spinoza or Darwin works within the lines of nature, and clarifies some part of that familiar object, that fact is the ground of my attachment to them: they have the savour of truth; but what the savour of truth is, I know very well without their help. Consequently there is no opposition in my mind between materialism and a Platonic or even Indian discipline of the spirit. The recognition of the material world and of the conditions of existence in it merely enlightens the spirit concerning the source of its troubles and the means to its happiness or deliverance: and it was happiness or deliverance, the supervening supreme expression of human will and imagination, that alone really concerned me. This alone was genuine philosophy: this alone was the life of reason.

Had the life of reason ever been cultivated in the world by people with a sane imagination? Yes, once, by the Greeks. Of the Greeks, however, I knew very little: the philosophical and political departments at Harvard had not yet discovered Plato and Aristotle. It was with the greater pleasure that I heard Paulsen in Berlin expounding Greek ethics with a sweet reasonableness altogether worthy of the subject: here at last was a vindication of order and beauty in the institutions of men and in their ideas. Here, through the pleasant medium of transparent myths or of summary scientific images, like the water of Thales, nature was essentially understood and honestly described; and here, for that very reason, the free mind could disentangle its true good, and could express it in art, in manners, and even in the most refined or the most austere spiritual discipline. Yet, although I knew henceforth that in the Greeks I should find the natural support and point of attachment for my own philosophy, I was not then collected or mature enough to pursue the matter; not until ten years later, in 1896-1897, did I take the opportunity of a year's leave of absence to go to England and begin a systematic reading of Plato and Aristotle under Doctor Henry Jackson of Trinity College, Cambridge. I am not conscious of any change of opinion supervening, nor of any having occurred earlier; but by that study and change of scene my mind was greatly enriched; and the composition of *The Life of Reason* was the consequence.

This book was intended to be a summary history of the human imagination, expressly distinguishing those phases of it which showed what Herbert Spencer called an adjustment of inner to outer relations; in other words, an adaptation of fancy and habit to material facts and opportunities. On the one hand, then, my subject being the imagination, I was never called on to step beyond the subjective sphere. I set out to describe, not nature or God, but the ideas of God or nature bred in the human mind. On the other hand, I was not concerned with these ideas for their own sake, as in a work of pure poetry or erudition, but I meant to consider them in their natural genesis and significance; for I assumed throughout that the whole life of reason was generated and controlled by the animal life of man in the bosom of nature. Human ideas had, accordingly, a symptomatic, expressive, and symbolic value: they were the inner notes sounded by man's passions and by his arts: and they became rational partly by their vital and inward harmony—for reason is a harmony of the passions—and partly by their adjustment to external facts and possibilities—for reason is a harmony of the inner life with truth and with fate. I was accordingly concerned to discover what wisdom is possible to an animal whose mind, from beginning to end, is poetical: and I found that this could not lie in discarding poetry in favour of a science supposed to be clairvoyant and literally true. Wisdom lay rather in taking everything good-humouredly, with a grain of salt. In science there was an element of poetry, pervasive, inevitable, and variable: it was strictly scientific and true only in so far as it involved a close and prosperous adjustment to the surrounding world, at first by its origin in observation and at last by its application in action. Science was the mental accompaniment of art.

Here was a sort of pragmatism: the same which I have again expressed, I hope more clearly, in one of the *Dialogues in Limbo* entitled "Normal Madness." The human mind is a faculty of dreaming awake, and its dreams are kept relevant to its environment and to its fate only by the external control exercised over them by Punishment, when the accompanying conduct brings ruin, or by Agreement, when it brings prosperity. In the latter case it is possible to establish correspondences between one part of a dream and another, or between the dreams of separate minds, and so create the world of literature, or the life of reason. I am not sure whether this notion, that thought is a controlled and consistent madness, appears among the thirteen pragmatisms which have been distinguished, but I have reason to think that I came to it under the influence of William James; nevertheless, when his book on *Pragmatism* appeared about the same time as my *Life of Reason,* it gave me a rude shock. I could not stomach that way of speaking about truth; and the continual substitution of human psychology—normal madness, in my view—for the universe, in which man is but one distracted and befuddled animal, seemed to me a confused remnant of idealism, and not serious.

The William James who had been my master was not this William James of the later years, whose pragmatism and pure empiricism and romantic metaphysics have made such a stir in the world. It was rather the puzzled but brilliant doctor, impatient of metaphysics, whom I had known in my undergraduate days, one of whose maxims was that to study the abnormal was the

best way of understanding the normal; or it was the genial author of *The Principles of Psychology*, chapters of which we read
from the manuscript and discussed with a small class of us in
1889. Even then what I learned from him was perhaps chiefly
things which explicitly he never taught, but which I imbibed
from the spirit and background of his teaching. Chief of these, I
should say, was a sense for the immediate: for the unadulterated,
unexplained, instant fact of experience. Actual experience, for
William James, however varied or rich its assault might be, was
always and altogether of the nature of a sensation: it possessed a
vital, leaping, globular unity which made the only fact, the flying fact, of our being. Whatever continuities of quality might be
traced in it, its existence was always momentary and self-war-
ranted. A man's life or soul borrowed its reality and imputed
wholeness from the intrinsic actuality of its successive parts;
existence was a perpetual re-birth, a travelling light to which
the past was lost and the future uncertain. The element of indetermination which James felt so strongly in this flood of existence was precisely the pulse of fresh unpredictable sensation,
summoning attention hither and thither to unexpected facts.
Apprehension in him being impressionistic—that was the age
of impressionism in painting too—and marvellously free from
intellectual assumptions or presumptions, he felt intensely the
fact of contingency, or the contingency of fact. This seemed to
me not merely a peculiarity of temperament in him, but a profound insight into existence, in its inmost irrational essence.
Existence, I learned to see, is intrinsically dispersed, seated in its
distributed moments, and arbitrary not only as a whole, but in the
character and place of each of its parts. Change the bits, and
you change the mosaic: nor can we count or limit the elements,
as in a little closed kaleidoscope, which may be shaken together
into the next picture. Many of them, such as pleasure and pain,
or the total picture itself, cannot possibly have pre-existed.

But, said I to myself, were these novelties for that reason
unconditioned? Was not sensation, by continually surprising
us, a continual warning to us of fatal conjunctions occurring
outside? And would not the same conjunctions, but for memory and habit, always produce the same surprises? Experience
of indetermination was no proof of indeterminism; and when

James proceeded to turn immediate experience into ultimate physics, his thought seemed to me to lose itself in words or in confused superstitions. Free will, a deep moral power contrary to a romantic indetermination in being, he endeavoured to pack into the bias of attention—the most temperamental of accidents. He insisted passionately on the efficacy of consciousness, and invoked Darwinian arguments for its utility—arguments which assumed that consciousness was a material engine absorbing and transmitting energy: so that it was no wonder that presently he doubted whether consciousness existed at all. He suggested a new physics or metaphysics in which the essences given in immediate experience should be deployed and hypostatised into the constituents of nature: but this pictorial cosmology had the disadvantage of abolishing the human imagination, with all the pathos and poetry of its animal status. James thus renounced that gift for literary psychology, that romantic insight, in which alone he excelled; and indeed his followers are without it. I pride myself on remaining a disciple of his earlier unsophisticated self, when he was an agnostic about the universe, but in his diagnosis of the heart an impulsive poet: a master in the art of recording or divining the lyric quality of experience as it actually came to him or to me.

Lyric experience and literary psychology, as I have learned to conceive them, are chapters in the life of one race of animals, in one corner of the natural world. But before relegating them to that modest station (which takes nothing away from their spiritual prerogatives) I was compelled to face the terrible problem which arises when, as in modern philosophy, literary psychology and lyric experience are made the fulcrum or the stuff of the universe. Has this experience any external conditions? If it has, are they knowable? And if it has not, on what principle are its qualities generated or its episodes distributed? Nay, how can literary psychology or universal experience have any seat save the present fancy of the psychologist or the historian? Although James had been bothered and confused by these questions, and Royce had enthroned his philosophy upon them, neither of these my principal teachers seemed to have come to clearness on the subject: it was only afterwards, when I read Fichte and Schopenhauer, that I began to see my way to a solution. We must oscillate between a radical transcendentalism, frankly reduced to a solipsism of the living moment, and a materialism posited as a presupposition of conventional sanity. There was no contradiction in joining together a scepticism which was not a dogmatic negation of anything and an animal faith which avowedly was a mere assumption in action and description. Yet such oscillation, if it was to be justified and rendered coherent, still demanded some understanding of two further points: what, starting from immediate experience, was the *causa cognoscendi* of the natural world; and what, starting from the natural world, was the *causa fiendi* of immediate experience?

On this second point (in spite of the speculations of my friend Strong) I have not seen much new light. I am constrained merely to register as a brute fact the emergence of consciousness in animal bodies. A psyche, or nucleus of hereditary organisation, gathers and governs these bodies, and at the same time breeds within them a dreaming, suffering, and watching mind. Such investigations as those of Fraser and of Freud have shown how rich and how mad a thing the mind is fundamentally, how pervasively it plays about animal life, and how remote its first and deepest intuitions are from any understanding of their true occasions. An interesting and consistent complement to these discoveries is furnished by behaviourism, which I heartily accept on its positive biological side: the hereditary life of the body, modified by accident or training, forms a closed cycle of habits and actions. Of this the mind is a concomitant spiritual expression, invisible, imponderable, and epiphenomenal, or, as I prefer to say, hypostatic: for in it the moving unities and tensions of animal life are synthesised on quite another plane of being, into actual intuitions and feelings. This spiritual fertility in living bodies is the most natural of things. It is unintelligible only as all existence, change, or genesis is unintelligible; but it might be better understood, that is, better assimilated to other natural miracles, if we understood better the life of matter everywhere, and that of its different aggregates.

On the other point raised by my naturalism, namely on the grounds of faith in the natural world, I have reached more positive conclusions. Criticism, I think, must first be invited to do its worst: nothing is more dangerous here than timidity or convention. A pure and radical transcendentalism will disclaim all knowledge of fact. Nature, history, the self become ghostly presences, mere notions of such things; and the being of these images becomes purely internal to them; they exist in no environing space or time; they possess no substance or hidden parts, but are all surface, all appearance. Such a being, or quality of being, I call an essence; and to the consideration of essences, composing of themselves an eternal and infinite realm, I have lately devoted much attention. To that sphere I transpose the familiar pictures painted by the senses, or by traditional science and religion. Taken as essences, all ideas are compatible and supplementary to one another, like the various arts of expression; it is possible to perceive, up to a certain point, the symbolic burden of each of them, and to profit by the spiritual criticism of experience which it may embody. In particular, I recognise this spiritual truth in the Neo-Platonic and Indian systems, without admitting their fabulous side: after all, it is an old maxim with me that many ideas may be convergent as poetry which would be divergent as dogmas. This applies, in quite another quarter, to that revolution in physics which is now loudly announced, sometimes as the bankruptcy of science, sometimes as the breakdown of materialism. This revolution becomes, in my view, simply a change in notation. Matter may be called gravity or an electric charge or a tension in an ether; mathematics may readjust its equations to more accurate observations; any fresh description of nature which may result will still be a product of human wit, like the Ptolemaic and the Newtonian systems, and nothing but an intellectual symbol for man's contacts with matter, in so far as they have gone or as he has become distinctly sensitive to them. The real matter, within him and without, will meantime continue to rejoice in its ancient ways, or to adopt new ones, and incidentally to create these successive notions of it in his head.

When all the data of immediate experience and all the constructions of thought have thus been purified and reduced to what they are intrinsically, that is, to eternal essences, by a sort of counterblast the sense of existence, of action, of ambushed reality everywhere about us, becomes all the clearer and more imperious. This assurance of the not-given is involved in action, in expectation, in fear, hope, or want: I call it animal faith. The object of this faith is the substantial energetic thing encountered in action, whatever this thing may be in itself; by moving, devouring, or transforming this thing I assure myself of its existence; and at the same time my respect for it becomes enlightened and proportionate to its definite powers. But throughout, for the description of it in fancy, I have only the essences which my senses or thought may evoke in its presence; these are my inevitable signs and names for that object. Thus the whole sensuous and intellectual furniture of the mind becomes a store whence I may fetch terms for the description of nature, and may compose the silly home-poetry in which I talk to myself about everything. All is a tale told, if not by an idiot, at least by a dreamer; but it is far from signifying nothing. Sensations are rapid dreams: perceptions are dreams sustained and developed at will; sciences are dreams abstracted, controlled, measured, and rendered scrupulously proportional to their occasions. Knowledge accordingly always remains a part of imagination in its terms and in its seat; yet by virtue of its origin and intent it becomes a memorial and a guide to the fortunes of man in nature.

In the foregoing I have said nothing about my sentiments concerning æsthetics or the fine arts; yet I have devoted two volumes to those subjects, and I believe that to some people my whole philosophy seems to be little but rhetoric or prose poetry. I must frankly confess that I have written some verses; and at one time I had thoughts of becoming an architect or even a painter. The decorative and poetic aspects of art and nature have always fascinated me and held my attention above everything else. But in philosophy I recognise no separable thing called æsthetics; and what has gone by the name of the philosophy of art, like the so-called philosophy of history, seems to me sheer verbiage. There is in art nothing but manual knack and professional tradition on the practical side, and on the contemplative side pure intuition of essence, with the inevitable intellectual or luxurious pleasure which pure intuition involves. I can draw no distinction—save for academic programmes—between moral and æsthetic values: beauty, being a good, is a moral good; and the practice and enjoyment of art, like all practice and all enjoyment, fall within the sphere of morals—at least if by morals we understand moral economy and not moral superstition. On the other hand, the good, when actually realised and not merely pursued from afar, is a joy in the immediate; it is possessed with wonder and is in that sense æsthetic. Such pure joy when blind is called pleasure, when centred in some sensible image is called beauty, and when diffused over the thought of ulterior propitious things is called happiness, love, or religious rapture. But where all is manifest, as it is in intuition, classifications are pedantic. Harmony, which might be called an æsthetic principle, is also the principle of health, of justice, and of happiness. Every impulse, not the æsthetic mood alone, is innocent and irresponsible in its origin and precious in its own eyes; but every impulse or indulgence, including the æsthetic, is evil in its effect, when it renders harmony impossible in the general tenor of life, or produces in the soul division and ruin. There is no lack of folly in the arts; they are full of inertia and affectation and of what must seem ugliness to a cultivated taste; yet there is no need of bringing the catapult of criticism against it: indifference is enough. A society will breed the art which it is capable of, and which it deserves; but even in its own eyes this art will hardly be important or beautiful unless it engages deeply the resources of the soul. The arts may die of triviality, as they were born of enthusiasm. On the other hand, there will always be beauty, or a transport akin to the sense of beauty, in any high contemplative moment. And it is only in contemplative moments that life is truly vital, when routine gives place to intuition, and experience is synthesised and brought before the spirit in its sweep and truth. The intention of my philosophy has certainly been to attain, if possible, such wide intuitions, and to celebrate the emotions with which they fill the mind. If this object be æsthetic and merely poetical, well and good: but it is a poetry or æstheticism which shines by disillusion and is simply intent on the unvarnished truth.

II

The American Intellect

✌ Tradition and Practice*

At a moment like this, when some of you stand on the very mountain-top of youth, your traditional education spread out on one side beneath you, on the other the prospect of practical life, and when the rest of us also stand there with you, in thought and by force of sympathy,—it might not be unnatural for some wise man, who had descended long since into the plains, if he were a practical man and something of a reformer, to speak to you in the following manner: "My young friends; you may think you have completed your education; you are mistaken; you are going to begin it. What you have hitherto learned is verbal and, even if true in its way, is not understood by you in its real or human value. The first thing you will have to do is to forget it all, and to learn the alphabet of hard fact, and the arithmetic of practical forces. Your character, if you have acquired a good one, will help you in the world; but your learning and your budding ideas will fade year by year, crowded out by a new wisdom which as yet you know nothing of."

It is in some such way that a man schooled in affairs might perhaps address you; but being nothing but an academic person myself I may be excused if I put the matter somewhat differently. Life, after all, is made up of all its periods and the world of all its

* Commencement Address at the Seventy-first Commencement of Oberlin College; printed subsequently in *The Oberlin Alumni Magazine*, I, No. 1 (October, 1904), 4-14.

activities; and youth, too, has its ultimate moments. College is a
part of the world, containing in miniature almost all its problems,
and the world, if we use it intelligently, is nothing but a second
university, another school of friendship, labour, and thought. In
this half-hour in which I have the privilege of addressing you,
I should like to dwell on this affinity between education and life,
between tradition and practice. There is naturally a close connection between receiving something important from society
and the past and rendering back something useful to society
and to the future. You have heard a thousand times the demand
that education should be practical, that traditions should not
be insisted on and kept alive artificially, when they have no further function in actual life. You have also heard a thousand times,
I am sure, that a man's life should be one of service to the world,
that he should measure his own success by the degree in which
it enables him to help others. As I repeat these familiar maxims
I may seem to be turning a discourse, which presumably ought
to be festive, into a class-room lecture or a downright sermon.
But perhaps if we put those two commonplaces together we may
get a somewhat more speculative idea, one that may well serve
to light up the double vista greeting us on this occasion. This
idea is that while tradition is only valuable when it is helpful in
practice, practice itself is only valuable when it is fertile in tradition—that is, when it helps to create or bring to light something
ideal, which can be transmitted from man to man, and from generation to generation.

In the modern world, and especially in America, tradition and
practice appear in an anomalous relation. Both exist; both are
powerful and complicated; yet they are in a way separated.
Tradition flourishes almost unchallenged in the mind, while practice concerns itself chiefly with things material. The historical
ground for this anomaly is very clear: if we divide tradition into
three great streams—the literary, the religious, and the scientific
—only the last, the scientific or economic tradition, which is a
short tradition as yet, is native to our society: the other two come
to us from alien races and remote periods of history. They were
vital elements in civilizations which as a whole are dead; and
surviving, as they do, in ours, they have in them something ab-

stract and adventitious; we have to learn them like a foreign
tongue. They influence our life, rather than express it; they endure as traditions to which we may give ourselves up more or
less heartily; but the more we do so the more we seem to withdraw from practice and its suggestions, to the abstract mind and
its traditional lore. Here are two most remarkable facts—anoma-
lies if we compare them with what is the case in most nations,
and what must be the case with humanity at large—that our literary models are in dead and foreign languages, and that our
religion is one to which our ancestors had to be converted, and
which we need to be instructed in. Neither tradition is native;
neither flows inevitably and of itself from our contact with nature and the spontaneous reflections of our minds. Only the third
great stream of tradition—the scientific and economic—has
grown up in our race under conditions such as those we still live
in; and accordingly this third tradition hardly seems such; it
seems rather part and parcel of the constitution of things. But
science is a tradition, as government is: and if you or I had to
begin a survey of nature for ourselves we should never arrive
at a hundredth part of the knowledge needed to invent and construct a steam-engine, or to have our lives insured.

All tradition might conceivably be native in this same way.
When a child is born he begins at once to educate his senses; he
learns by groping to spell the external world and to attach
himself to whatever in it helps to awaken his instincts, and to satisfy them. He explores house and field; he makes experiments
in social intercourse, establishing his firm little allegiances and
enmities—to parents, playfellows, strangers, and dolls. If we
could imagine him growing up quite independently, yet shielded
from all dangers as yet too grave for him, he would soon have a
poetry, a science, and a morality of his own. Fantastic as these
would doubtless be in their form, they would all centre around
actual experience and somehow express it: his life, practical
and imaginative, would be all of a piece. So poets actually feel
the world. Convention has little power over them, either to impress on them useful things for which they do not care, or to
choke off their native insights. It was largely in this way that the
Greeks, that childlike and self-taught people, worked out their

myths and their science; so that both were beautiful and legitimate, and even true, in so far as experience could as yet avail to
control them.

What happens to our children, what happened to ourselves,
when we embarked in childhood on this great voyage of discovery? We were led aside—of course, to be instructed—but we were
led aside into regions not contiguous to what we could see or
appreciate; our souls were transplanted from their native soil and
bidden to bear fruits of very singular and alien grafting. I suspect
that much of what I have in mind may not have fallen to your
lot in the same aggravated form in which it fell to mine. Your
teachers have, in many ways, brought education nearer to experience; they have sought in kindergartens and in nature-stud-
ies, in manual and economic training, to develop what was present to your senses and lead up without break to activities which
were to be yours in future. It is a merit of Protestant Christianity
to solicit religion rather than to impose it. It knows how to
mould creeds to moral feeling, as this changes its emphasis, and
it strives to represent throughout an inner personal impulsion.
But suppose that these reforms had not taken place—and at best
they are only partial—what would have happened to the child
when he went to school and began to absorb tradition? He would
have been ushered into hearsay worlds, real perhaps in themselves, but coming to him in the guise of superfluous fictions.
These reports may find his imagination more or less receptive;
they may entice him, as fairy-tales do, and make him wish he
might wake up some fine morning in the world they describe;
but I am not sure that it is when they are most welcome that they
are most beneficial. Suppose he hears, as I did in my boyhood—
and very gladly too—that in this world which he had just begun
to spell out and find his place in, there is nothing really important; that to be dissatisfied here is only what is to be expected, for
he is a pilgrim and stranger; that the earth is a vale of tears; that
close above it, accessible at every turn, there is a supernatural
realm, where his true pleasures should live; that there he can
have his real friends and his real conversations; that there all
his fortunes are mysteriously prepared and will have their miraculous and incalculable issues; so that he begins to walk the earth
with a certain incredulity, and to translate its facts, as he meets

them, into his own mystical language, reading into them values directly contrary, possibly, to those which they ostensibly have. This new mystical life may offer a congenial fourth dimension for his fancy to spread in; in those supernatural vistas he may discover something kindly and good, a needful refuge from his impotence or loneliness in the real world. But what a struggle in his heart! What an oscillation there must be in his allegiance between this world, in which he cannot well play his part without taking it seriously, and the other world, which he has been drawn into by an incidental tradition! But this is only the beginning of his distraction; another tradition remains behind.

Scarcely, indeed, has he accustomed himself to his double life and learned to speak his two languages together in a way intelligible, at least to himself, when he is led into a third universe. He begins to study the history and literature, perhaps even the philosophy, of Greece and Rome. As most often happens, the boy is merely pestered with what to him is a blind labour, producing a formal sort of knowledge soon happily to be unloaded on an examination paper and forgotten: but if he is quick and imaginative, with some premonitions in him of what a pure humanity might be, he very likely feels attracted to those masterpieces, and falls in love with that civilization, ancient in date, but more than modern, where moral interests are concerned, by its enterprise and freedom. But these classic memories and suggestions cannot be connected in the student's mind either with his own experience or with his religious instruction. Those early heroes are not pictured as doing anything which he himself might do. Those poetic and rhetorical passions do not express his family life, his public duties, nor his private problems and destiny. All is a mere fairyland, a literary tradition about exotic and distant things, surely not uninteresting in themselves, eloquent, very likely, to his speculative mind, but out of all relation to his practical existence.

Such was not the situation out of which those masterpieces themselves first grew. They were the work of young people, like the American, but people who, unlike the American, had no conscious traditions reaching far behind their youth. They were native products, in every fibre expressions of human nature at first hand. Suppose a copy of Virgil, such as our school-children use, could reach the poet in whatever honourable limbo we may fancy his spirit to inhabit. Would he not be at a loss to understand how things could have come to such a pass among us that we should compel ourselves to study a dead language and to read hundreds of verses none of which can have a native ring in our ears? "Is it possible," he might ask, "that you pretend to form your taste and mind by reading poets in a foreign language? What profit can you find in so artificial an exercise? Is it that you value our religion? No. Rome and the world it conquered perished more than a thousand years ago, and the piety with which I tried to express, in myths which to you have lost all their sanctity, her origin and spirit, is not piety for you: it is archaeology. Have you, then, no poets of your own to recast my patriotism and wisdom, so dressed that you may relish them—for the high passion and dignity of my lines must have been lost with their music? One would think your nations to be without arts: yet if you were wholly barbarous, how could you know the value of culture or go to the extreme pains which so tortured and sterile an education must involve? We Romans, to be sure, used to study Greek; but it was then a living tongue, spoken widely in our own dominions: we had nurses and native masters to teach it to us; we learned to speak it glibly, and found it afterwards useful when we became praetors and proconsuls in the East. Besides, we and the Greeks were kindred peoples, with a similar religion and polity, which in many ways had been developed in Greece more perfectly than in Latium, so that to us Greek literature was something better than native and more truly appealing—it was ideal. But you, to my astonishment, seem to sacrifice for a glimpse of unattainable excellence, and philosophies which you cannot apply to your affairs, whatever comfort, strength, and solid religion a homely education might bring. The Gauls and Germans, the Iberians and Britons of my day, though rude and unhappy, had an honest, patriotic pride which I cannot discover in you. They despised our traditions, so long as they defied our arms. No one among them, unless he wished to flatter Rome and was at heart a traitor, would have given his sons my poems to read. How comes it that your peoples, who have nothing to fear from our power, are still enslaved by our minds?"

What could we say to Virgil if he spoke to us in this way (as

in all seriousness I believe he would) and what apology could we
offer for the fact that we still read him? We should have to explain to him the whole riddle of our history: we should have to
confess that only our young scientific and economic tradition
is the fruit of our own genius: that for high things in literature
and religion we still lean upon antiquity, sometimes, as in religion, venturing to adapt that tradition to our needs, and seeking to
apply it in practice, sometimes, as in literature, almost abandoning the attempt to continue what we accept from the past, but
keeping that past mummified and lifeless, to be the object of a
contemplation called philology. And when he protested again
at such behavior on our part, and threatened to hurl the word
barbarous at us once more, not for our science and machinery,
which he would immensely respect, but for our philology and
our dependence on dead tradition—we should have to add this
further explanation. We do not cling to tradition because it is
old; it is not the barbarian's conservatism that makes us worship
something conventional apart from ideal uses which it may have
had in our own day. No: it is our incapacity so to exhaust and
digest experience for ourselves as to rediscover what is eternally
true in those traditions, that in them which is still vital in the
world. We are in too great haste to understand ourselves, hence
we must take for self-expression, and as a substitute for a mastery
of experience which we dare not attempt, the self-expression
and mastery of ancient, calmer spirits: we must let them still
speak for us, because they still speak for us better than we are
able to speak for ourselves. Virgil would be less surprised that we
puzzle over his pages, if he knew the character of our own literature. Even seen through a veil, his world is clearer and more
beautiful than ours. Even disfigured by our pedantic approach
to it, his mind seems so majestic, exquisite, and true, that we
can find nothing better for a model. His verses, sputtered in a
barbarous mouth, are still our standard of excellence: his country's ruins are our best type of greatness: his religion, though not
sacred to us as to him, remains the mould of our fancy, without
which thought would lose half its symbols and nature half her
amenity.

If our traditions, then, are in any way burdensome, if we are
obliged to lean on them too much, it is only because we have not

learned to draw tradition enough from our own practice. It is
because the present yields so little as yet to the spirit, that the
spirit looks behind to those heroic nations which knew how to
make all things pay tribute to the mind. It was a smaller world,
a quieter world, perhaps, that they were able to master: it
brought them, for that very reason, more quickly to ultimate
things. And for that reason, too, it is not possible for us to profit
by their dominion directly. The principle of it we can adopt and
reapply: the solution they gave is, in its form, inapplicable to
us. Therefore, when we adopt it literally, it is apt to remain in the
region of mere words. This, as it seems to me, is the great defect
of our traditional education: it is a verbal education. And this is
not because the objects with which our literature deals—be it
sacred or profane—were themselves empty: no thought is further
from my mind than that. The subject matter in both cases was
living, it was momentous, it was engrossing; so engrossing, momentous, and living, that it made up, in each case, a whole world,
with its own morality and civilization, with its own complete philosophy. But as neither of those worlds is ours, the literatures that
express them do not educate us for our own life. They annex
something to it; but this something is apt to remain a dead letter, seeing that we should have to transport ourselves out of our
age and clime, if we were really to accept it practically and intelligently.

And what happens? We agitate ourselves amid these influences
for a few years, while our verbal education is going on; but grad-
uation comes: the real and sunlit world beckons us to begin an
education through action. This is the point you have reached to-
day; and many of you, I am sure, without any conscious dissatisfaction with what has gone before, look forward to the change
with a high emotion, with the sense of power now for the first
time to be really exerted, and real forces now for the first time
to be met. You are eager to be done with tradition: it is practice
you feel that will free your souls. Such a premonition cannot well
be deceptive. It may be frustrated by chance in one or another
of you, for in the most brilliant victories many fall by the way;
but it can hardly be frustrated on the whole for a race and a generation that feels it distinctly. Much less can it be frustrated in
America, where an altogether unprecedented career is open to

human effort. This country has had the privilege of beginning with all the advantages of tradition and with none of its trammels. The advantages were a seasoned moral character, a religion free from gross superstition, possessed of the various practical arts and crafts current in Europe, and an almost empty continent in the temperate zone. Under such conditions practice ought to yield fruit quickly, and not to be much misinterpreted by the traditions to which it gives rise. Such traditions have in fact arisen —first in politics, and industry. New and appropriate moulds have been given to political and industrial life which not only secure efficiency but which engross intellect and inspire emotion. American life, every one has heard, has extraordinary intensity; it goes at a great rate. This is not due, I should say, to any particular urgency in the object pursued. Other nations have more pressing motives to bestir themselves than America has; and it is observable that not all the new nations, in either hemisphere, are energetic. This energy can hardly spring either from unusually intolerable conditions which people wish to overcome, nor from unusually important objects which they wish to attain. It springs, I should venture to say, from the harmony which subsists between the task and the spirit, between the mind's vitality and the forms which, in America, political and industrial tradition has taken on. It is sometimes said that the ruling passion in America is the love of money. That seems to me a complete mistake. The ruling passion is the love of *business*, which is something quite different. The lover of money would be jealous of it; he would spend it carefully, he would study to get out of it the most he could. But the lover of business, when he is successful, does not much change his way of living, he does not think out what further advantages he can get out of his success. His joy is in that business itself and in its further operation, in making it greater and better organized and a mightier engine in the general life. The adventitious personal profit in it is the last thing he thinks of, the last thing he is skillful in bringing about; and the same zeal and intensity is applied in managing a college, or a public office, or a naval establishment, as is lavished on private business, for it is not a motive of personal gain that stimulates to such exertions. It is the absorbing, satisfying character of the activities themselves: it is the art, the happiness, the greatness of them. So that in beginning life in such a society, which has developed a native and vital tradition out of its practice, you have good reason to feel that your spirit will be freed, that you will begin to realize a part of what you are living for.

At the same time, these congenial and ideal activities into which you will pass—what is called business, in the widest sense of the word—will still fail to contain all that would be ideal and congenial, it will leave certain powers in you unexercised, powers which in college, perhaps, you once felt you possessed and had begun to exercise. Your business, even if it be the business of teaching or of managing a college, will, as things now stand, look chiefly to material results. The question will be how many buildings you can put up, how many graduates you can turn out, how many books you can publish, and how many athletic victories you can score. To gain material results of this sort is itself an ideal object: without a material basis nothing spiritual can exist, or can reach expression; but the material basis is a basis only, as the body is in personal life, and when that has been rendered vigorous and healthy, the question still remains what further functions you are to give to your soul. There is, as the ancients said, a vegetative soul: it was very profound in them to see that vegetation also is spiritual, and that to perfect material instruments is already to embody an ideal. But the vegetative soul, in man, is only a background and a potentiality: the moral and intellectual functions must be superposed upon it. Will your business life, as you are likely to find it, supply adequately these moral and intellectual functions? Will you never have a pause, as for a Sabbath, and turn a speculative eye upon regions distant and serene? Will you not long sometimes for a holiday in the country, for solitude, for abstraction: thinking in that way to revert to something deeper and higher than your ordinary thoughts? Probably you will: and it is then that at church or in your library or in the woods, you will call back those sacred and remote traditions into which you were initiated in your youth: you will feel the need of them, and sigh, perhaps, for their painted worlds. In that case one thing will be plain: the tradition grounded on your daily practice and embodied there—the scientific, economic, political tradition of our age—will not have sufficed for your daily life. You will need something more, and the question is how you are going to get it.

And at this point, in bringing my discourse to a head, there is one thought I would urge upon you. You will never solve the problem satisfactorily or in a stable manner, you will never contribute to a truly sacred human tradition, so long as you are content to append your higher ideals, like postscripts, to your life. I once had a friend who feeling that there might be something narrow in his profession of glass-blower, thought he would go to Europe, as he expressed it, to pick up culture in the galleries. He went; but I could observe no conspicuous culture sticking to him on his return, and he is now blowing glass without it. Even if he had acquired it, it would have been a private possession, that would have gone with him to his grave. Suppose instead he had stayed at home and spent his savings in buying books about glassware, and making experiments in more beautiful and appropriate forms to be given to glasses and bowls; he would have become a really cultivated man, one whose conversation any one would have been glad to listen to, and he would have established a better tradition in his art, one that might have made a difference for generations. Many a man, to take another example, absorbed in business and carrying it on in total abstraction from human feeling, may be most affectionate at home: he makes up to himself there for the inhumanity which he shows to the world. To the world, however, he never makes it up. His affectionate feelings are his self-indulgence, his self-deception: out of his public practice there flows no sweeter or kindlier tradition. It is time, perhaps, that by way of exception some great employer should deny himself a home and a family, as the monks did; that he should live among his workmen, in sight of the factory, so that his humanity might have a chance to spread itself out there, to beautify the places where life is at white heat; and such an employer, when his friends asked him where he lived and what was his family, might point like a sort of a masculine Cornelia to the happier colony about him and say: "These are my children." The principle is the same which the Apostle expresses when he says that whether we eat or drink we should do it for the glory of God: and while a certain alternation and

rhythm is necessary in human life, and we must intensify our
religion at certain moments, giving it more marked expression
on some days and on some occasions than on others, that is merely
a physical necessity: it is not the ideal of religion that it should be
a thing apart and an escapade, as it were, from existence. Nor is
that the ideal of any art; yet there are some people so ill-educated
that when they have something to say, say it in the most imperfect and bungling fashion, and then, when their matter is exhausted, put in a rhetorical peroration, by way of showing that
they too can be eloquent if they choose. But they prove the
opposite, for their mouthings are as little eloquent as their crudi-
ties were; since eloquence does not consist in displaying a vocabulary when there is nothing to say. Eloquence is rather the essential rounding out of a thought, as you bring clearly to light the
facts and emotions that justify it. You cannot be eloquent unless
you are intelligent, and if you seem so, it will be only to those
who are unintelligent themselves. Eloquence and art, religion
and kindness, do not flourish in water-tight compartments: there
needs to be a vital circulation among them if any of them is
really to live.

It would therefore be a mere expedient, a sop thrown to
Cerberus, if you appended one or more ideal interests to your
practical life. In so far as you do so, you merely chill your practice, making it vulgar, unfruitful in liberal traditions, while at the
same time you keep your ideality visionary and thin. The remedy, which it will take centuries to make thoroughly efficacious,
but which every one may apply in a measure for himself, is simply to deepen practical life, to make it express all its possible affinities, all its latent demands. Were that done, we should find ourselves in unexpected and spontaneous harmony with the traditions which we might seem to have disregarded. For those ancient
and alien traditions have survived because they express, each in
its language, something which has a meaning at all times, something essentially human. Had our humanity, under its own conditions, found a full expression, it would have repeated unawares
those accepted truths. If we then read Virgil, having come round
to him in the natural development of our interest for all things
human, we should love him for celebrating so loyally things also
interesting to us: agriculture, and its cosmic emotions; nationality,

with its deep springs and sacred responsibilities. For that is what Virgil is talking about: that is what Virgil is, not a labyrinth of syntax and prosody. In the same way our religious traditions would recover their rights, in the measure in which we found them prophetic of our deepest necessities. All traditions have been founded on practice: in practice the most ideal of them regain their authority, when practice really deals with reality, and faces the world squarely, in the interests of the whole soul. To bring the whole soul to expression is what all civilization is after. We must therefore be patient, for the task is long; but the fields are always white for the harvest, and the yield cannot be insignificant when labourers go forth into the harvest with the high and diligent spirit which we divine in you.

The Genteel Tradition in American Philosophy*

Ladies and Gentlemen,— The privilege of addressing you to-day is very welcome to me, not merely for the honour of it, which is great, nor for the pleasures of travel, which are many, when it is California that one is visiting for the first time, but also because there is something I have long wanted to say which this occasion seems particularly favourable for saying. America is still a young country, and this part of it is especially so; and it would have been nothing extraordinary if, in this young country, material preoccupations had altogether absorbed people's minds, and they had been too much engrossed in living to reflect upon life, or to have any philosophy. The opposite, however, is the case. Not only have you already found time to philosophise in California, as your society proves, but the eastern colonists from the very beginning were a sophisticated race. As much as in clearing the land and fighting the Indians they were occupied, as they expressed it, in wrestling with the Lord. The country was new, but the race was tried, chastened, and full of solemn memories. It was an old wine in new bottles; and America did not have to wait for its present universities, with their departments of academic philosophy, in order to possess a living philosophy—to have a distinct vision of the universe and definite convictions about human destiny.

* From *Winds of Doctrine: Studies in Contemporary Opinion* (New York: Charles Scribner's Sons, 1913).

Now this situation is a singular and remarkable one, and has many consequences, not all of which are equally fortunate. America is a young country with an old mentality: it has enjoyed the advantages of a child carefully brought up and thoroughly indoctrinated; it has been a wise child. But a wise child, an old head on young shoulders, always has a comic and an unpromising side. The wisdom is a little thin and verbal, not aware of its full meaning and grounds; and physical and emotional growth may be stunted by it, or even deranged. Or when the child is too vigorous for that, he will develop a fresh mentality of his own, out of his observations and actual instincts; and this fresh mentality will interfere with the traditional mentality, and tend to reduce it to something perfunctory, conventional, and perhaps secretly despised. A philosophy is not genuine unless it inspires and expresses the life of those who cherish it. I do not think the hereditary philosophy of America has done much to atrophy the natural activities of the inhabitants; the wise child has not missed the joys of youth or of manhood; but what has happened is that the hereditary philosophy has grown stale, and that the academic philosophy afterwards developed has caught the stale odour from it. America is not simply, as I said a moment ago, a young country with an old mentality: it is a country with two mentalities, one a survival of the beliefs and standards of the fathers, the other an expression of the instincts, practice, and discoveries of the younger generations. In all the higher things of the mind— in religion, in literature, in the moral emotions—it is the hereditary spirit that still prevails, so much so that Mr. Bernard Shaw finds that America is a hundred years behind the times. The truth is that one-half of the American mind, that not occupied intensely in practical affairs, has remained, I will not say high-and-dry, but slightly becalmed; it has floated gently in the backwater, while, alongside, in invention and industry and social organisation, the other half of the mind was leaping down a sort of Niagara Rapids. This division may be found symbolised in American architecture: a neat reproduction of the colonial mansion—with some modern comforts introduced surreptitiously—stands beside the sky-scraper. The American Will inhabits the sky-scraper; the American Intellect inhabits the colonial mansion. The one is the sphere of the American man; the other, at

least predominantly, of the American woman. The one is all
aggressive enterprise; the other is all genteel tradition.

Now, with your permission, I should like to analyse more
fully how this interesting situation has arisen, how it is qualified,
and whither it tends. And in the first place we should remember
what, precisely, that philosophy was which the first settlers
brought with them into the country. In strictness there was
more than one; but we may confine our attention to what I will
call Calvinism, since it is on this that the current academic philosophy has been grafted. I do not mean exactly the Calvinism of
Calvin, or even of Jonathan Edwards; for in their systems there
was much that was not pure philosophy, but rather faith in the
externals and history of revelation. Jewish and Christian revelation was interpreted by these men, however, in the spirit of a
particular philosophy, which might have arisen under any sky,
and been associated with any other religion as well as with Protestant Christianity. In fact, the philosophical principle of Calvinism
appears also in the Koran, in Spinoza, and in Cardinal Newman;
and persons with no very distinctive Christian belief, like Carlyle
or like Professor Royce, may be nevertheless, philosophically,
perfect Calvinists. Calvinism, taken in this sense, is an expression
of the agonised conscience. It is a view of the world which an
agonised conscience readily embraces, if it takes itself seriously,
as, being agonised, of course it must. Calvinism, essentially, asserts three things: that sin exists, that sin is punished, and that it is
beautiful that sin should exist to be punished. The heart of the
Calvinist is therefore divided between tragic concern at his own
miserable condition, and tragic exultation about the universe at
large. He oscillates between a profound abasement and a paradoxical elation of the spirit. To be a Calvinist philosophically
is to feel a fierce pleasure in the existence of misery, especially
of one's own, in that this misery seems to manifest the fact that
the Absolute is irresponsible or infinite or holy. Human nature,
it feels, is totally depraved: to have the instincts and motives that
we necessarily have is a great scandal, and we must suffer for it;
but that scandal is requisite, since otherwise the serious importance of being as we ought to be would not have been vindi-
cated.

To those of us who have not an agonised conscience this system may seem fantastic and even unintelligible; yet it is logically and intently thought out from its emotional premises. It can take permanent possession of a deep mind here and there, and under certain conditions it can become epidemic. Imagine, for instance, a small nation with an intense vitality, but on the verge of ruin, ecstatic and distressful, having a strict and minute code of laws, that paints life in sharp and violent chiaroscuro, all pure righteousness and black abominations, and exaggerating the consequences of both perhaps to infinity. Such a people were the Jews after the exile, and again the early Protestants. If such a people is philosophical at all, it will not improbably be Calvinistic. Even in the early American communities many of these conditions were fulfilled. The nation was small and isolated; it lived under pressure and constant trial; it was acquainted with but a small range of goods and evils. Vigilance over conduct and an absolute demand for personal integrity were not merely traditional things, but things that practical sages, like Franklin and Washington, recommended to their countrymen, because they were virtues that justified themselves visibly by their fruits. But soon these happy results themselves helped to relax the pressure of external circumstances, and indirectly the pressure of the agonised conscience within. The nation became numerous; it ceased to be either ecstatic or distressful; the high social morality which on the whole it preserved took another colour; people remained honest and helpful out of good sense and good will rather than out of scrupulous adherence to any fixed principles. They retained their instinct for order, and often created order with surprising quickness; but the sanctity of law, to be obeyed for its own sake, began to escape them; it seemed too unpractical a notion, and not quite serious. In fact, the second and native-born American mentality began to take shape. The sense of sin totally evaporated. Nature, in the words of Emerson, was all beauty and commodity; and while operating on it laboriously, and drawing quick returns, the American began to drink in inspiration from it æsthetically. At the same time, in so broad a continent, he had elbow-room. His neighbours helped more than they hindered him; he wished their number to increase. Good will became the great American virtue; and a passion arose for counting heads, and square miles, and cubic feet, and minutes saved—as if there had been anything to save them for. How strange to the American now that saying of Jonathan Edwards, that men are naturally God's enemies! Yet that is an axiom to any intelligent Calvinist, though the words he uses may be different. If you told the modern American that he is totally depraved, he would think you were joking, as he himself usually is. He is convinced that he always has been, and always will be, victorious and blameless.

Calvinism thus lost its basis in American life. Some emotional natures, indeed, reverted in their religious revivals or private searchings of heart to the sources of the tradition; for any of the radical points of view in philosophy may cease to be prevalent, but none can cease to be possible. Other natures, more sensitive to the moral and literary influences of the world, preferred to abandon parts of their philosophy, hoping thus to reduce the distance which should separate the remainder from real life.

Meantime, if anybody arose with a special sensibility or a technical genius, he was in great straits; not being fed sufficiently by the world, he was driven in upon his own resources. The three American writers whose personal endowment was perhaps the finest—Poe, Hawthorne, and Emerson—had all a certain starved and abstract quality. They could not retail the genteel tradition; they were too keen, too perceptive, and too independent for that. But life offered them little digestible material, nor were they naturally voracious. They were fastidious, and under the circumstances they were starved. Emerson, to be sure, fed on books. There was a great catholicity in his reading; and he showed a fine tact in his comments, and in his way of appropriating what he read. But he read transcendentally, not historically, to learn what he himself felt, not what others might have felt before him. And to feed on books, for a philosopher or a poet, is still to starve. Books can help him to acquire form, or to avoid pitfalls; they cannot supply him with substance, if he is to have any. Therefore the genius of Poe and Hawthorne, and even of Emerson, was employed on a sort of inner play, or digestion of vacancy. It was a refined labour, but it was in danger of being morbid, or tinkling, or self-indulgent. It was a play of intra-mental rhymes. Their mind was like an old music-box, full of tender echoes and quaint fancies. These fancies expressed their personal genius sincerely, as dreams may; but they were arbitrary fancies in comparison with what a real observer would have said in the premises. Their manner, in a word, was subjective. In their own persons they escaped the mediocrity of the genteel tradition, but they supplied nothing to supplant it in other minds.

The churches, likewise, although they modified their spirit, had no philosophy to offer save a new emphasis on parts of what Calvinism contained. The theology of Calvin, we must remember, had much in it besides philosophical Calvinism. A Christian tenderness, and a hope of grace for the individual, came to mitigate its sardonic optimism; and it was these evangelical elements that the Calvinistic churches now emphasised, seldom and with blushes referring to hell-fire or infant damnation. Yet philosophic Calvinism, with a theory of life that would perfectly justify hell-fire and infant damnation if they happened to exist, still dominates the traditional metaphysics. It is an ingredient, and the decisive ingredient, in what calls itself idealism. But in order to see just what part Calvinism plays in current idealism, it will be necessary to distinguish the other chief element in that complex system, namely, transcendentalism.

Transcendentalism is the philosophy which the romantic era produced in Germany, and independently, I believe, in America also. Transcendentalism proper, like romanticism, is not any particular set of dogmas about what things exist; it is not a system of the universe regarded as a fact, or as a collection of facts. It is a method, a point of view, from which any world, no matter what it might contain, could be approached by a self-conscious observer. Transcendentalism is systematic subjectivism. It studies the perspectives of knowledge as they radiate from the self; it is a plan of those avenues of inference by which our ideas of things must be reached, if they are to afford any systematic or distant vistas. In other words, transcendentalism is the critical logic of science. Knowledge, it says, has a station, as in a watchtower; it is always seated here and now, in the self of the moment. The past and the future, things inferred and things conceived, lie around it, painted as upon a panorama. They cannot be lighted up save by some centrifugal ray of attention and present interest, by some active operation of the mind.

This is hardly the occasion for developing or explaining this delicate insight; suffice it to say, lest you should think later that I

disparage transcendentalism, that as a method I regard it as correct and, when once suggested, unforgettable. I regard it as
the chief contribution made in modern times to speculation. But
it is a method only, an attitude we may always assume if we
like and that will always be legitimate. It is no answer, and involves no particular answer, to the question: What exists; in what
order is what exists produced; what is to exist in the future? This
question must be answered by observing the object, and tracing
humbly the movement of the object. It cannot be answered at
all by harping on the fact that this object, if discovered, must be
discovered by somebody, and by somebody who has an interest
in discovering it. Yet the Germans who first gained the full transcendental insight were romantic people; they were more or less
frankly poets; they were colossal egotists, and wished to make
not only their own knowledge but the whole universe centre
about themselves. And full as they were of their romantic isolation and romantic liberty, it occurred to them to imagine that all
reality might be a transcendental self and a romantic dreamer
like themselves; nay, that it might be just their own transcendental self and their own romantic dreams extended indefinitely.
Transcendental logic, the method of discovery for the mind, was
to become also the method of evolution in nature and history.
Transcendental method, so abused, produced transcendental
myth. A conscientious critique of knowledge was turned into a
sham system of nature. We must therefore distinguish sharply
the transcendental grammar of the intellect, which is significant
and potentially correct, from the various transcendental systems of the universe, which are chimeras.

In both its parts, however, transcendentalism had much to recommend it to American philosophers, for the transcendental
method appealed to the individualistic and revolutionary temper of their youth, while transcendental myths enabled them to
find a new status for their inherited theology, and to give what
parts of it they cared to preserve some semblance of philosophical backing. This last was the use to which the transcendental
method was put by Kant himself, who first brought it into
vogue, before the terrible weapon had got out of hand, and become the instrument of pure romanticism. Kant came, he himself
said, to remove knowledge in order to make room for faith,

which in his case meant faith in Calvinism. In other words, he applied the transcendental method to matters of fact, reducing them thereby to human ideas, in order to give to the Calvinistic postulates of conscience a metaphysical validity. For Kant had a genteel tradition of his own, which he wished to remove to a place of safety, feeling that the empirical world had become too hot for it; and this place of safety was the region of transcendental myth. I need hardly say how perfectly this expedient suited the needs of philosophers in America, and it is no accident if the influence of Kant soon became dominant here. To embrace this philosophy was regarded as a sign of profound metaphysical insight, although the most mediocre minds found no difficulty in embracing it. In truth it was a sign of having been brought up in the genteel tradition, of feeling it weak, and of wishing to save it.

But the transcendental method, in its way, was also sympathetic to the American mind. It embodied, in a radical form, the spirit of Protestantism as distinguished from its inherited doctrines; it was autonomous, undismayed, calmly revolutionary; it felt that Will was deeper than Intellect; it focussed everything here and now, and asked all things to show their credentials at the bar of the young self, and to prove their value for this latest born moment. These things are truly American; they would be characteristic of any young society with a keen and discursive intelligence, and they are strikingly exemplified in the thought and in the person of Emerson. They constitute what he called self-trust. Self-trust, like other transcendental attitudes, may be expressed in metaphysical fables. The romantic spirit may imagine itself to be an absolute force, evoking and moulding the plastic world to express its varying moods. But for a pioneer who is actually a world-builder this metaphysical illusion has a partial warrant in historical fact; far more warrant than it could boast of in the fixed and articulated society of Europe, among the moonstruck rebels and sulking poets of the romantic era. Emerson was a shrewd Yankee, by instinct on the winning side; he was a cheery, child-like soul, impervious to the evidence of evil, as of everything that it did not suit his transcendental individuality to appreciate or to notice. More, perhaps, than anybody that has ever lived, he practised the transcendental method in all its purity. He had no system. He opened his eyes on the world ev-

ery morning with a fresh sincerity, marking how things seemed
to him then, or what they suggested to his spontaneous fancy.
This fancy, for being spontaneous, was not always novel; it was
guided by the habits and training of his mind, which were those
of a preacher. Yet he never insisted on his notions so as to turn
them into settled dogmas; he felt in his bones that they were
myths. Sometimes, indeed, the bad example of other transcendentalists, less true than he to their method, or the pressing
questions of unintelligent people, or the instinct we all have to
think our ideas final, led him to the very verge of system-making;
but he stopped short. Had he made a system out of his notion
of compensation, or the over-soul, or spiritual laws, the result
would have been as thin and forced as it is in other transcendental systems. But he coveted truth; and he returned to experience, to history, to poetry, to the natural science of his day, for
new starting-points and hints toward fresh transcendental mus-
ings.

To covet truth is a very distinguished passion. Every philosopher says he is pursuing the truth, but this is seldom the case. As
Mr. Bertrand Russell has observed, one reason why philosophers often fail to reach the truth is that often they do not desire
to reach it. Those who are genuinely concerned in discovering
what happens to be true are rather the men of science, the naturalists, the historians; and ordinarily they discover it, according
to their lights. The truths they find are never complete, and are
not always important; but they are integral parts of the truth,
facts and circumstances that help to fill in the picture, and that no
later interpretation can invalidate or afford to contradict. But
professional philosophers are usually only apologists: that is,
they are absorbed in defending some vested illusion or some eloquent idea. Like lawyers or detectives, they study the case for
which they are retained, to see how much evidence or semblance
of evidence they can gather for the defence, and how much prejudice they can raise against the witnesses for the prosecution;
for they know they are defending prisoners suspected by the
world, and perhaps by their own good sense, of falsification.
They do not covet truth, but victory and the dispelling of their
own doubts. What they defend is some system, that is, some view
about the totality of things, of which men are actually ignorant.

No system would have ever been framed if people had been simply interested in knowing what is true, whatever it may be. What produces systems is the interest in maintaining against all comers that some favourite or inherited idea of ours is sufficient and right. A system may contain an account of many things which, in detail, are true enough; but as a system, covering infinite possibilities that neither our experience nor our logic can prejudge, it must be a work of imagination and a piece of human soliloquy. It may be expressive of human experience, it may be poetical; but how should any one who really coveted truth suppose that it was true?

Emerson had no system; and his coveting truth had another exceptional consequence: he was detached, unworldly, contemplative. When he came out of the conventicle or the reform meeting, or out of the rapturous close atmosphere of the lecture-room, he heard Nature whispering to him: "Why so hot, little sir?" No doubt the spirit or energy of the world is what is acting in us, as the sea is what rises in every little wave; but it passes through us, and cry out as we may, it will move on. Our privilege is to have perceived it as it moves. Our dignity is not in what we do, but in what we understand. The whole world is doing things. We are turning in that vortex; yet within us is silent observation, the speculative eye before which all passes, which bridges the distances and compares the combatants. On this side of his genius Emerson broke away from all conditions of age or country and represented nothing except intelligence itself.

There was another element in Emerson, curiously combined with transcendentalism, namely, his love and respect for Nature. Nature, for the transcendentalist, is precious because it is his own work, a mirror in which he looks at himself and says (like a poet relishing his own verses), "What a genius I am! Who would have thought there was such stuff in me?" And the philosophical egotist finds in his doctrine a ready explanation of whatever beauty and commodity Nature actually has. No wonder, he says to himself, that Nature is sympathetic, since I made it. And such a view, one-sided and even fatuous as it may be, undoubtedly sharpens the vision of a poet and a moralist to all that is inspiring and symbolic in the natural world. Emerson was particularly ingenious and clear-sighted in feeling the spiritual uses of fellow-

ship with the elements. This is something in which all Teutonic
poetry is rich and which forms, I think, the most genuine and
spontaneous part of modern taste, and especially of American
taste. Just as some people are naturally enthralled and refreshed
by music, so others are by landscape. Music and landscape make
up the spiritual resources of those who cannot or dare not express
their unfulfilled ideals in words. Serious poetry, profound religion (Calvinism, for instance), are the joys of an unhappiness
that confesses itself; but when a genteel tradition forbids people
to confess that they are unhappy, serious poetry and profound
religion are closed to them by that; and since human life, in its
depths, cannot then express itself openly, imagination is driven
for comfort into abstract arts, where human circumstances are
lost sight of, and human problems dissolve in a purer medium.
The pressure of care is thus relieved, without its quietus being
found in intelligence. To understand oneself is the classic form
of consolation; to elude oneself is the romantic. In the presence
of music or landscape human experience eludes itself; and thus
romanticism is the bond between transcendental and naturalistic
sentiment. The winds and clouds come to minister to the solitary
ego.

Have there been, we may ask, any successful efforts to escape
from the genteel tradition, and to express something worth expressing behind its back? This might well not have occurred as
yet; but America is so precocious, it has been trained by the
genteel tradition to be so wise for its years, that some indications
of a truly native philosophy and poetry are already to be found.
I might mention the humourists, of whom you here in California
have had your share. The humourists, however, only half escape
the genteel tradition; their humour would lose its savour if they
had wholly escaped it. They point to what contradicts it in the
facts; but not in order to abandon the genteel tradition, for they
have nothing solid to put in its place. When they point out
how ill many facts fit into it, they do not clearly conceive that
this militates against the standard, but think it a funny perversity
in the facts. Of course, did they earnestly respect the genteel
tradition, such an incongruity would seem to them sad, rather
than ludicrous. Perhaps the prevalence of humour in America,
in and out of season, may be taken as one more evidence that

the genteel tradition is present pervasively, but everywhere weak. Similarly in Italy, during the Renaissance, the Catholic tradition could not be banished from the intellect, since there was nothing articulate to take its place; yet its hold on the heart was singularly relaxed. The consequence was that humourists could regale theselves with the foibles of monks and of cardinals, with the credulity of fools, and the bogus miracles of the saints; not intending to deny the theory of the church, but caring for it so little at heart that they could find it infinitely amusing that it should be contradicted in men's lives and that no harm should come of it. So when Mark Twain says, "I was born of poor but dishonest parents," the humour depends on the parody of the genteel Anglo-Saxon convention that it is disreputable to be poor; but to hint at the hollowness of it would not be amusing if it did not remain at bottom one's habitual conviction.

The one American writer who has left the genteel tradition entirely behind is perhaps Walt Whitman. For this reason educated Americans find him rather an unpalatable person, who they sincerely protest ought not to be taken for a representative of their culture; and he certainly should not, because their culture is so genteel and traditional. But the foreigner may sometimes think otherwise, since he is looking for what may have arisen in America to express, not the polite and conventional American mind, but the spirit and the inarticulate principles that animate the community, on which its own genteel mentality seems to sit rather lightly. When the foreigner opens the pages of Walt Whitman, he thinks that he has come at last upon something representative and original. In Walt Whitman democracy is carried into psychology and morals. The various sights, moods, and emotions are given each one vote; they are declared to be all free and equal, and the innumerable commonplace moments of life are suffered to speak like the others. Those moments formerly reputed great are not excluded, but they are made to march in the ranks with their companions—plain foot-soldiers and servants of the hour. Nor does the refusal to discriminate stop there; we must carry our principle further down, to the animals, to inanimate nature, to the cosmos as a whole. Whitman became a pantheist; but his pantheism, unlike that of the Stoics and of Spinoza, was unintellectual, lazy, and self-indulgent; for he simply felt jovially that everything real was good enough, and that he was good enough himself. In him Bohemia rebelled against the genteel tradition; but the reconstruction that alone can justify revolution did not ensue. His attitude, in principle, was utterly disintegrating; his poetic genius fell back to the lowest level, perhaps, to which it is possible for poetic genius to fall. He reduced his imagination to a passive sensorium for the registering of impressions. No element of construction remained in it, and therefore no element of penetration. But his scope was wide; and his lazy, desultory apprehension was poetical. His work, for the very reason that it is so rudimentary, contains a beginning, or rather many beginnings, that might possibly grow into a noble moral imagination, a worthy filling for the human mind. An American in the nineteenth century who completely disregarded the genteel tradition could hardly have done more.

But there is another distinguished man, lately lost to this country, who has given some rude shocks to this tradition and who, as much as Whitman, may be regarded as representing the genuine, the long silent American mind—I mean William James. He and his brother Henry were as tightly swaddled in the genteel tradition as any infant geniuses could be, for they were born before 1850, and in a Swedenborgian household. Yet they burst those bands almost entirely. The ways in which the two brothers freed themselves, however, are interestingly different. Mr. Henry James has done it by adopting the point of view of the outer world, and by turning the genteel American tradition, as he turns everything else, into a subject-matter for analysis. For him it is a curious habit of mind, intimately comprehended, to be compared with other habits of mind, also well known to him. Thus he has overcome the genteel tradition in the classic way, by understanding it. With William James too this infusion of worldly insight and European sympathies was a potent influence, especially in his earlier days; but the chief source of his liberty was another. It was his personal spontaneity, similar to that of Emerson, and his personal vitality, similar to that of nobody else. Convictions and ideas came to him, so to speak, from the subsoil. He had a prophetic sympathy with the dawning sentiments of the age, with the moods of the dumb majority. His scattered words caught fire in many parts of the world. His way of thinking and feeling represented the true America, and represented in a measure the whole ultra-modern, radical world. Thus he eluded the genteel tradition in the romantic way, by continuing it into its opposite. The romantic mind, glorified in Hegel's dialectic (which is not dialectic at all, but a sort of tragi-comic history of experience), is always rendering its thoughts unrecognisable through the infusion of new insights, and through the insensible transformation of the moral feeling that accompanies them, till at last it has completely reversed its old judgments under cover of expanding them. Thus the genteel tradition was led a merry dance when it fell again into the hands of a genuine and vigorous romanticist like William James. He restored their revolutionary force to its neutralised elements, by picking them out afresh, and emphasising them separately, according to his personal predilections.

For one thing, William James kept his mind and heart wide open to all that might seem, to polite minds, odd, personal, or visionary in religion and philosophy. He gave a sincerely respectful hearing to sentimentalists, mystics, spiritualists, wizards, cranks, quacks, and impostors—for it is hard to draw the line, and James was not willing to draw it prematurely. He thought, with his usual modesty, that any of these might have something to teach him. The lame, the halt, the blind, and those speaking with tongues could come to him with the certainty of finding sympathy; and if they were not healed, at least they were comforted, that a famous professor should take them so seriously; and they began to feel that after all to have only one leg, or one hand, or one eye, or to have three, might be in itself no less beauteous than to have just two, like the stolid majority. Thus William James became the friend and helper of those groping, nervous, half-educated, spiritually disinherited, passionately hungry individuals of which America is full. He became, at the same time, their spokesman and representative before the learned world; and he made it a chief part of his vocation to recast what the learned world has to offer, so that as far as possible it might serve the needs and interests of these people.

Yet the normal practical masculine American, too, had a friend in William James. There is a feeling abroad now, to which biology and Darwinism lend some colour, that theory is simply an instrument for practice, and intelligence merely a help toward material survival. Bears, it is said, have fur and claws, but poor naked man is condemned to be intelligent, or he will perish. This feeling William James embodied in that theory of thought and of truth which he called pragmatism. Intelligence, he thought, is no miraculous, idle faculty, by which we mirror passively any or everything that happens to be true, reduplicating the real world to no purpose. Intelligence has its roots and its issue in the context of events; it is one kind of practical adjustment, an experimental act, a form of vital tension. It does not essentially serve to picture other parts of reality, but to connect them. This view was not worked out by William James in its psychological and historical details; unfortunately he developed it chiefly in controversy against its opposite, which he called intellectualism, and which he hated with all the hatred of which his kind heart was capable. Intellectualism, as he conceived it, was pure pedantry; it impoverished and verbalised everything, and tied up nature in red tape. Ideas and rules that may have been occasionally useful it put in the place of the full-blooded irrational movement of life which had called them into being; and these abstractions, so soon obsolete, it strove to fix and to worship for ever. Thus all creeds and theories and all formal precepts sink in the estimation of the pragmatist to a local and temporary grammar of action; a grammar that must be changed slowly by time, and may be changed quickly by genius. To know things as a whole, or as they are eternally, if there is anything eternal in them, is not only beyond our powers, but would prove worthless, and perhaps even fatal to our lives. Ideas are not mirrors, they are weapons; their function is to prepare us to meet events, as future experience may unroll them. Those ideas that disappoint us are false ideas; those to which events are true are true themselves.

This may seem a very utilitarian view of the mind; and I confess I think it a partial one, since the logical force of beliefs and ideas, their truth or falsehood as assertions, has been overlooked altogether, or confused with the vital force of the material processes which these ideas express. It is an external view only, which marks the place and condition of the mind in nature, but neglects its specific essence; as if a jewel were defined as a round hole in a ring. Nevertheless, the more materialistic the pragmatist's theory of the mind is, the more vitalistic his theory of nature will have to become. If the intellect is a device produced in organic bodies to expedite their processes, these organic bodies must have interests and a chosen direction in their life; otherwise their life could not be expedited, nor could anything be useful to it. In other words—and this is a third point at which the philosophy of William James has played havoc with the genteel tradition, while ostensibly defending it—nature must be conceived anthropomorphically and in psychological terms. Its purposes are not to be static harmonies, self-unfolding destinies, the logic of spirit, the spirit of logic, or any other formal method and abstract law; its purposes are to be concrete endeavours, finite efforts of souls living in an environment which they transform and by which they, too, are affected. A spirit, the divine spirit as much as the human, as this new animism conceives it, is a romantic adventurer. Its future is undetermined. Its scope, its duration, and the quality of its life are all contingent. This spirit grows; it buds and sends forth feelers, sounding the depths around for such other centres of force or life as may exist there. It has a vital momentum, but no predetermined goal. It uses its past as a stepping-stone, or rather as a diving-board, but has an absolutely fresh will at each moment to plunge this way or that into the unknown. The universe is an experiment; it is unfinished. It has no ultimate or total nature, because it has no end. It embodies no formula or statable law; any formula is at best a poor abstraction, describing what, in some region and for some time, may be the most striking characteristic of existence; the law is a description *a posteriori* of the habit things have chosen to acquire, and which they may possibly throw off altogether. What a day may bring forth is uncertain; uncertain even to God. Omniscience is impossible; time is real; what had been omniscience hitherto might discover something more to-day. "There shall be news," William James was fond of saying with rapture, quoting from the unpublished poem of an obscure friend, "there shall be news in heaven!" There is almost certainly, he thought, a God now; there may be several gods, who might exist together, or one after the other. We might, by our conspiring sympathies, help to make a new one. Much in us is doubtless immortal; we survive death for some time in a recognisable form; but what our career and trans-

formations may be in the sequel we cannot tell, although we may
help to determine them by our daily choices. Observation must
be continual if our ideas are to remain true. Eternal vigilance is
the price of knowledge; perpetual hazard, perpetual experiment
keep quick the edge of life.

This is, so far as I know, a new philosophical vista; it is a conception never before presented, although implied, perhaps, in
various quarters, as in Norse and even Greek mythology. It is a
vision radically empirical and radically romantic; and as William
James himself used to say, the visions and not the arguments of
a philosopher are the interesting and influential things about him.
William James, rather too generously, attributed this vision to
M. Bergson, and regarded him in consequence as a philosopher
of the first rank, whose thought was to be one of the turning-
points in history. M. Bergson had killed intellectualism. It was his
book on creative evolution, said James with humourous emphasis, that had come at last to *"écraser l'infâme."* We may suspect,
notwithstanding, that intellectualism, infamous and crushed,
will survive the blow; and if the author of the Book of Ecclesiastes were now alive, and heard that there shall be news in
heaven, he would doubtless say that there may possibly be news
there, but that under the sun there is nothing new—not even
radical empiricism or radical romanticism, which from the beginning of the world has been the philosophy of those who as
yet had had little experience; for to the blinking little child it is
not merely something in the world that is new daily, but everything is new all day.

I am not concerned with the rights and wrongs of that controversy; my point is only that William James, in this genial evo-
lutionary view of the world, has given a rude shock to the genteel tradition. What! The world a gradual improvisation? Creation unpremeditated? God a sort of young poet or struggling
artist? William James is an advocate of theism; pragmatism adds
one to the evidences of religion; that is excellent. But is not the
cool abstract piety of the genteel getting more than it asks for?
This empirical naturalistic God is too crude and positive a force;
he will work miracles, he will answer prayers, he may inhabit
distinct places, and have distinct conditions under which alone he
can operate; he is a neighbouring being, whom we can act upon,

and rely upon for specific aids, as upon a personal friend, or a physician, or an insurance company. How disconcerting! Is not this new theology a little like superstition? And yet how interesting, how exciting, if it should happen to be true! I am far from wishing to suggest that such a view seems to me more probable than conventional idealism or than Christian orthodoxy. All three are in the region of dramatic system-making and myth to which probabilities are irrelevant. If one man says the moon is sister to the sun, and another that she is his daughter, the question is not which notion is more probable, but whether either of them is at all expressive. The so-called evidences are devised afterwards, when faith and imagination have prejudged the issue. The force of William James's new theology, or romantic cosmology, lies only in this: that it has broken the spell of the genteel tradition, and enticed faith in a new direction, which on second thoughts may prove no less alluring than the old. The important fact is not that the new fancy might possibly be true—who shall know that?—but that it has entered the heart of a leading American to conceive and to cherish it. The genteel tradition cannot be dislodged by these insurrections; there are circles to which it is still congenial, and where it will be preserved. But it has been challenged and (what is perhaps more insidious) it has been discovered. No one need be browbeaten any longer into accepting it. No one need be afraid, for instance, that his fate is sealed because some young prig may call him a dualist; the pint would call the quart a dualist, if you tried to pour the quart into him. We need not be afraid of being less profound, for being direct and sincere. The intellectual world may be traversed in many directions; the whole has not been surveyed; there is a great career in it open to talent. That is a sort of knell, that tolls the passing of the genteel tradition. Something else is now in the field; something else can appeal to the imagination, and be a thousand times more idealistic than academic idealism, which is often simply a way of white-washing and adoring things as they are. The illegitimate monopoly which the genteel tradition had established over what ought to be assumed and what ought to be hoped for has been broken down by the first-born of the family, by the genius of the race. Henceforth there can hardly be the same peace and the same pleasure in hugging the old pro-

prieties. Hegel will be to the next generation what Sir William
Hamilton was to the last. Nothing will have been disproved, but
everything will have been abandoned. An honest man has spoken,
and the cant of the genteel tradition has become harder for
young lips to repeat.

With this I have finished such a sketch as I am here able to offer you of the genteel tradition in American philosophy. The
subject is complex, and calls for many an excursus and qualifying
footnote; yet I think the main outlines are clear enough. The
chief fountains of this tradition were Calvinism and transcendentalism. Both were living fountains; but to keep them alive they required, one an agonised conscience, and the other a radical subjective criticism of knowledge. When these rare metaphysical
preoccupations disappeared—and the American atmosphere is
not favourable to either of them—the two systems ceased to be
inwardly understood; they subsisted as sacred mysteries only;
and the combination of the two in some transcendental system of
the universe (a contradiction in principle) was doubly artificial. Besides, it could hardly be held with a single mind. Natural
science, history, the beliefs implied in labour and invention,
could not be disregarded altogether; so that the transcendental philosopher was condemned to a double allegiance, and to
not letting his left hand know the bluff that his right hand was
making. Nevertheless, the difficulty in bringing practical inarticulate convictions to expression is very great, and the genteel
tradition has subsisted in the academic mind for want of anything equally academic to take its place.

The academic mind, however, has had its flanks turned. On
the one side came the revolt of the Bohemian temperament, with
its poetry of crude naturalism; on the other side came an impassioned empiricism, welcoming popular religious witnesses to the
unseen, reducing science to an instrument of success in action,
and declaring the universe to be wild and young, and not to be
harnessed by the logic of any school.

This revolution, I should think, might well find an echo
among you, who live in a thriving society, and in the presence
of a virgin and prodigious world. When you transform nature to
your uses, when you experiment with her forces, and reduce
them to industrial agents, you cannot feel that nature was made

by you or for you, for then these adjustments would have been
pre-established. Much less can you feel it when she destroys your
labour of years in a momentary spasm. You must feel, rather, that
you are an offshoot of her life; one brave little force among her
immense forces. When you escape, as you love to do, to your for-
ests and your sierras, I am sure again that you do not feel you
made them, or that they were made for you. They have grown,
as you have grown, only more massively and more slowly. In
their non-human beauty and peace they stir the sub-human
depths and the superhuman possibilities of your own spirit. It is
no transcendental logic that they teach; and they give no sign
of any deliberate morality seated in the world. It is rather
the vanity and superficiality of all logic, the needlessness of argument, the relativity of morals, the strength of time, the fertility
of matter, the variety, the unspeakable variety, of possible life.
Everything is measurable and conditioned, indefinitely repeated,
yet, in repetition, twisted somewhat from its old form. Everywhere is beauty and nowhere permanence, everywhere an incipient harmony, nowhere an intention, nor a responsibility, nor
a plan. It is the irresistible suasion of this daily spectacle, it is the
daily discipline of contact with things, so different from the verbal discipline of the schools, that will, I trust, inspire the philosophy of your children. A Californian whom I had recently the
pleasure of meeting observed that, if the philosophers had lived
among your mountains their systems would have been different
from what they are. Certainly, I should say, very different
from what those systems are which the European genteel tradition has handed down since Socrates; for these systems are egotistical; directly or indirectly they are anthropocentric, and inspired by the conceited notion that man, or human reason, or
the human distinction between good and evil, is the centre and
pivot of the universe. That is what the mountains and the woods
should make you at last ashamed to assert. From what, indeed,
does the society of nature liberate you, that you find it so sweet?
It is hardly (is it?) that you wish to forget your past, or your
friends, or that you have any secret contempt for your present
ambitions. You respect these, you respect them perhaps too much;
you are not suffered by the genteel tradition to criticise or to
reform them at all radically. No; it is the yoke of this genteel

tradition itself that these primeval solitudes lift from your shoulders. They suspend your forced sense of your own importance not merely as individuals, but even as men. They allow you, in one happy moment, at once to play and to worship, to take yourselves simply, humbly, for what you are, and to salute the wild, indifferent, non-censorious infinity of nature. You are admonished that what you can do avails little materially, and in the end nothing. At the same time, through wonder and pleasure, you are taught speculation. You learn what you are really fitted to do, and where lie your natural dignity and joy, namely, in representing many things, without being them, and in letting your imagination, through sympathy, celebrate and echo their life. Because the peculiarity of man is that his machinery for reaction on external things has involved an imaginative transcript of these things, which is preserved and suspended in his fancy; and the interest and beauty of this inward landscape, rather than any fortunes that may await his body in the outer world, constitute his proper happiness. By their mind, its scope, quality, and temper, we estimate men, for by the mind only do we exist as men, and are more than so many storage-batteries for material energy. Let us therefore be frankly human. Let us be content to live in the mind.

⤷ The Moral Background*

About the middle of the nineteenth century, in the quiet sunshine of provincial prosperity, New England had an Indian summer of the mind; and an agreeable reflective literature showed
how brilliant that russet and yellow season could be. There were
poets, historians, orators, preachers, most of whom had studied
foreign literatures and had travelled; they demurely kept up with
the times; they were universal humanists. But it was all a harvest
of leaves; these worthies had an expurgated and barren conception of life; theirs was the purity of sweet old age. Sometimes
they made attempts to rejuvenate their minds by broaching
native subjects; they wished to prove how much matter for poetry the new world supplied, and they wrote "Rip van Winkle,"
"Hiawatha," or "Evangeline"; but the inspiration did not seem
much more American than that of Swift or Ossian or Château-
briand. These cultivated writers lacked native roots and fresh sap
because the American intellect itself lacked them. Their culture
was half a pious survival, half an intentional acquirement; it was
not the inevitable flowering of a fresh experience. Later there
have been admirable analytic novelists who have depicted American life as it is, but rather bitterly, rather sadly; as if the joy and
the illusion of it did not inspire them, but only an abstract interest in their own art. If any one, like Walt Whitman, penetrated

* Chapter I of *Character and Opinion in the United States* (New York:
Charles Scribner's Sons, 1920).

to the feelings and images which the American scene was able to breed out of itself, and filled them with a frank and broad afflatus of his own, there is no doubt that he misrepresented the conscious minds of cultivated Americans; in them the head as yet did not belong to the trunk.

Nevertheless, *belles-lettres* in the United States—which after all stretch beyond New England—have always had two points of contact with the great national experiment. One point of contact has been oratory, with that sort of poetry, patriotic, religious, or moral, which has the function of oratory. Eloquence is a republican art, as conversation is an aristocratic one. By eloquence at public meetings and dinners, in the pulpit or in the press, the impulses of the community could be brought to expression; consecrated maxims could be reapplied; the whole latent manliness and shrewdness of the nation could be mobilised. In the form of oratory, reflection, rising out of the problems of action, could be turned to guide or to sanction action, and sometimes could attain, in so doing, a notable elevation of thought. Although Americans, and many other people, usually say that thought is for the sake of action, it has evidently been in these high moments, when action became incandescent in thought, that they have been most truly alive, intensively most active, and although *doing* nothing, have found at last that their existence was worth while. Reflection is itself a turn, and the top turn, given to life. Here is the second point at which literature in America has fused with the activities of the nation: it has paused to enjoy them. Every animal has his festive and ceremonious moments, when he poses or plumes himself or thinks; sometimes he even sings and flies aloft in a sort of ecstasy. Somewhat in the same way, when reflection in man becomes dominant, it may become passionate; it may create religion or philosophy—adventures often more thrilling than the humdrum experience they are supposed to interrupt.

This pure flame of mind is nothing new, superadded, or alien in America. It is notorious how metaphysical was the passion that drove the Puritans to those shores; they went there in the hope of living more perfectly in the spirit. And their pilgrim's progress was not finished when they had founded their churches in the wilderness; an endless migration of the mind was still be-

fore them, a flight from those new idols and servitudes which
prosperity involves, and the eternal lure of spiritual freedom and
truth. The moral world always contains undiscovered or thinly
peopled continents open to those who are more attached to what
might or should be than to what already is. Americans are eminently prophets; they apply morals to public affairs; they are impatient and enthusiastic. Their judgments have highly speculative implications, which they often make explicit; they are men
with principles, and fond of stating them. Moreover, they have
an intense self-reliance; to exercise private judgment is not only
a habit with them but a conscious duty. Not seldom personal con-
versions and mystical experiences throw their ingrained faith into
novel forms, which may be very bold and radical. They are tra-
ditionally exercised about religion, and adrift on the subject more
than any other people on earth; and if religion is a dreaming
philosophy, and philosophy a waking religion, a people so wide
awake and so religious as the old Yankees ought certainly to have
been rich in philosophers.

In fact, philosophy in the good old sense of curiosity about the
nature of things, with readiness to make the best of them, has
not been absent from the practice of Americans or from their
humourous moods; their humour and shrewdness are sly comments on the shortcomings of some polite convention that everybody accepts tacitly, yet feels to be insecure and contrary to the
principles on which life is actually carried on. Nevertheless, with
the shyness which simple competence often shows in the presence of conventional shams, these wits have not taken their native wisdom very seriously. They have not had the leisure nor the
intellectual scope to think out and defend the implications of their
homely perceptions. Their fresh insight has been whispered in
parentheses and asides; it has been humbly banished, in alarm,
from their solemn moments. What people have respected have
been rather scraps of official philosophy, or entire systems, which
they have inherited or imported, as they have respected operas
and art museums. To be on speaking terms with these fine things
was a part of social respectability, like having family silver. High
thoughts must be at hand, like those candlesticks, probably can-
dleless, sometimes displayed as a seemly ornament in a room
blazing with electric light. Even in William James, spontaneous

and stimulating as he was, a certain underlying discomfort was discernible; he had come out into the open, into what should have been the sunshine, but the vast shadow of the temple still stood between him and the sun. He was worried about what *ought* to be believed and the awful deprivations of disbelieving. What he called the cynical view of anything had first to be brushed aside, without stopping to consider whether it was not the true one; and he was bent on finding new and empirical reasons for clinging to free-will, departed spirits, and tutelary gods. Nobody, except perhaps in this last decade, has tried to bridge the chasm between what he believes in daily life and the "problems" of philosophy. Nature and science have not been ignored, and "practice" in some schools has been constantly referred to; but instead of supplying philosophy with its data they have only constituted its difficulties; its function has been not to build on known facts but to explain them away. Hence a curious alternation and irrelevance, as between weekdays and Sabbaths, between American ways and American opinions.

That philosophy should be attached to tradition would be a great advantage, conducive to mutual understanding, to maturity, and to progress, if the tradition lay in the highway of truth. To deviate from it in that case would be to betray the fact that, while one might have a lively mind, one was not master of the subject. Unfortunately, in the nineteenth century, in America as elsewhere, the ruling tradition was not only erratic and far from the highway of truth, but the noonday of this tradition was over, and its classic forms were outgrown. A philosophy may have a high value, other than its truth to things, in its truth to method and to the genius of its author; it may be a feat of synthesis and imagination, like a great poem, expressing one of the eternal possibilities of being, although one which the creator happened to reject when he made this world. It is possible to be a master in false philosophy—easier, in fact, than to be a master in the truth, because a false philosophy can be made as simple and consistent as one pleases. Such had been the masters of the tradition prevalent in New England—Calvin, Hume, Fichte, not to mention others more relished because less pure; but one of the disadvantages of such perfection in error is that the illusion is harder to transmit to another age and country. If Jonathan Edwards, for instance, was a Calvinist of pristine force and perhaps the greatest *master* in false philosophy that America has yet produced, he paid the price by being abandoned, even in his lifetime, by his own sect, and seeing the world turn a deaf ear to his logic without so much as attempting to refute it. One of the peculiarities of recent speculation, especially in America, is that ideas are abandoned in virtue of a mere change of feeling, without any new evidence or new arguments. We do not nowadays refute our predecessors, we pleasantly bid them good-bye. Even if all our principles are unwittingly traditional we do not like to bow openly to authority. Hence masters like Calvin, Hume, or Fichte rose before their American admirers like formidable ghosts, foreign and unseizable. People refused to be encumbered with any system, even one of their own; they were content to imbibe more or less of the spirit of a philosophy and to let it play on such facts as happened to attract their attention. The originality even of Emerson and of William James was of this incidental character; they found new approaches to old beliefs or new expedients in old dilemmas. They were not in a scholastic sense pupils of anybody or masters in anything. They hated the scholastic way of saying what they meant, if they had heard of it; they insisted on a personal freshness of style, refusing to make their thought more precise than it happened to be spontaneously; and they lisped their logic, when the logic came.

We must remember that ever since the days of Socrates, and especially after the establishment of Christianity, the dice of thought have been loaded. Certain pledges have preceded inquiry and divided the possible conclusions beforehand into the acceptable and the inacceptable, the edifying and the shocking, the noble and the base. Wonder has no longer been the root of philosophy, but sometimes impatience at having been cheated and sometimes fear of being undeceived. The marvel of existence, in which the luminous and the opaque are so romantically mingled, no longer lay like a sea open to intellectual adventure, tempting the mind to conceive some bold and curious system of the universe on the analogy of what had been so far discovered. Instead, people were confronted with an orthodoxy—though not always the same orthodoxy—whispering mysteries and brandishing anathemas. Their wits were absorbed in solving traditional problems, many of them artificial and such as the ruling orthodoxy had created by its gratuitous assumptions. Difficulties were therefore found in some perfectly obvious truths; and obvious fables, if they were hallowed by association, were seriously weighed in the balance against one another or against the facts; and many an actual thing was proved to be impossible, or was hidden under a false description. In conservative schools the student learned and tried to fathom the received solutions; in liberal schools he was perhaps invited to seek solutions of his own, but still to the old questions. Freedom, when nominally allowed, was a provisional freedom; if your wanderings did not somehow bring you back to orthodoxy you were a misguided being, no matter how disparate from the orthodox might be the field from which you fetched your little harvest; and if you could not be answered you were called superficial. Most spirits are cowed by such disparagement; but even those who snap their fingers at it do not escape; they can hardly help feeling that in calling a spade a spade they are petulant and naughty; or if their inspiration is too genuine for that, they still unwittingly shape their opinions in contrast to those that claim authority, and therefore on the same false lines—a terrible tax to pay to the errors of others; and it is only here and there that a very great and solitary mind, like that of Spinoza, can endure obloquy without bitterness or can pass through perverse controversies without contagion.

Under such circumstances it is obvious that speculation can be frank and happy only where orthodoxy has receded, abandoning a larger and larger field to unprejudiced inquiry; or else (as has happened among liberal Protestants) where the very heart of orthodoxy has melted, has absorbed the most alien substances, and is ready to bloom into anything that anybody finds attractive. This is the secret of that extraordinary vogue which the transcendental philosophy has had for nearly a century in Great Britain and America; it is a method which enables a man to renovate all his beliefs, scientific and religious, from the inside, giving them a new status and interpretation as phases of his own experience or imagination; so that he does not seem to himself to reject anything, and yet is bound to nothing, except to his creative self. Many too who have no inclination to practise this transcendental method—a personal, arduous, and futile art, which requires to be renewed at every moment—have been impressed with the results or the maxims of this or that transcendental philosopher, such as that every opinion leads on to another that reinterprets it, or every evil to some higher good that contains it; and they have managed to identify these views with what still seemed to them vital in religion.

In spite of this profound mutation at the core, and much paring at the edges, traditional belief in New England retained its continuity and its priestly unction; and religious teachers and philosophers could slip away from Calvinism and even from Christianity without any loss of elevation or austerity. They found it so pleasant and easy to elude the past that they really had no quarrel with it. The world, they felt, was a safe place, watched over by a kindly God, who exacted nothing but cheerfulness and good-will from his children; and the American flag was a sort of rainbow in the sky, promising that all storms were over. Or if storms came, such as the Civil War, they would not be harder to weather than was necessary to test the national spirit and raise it to a new efficiency. The subtler dangers which we may now see threatening America had not yet come in sight—material restlessness was not yet ominous, the pressure of business enterprises was not yet out of scale with the old life or out of key with the old moral harmonies. A new type of American had not appeared—the untrained, pushing, cosmopolitan orphan, cock-sure in manner but not too sure in his morality, to whom the old Yankee, with his sour integrity, is almost a foreigner. Was not "increase," in the Bible, a synonym for benefit? Was not "abundance" the same, or almost the same, as happiness?

Meantime the churches, a little ashamed of their past, began to court the good opinion of so excellent a world. Although called evangelical, they were far, very far, from prophesying its end, or offering a refuge from it, or preaching contempt for it; they existed only to serve it, and their highest divine credential was that the world needed them. Irreligion, dissoluteness, and pessimism—supposed naturally to go together—could never prosper; they were incompatible with efficiency. That was the supreme test. "Be Christians," I once heard a president of Yale College cry to his assembled pupils, "be Christians and you will

be successful." Religion was indispensable and sacred, when not
carried too far; but theology might well be unnecessary. Why
distract this world with talk of another? Enough for the day was
the good thereof. Religion should be disentangled as much as
possible from history and authority and metaphysics, and made
to rest honestly on one's fine feelings, on one's indomitable optimism and trust in life. Revelation was nothing miraculous,
given once for all in some remote age and foreign country; it
must come to us directly, and with greater authority now than
ever before. If evolution was to be taken seriously and to include
moral growth, the great men of the past could only be stepping-
stones to our own dignity. To grow was to contain and sum up
all the good that had gone before, adding an appropriate incre-
ment. Undoubtedly some early figures were beautiful, and al-
lowances had to be made for local influences in Palestine, a place
so much more primitive and backward than Massachusetts.
Jesus was a prophet more winsome and nearer to ourselves than
his predecessors; but how could any one deny that the twenty
centuries of progress since his time must have raised a loftier
pedestal for Emerson or Channing or Phillips Brooks? It might
somehow not be in good taste to put this feeling into clear words;
one and perhaps two of these men would have deprecated it;
nevertheless it beamed with refulgent self-satisfaction in the lives
and maxims of most of their followers.

All this liberalism, however, never touched the centre of
traditional orthodoxy, and those who, for all their modernness,
felt that they inherited the faith of their fathers and were true
to it were fundamentally right. There was still an orthodoxy
among American highbrows at the end of the nineteenth century, dissent from which was felt to be scandalous; it consisted
in holding that the universe exists and is governed for the sake
of man or of the human spirit. This persuasion, arrogant as it
might seem, is at bottom an expression of impotence rather than
of pride. The soul is originally vegetative; it feels the weal and
woe of what occurs within the body. With locomotion and the
instinct to hunt and to flee, animals begin to notice external
things also; but the chief point noticed about them is whether
they are good or bad, friendly or hostile, far or near. The station of the animal and his interests thus become the measure of

all things for him, in so far as he knows them; and this aspect of them is, by a primitive fatality, the heart of them to him. It is only reason that can discount these childish perspectives, neutralise the bias of each by collating it with the others, and masterfully conceive the field in which their common objects are deployed, discovering also the principle of foreshortening or projection which produces each perspective in turn. But reason is a later comer into this world, and weak; against its suasion stands the mighty resistance of habit and of moral presumption. It is in their interest, and to rehabilitate the warm vegetative autonomy of the primitive soul, that orthodox religion and philosophy labour in the western world—for the mind of India cannot be charged with this folly. Although inwardly these systems have not now a good conscience and do not feel very secure (for they are retrograde and sin against the light), yet outwardly they are solemn and venerable; and they have incorporated a great deal of moral wisdom with their egotism or humanism—more than the Indians with their respect for the infinite. In deifying human interests they have naturally studied and expressed them justly, whereas those who perceive the relativity of human goods are tempted to scorn them—which is itself unreasonable—and to sacrifice them all to the single passion of worship or of despair. Hardly anybody, except possibly the Greeks at their best, has realised the sweetness and glory of being a rational animal.

The Jews, as we know, had come to think that it was the creator of the world, the God of the universe, who had taken them for his chosen people. Christians in turn had asserted that it was God in person who, having become a man, had founded their church. According to this Hebraic tradition, the dignity of man did not lie in being a mind (which he undoubtedly is) but in being a creature materially highly favoured, with a longer life and a brighter destiny than other creatures in the world. It is remarkable how deep, in the Hebraic religions, is this interest in material existence; so deep that we are surprised when we discover that, according to the insight of other races, this interest is the essence of irreligion. Some detachment from existence and from hopes of material splendour has indeed filtered into Christianity through Platonism. Socrates and his disciples admired this world, but they did not particularly covet it, or wish to live

long in it, or expect to improve it; what they cared for was an
idea or a good which they found expressed in it, something outside it and timeless, in which the contemplative intellect might
be literally absorbed. This philosophy was no less humanistic
than that of the Jews, though in a less material fashion: if it did
not read the universe in terms of thrift, it read it in terms of art.
The pursuit of a good, such as is presumably aimed at in human action, was supposed to inspire every movement in nature;
and this good, for the sake of which the very heavens revolved,
was akin to the intellectual happiness of a Greek sage. Nature was
a philosopher in pursuit of an idea. Natural science then took a
moralising turn which it has not yet quite outgrown. Socrates
required of astronomy, if it was to be true science, that it should
show why *it was best* that the sun and moon should be as
they are; and Plato, refining on this, assures us that the eyes are
placed in the front of the head, rather than at the back, because
the front is the nobler quarter, and that the intestines are long in
order that we may have leisure between meals to study philosophy. Curiously enough, the very enemies of final causes sometimes catch this infection and attach absolute values to facts in
an opposite sense and in an inhuman interest; and you often hear
in America that whatever is is right. These naturalists, while
they rebuke the moralists for thinking that nature is ruled magically for our good, think her adorable for being ruled, in scorn of
us, only by her own laws; and thus we oscillate between egotism
and idolatry.

The Reformation did not reform this belief in the cosmic
supremacy of man, or the humanity of God; on the contrary, it
took it (like so much else) in terrible German earnest, not suffering it any longer to be accepted somewhat lightly as a classical figure of speech or a mystery resting on revelation. The human race, the chosen people, the Christian elect were like tabernacle within tabernacle for the spirit; but in the holy of holies
was the spirit itself, one's own spirit and experience, which was
the centre of everything. Protestant philosophy, exploring the
domain of science and history with confidence, and sure of finding the spirit walking there, was too conscientious to misrepresent what it found. As the terrible facts could not be altered they
had to be undermined. By turning psychology into metaphysics

this could be accomplished, and we could reach the remarkable conclusion that the human spirit was not so much the purpose of the universe as its seat, and the only universe there was.

This conclusion, which sums up idealism on its critical or scientific side, would not of itself give much comfort to religious minds, that usually crave massive support rather than sublime independence; it leads to the heroic egotism of Fichte or Nietzsche rather than to any green pastures beside any still waters. But the critical element in idealism can be used to destroy belief in the natural world; and by so doing it can open the way to another sort of idealism, not at all critical, which might be called the higher superstition. This views the world as an oracle or charade, concealing a dramatic unity, or formula, or maxim, which all experience exists to illustrate. The habit of regarding existence as a riddle, with a surprising solution which we think we have found, should be the source of rather mixed emotions; the facts remain as they were, and rival solutions may at any time suggest themselves; and the one we have hit on may not, after all, be particularly comforting. The Christian may find himself turned by it into a heathen, the humanist into a pantheist, and the hope with which we instinctively faced life may be chastened into mere conformity. Nevertheless, however chilling and inhuman our higher superstition may prove, it will make us feel that we are masters of a mystical secret, that we have a faith to defend, and that, like all philosophers, we have taken a ticket in a lottery in which if we hit on the truth, even if it seems a blank, we shall have drawn the first prize.

Orthodoxy in New England, even so transformed and attenuated, did not of course hold the field alone. There are materialists by instinct in every age and country; there are always private gentlemen whom the clergy and the professors cannot deceive. Here and there a medical or scientific man, or a man of letters, will draw from his special pursuits some hint of the nature of things at large; or a political radical will nurse undying wrath against all opinions not tartly hostile to church and state. But these clever people are not organised, they are not always given to writing, nor speculative enough to make a system out of their convictions. The enthusiasts and the pedagogues naturally flock to the other camp. The very competence which scien-

tific people and connoisseurs have in their special fields disinclines
them to generalise, or renders their generalisations one-sided; so
that their speculations are extraordinarily weak and stammering.
Both by what they represent and by what they ignore they are
isolated and deprived of influence, since only those who are at
home in a subject can feel the force of analogies drawn from that
field, whereas any one can be swayed by sentimental and moral
appeals, by rhetoric and unction. Furthermore, in America the
materialistic school is without that support from popular passions
which it draws in many European countries from its association
with anti-clericalism or with revolutionary politics; and it also
lacks the maturity, self-confidence, and refinement proper in
older societies to the great body of Epicurean and disenchanted
opinion, where for centuries wits, critics, minor philosophers,
and men of the world have chuckled together over their Hor-
ace, their Voltaire, and their Gibbon. The horror which the theologians have of infidelity passes therefore into the average
American mind unmitigated by the suspicion that anything
pleasant could lie in that quarter, much less the open way to nature and truth and a secure happiness.

There is another handicap, of a more technical sort, under
which naturalistic philosophy labours in America, as it does in
England; it has been crossed by scepticism about the validity of
perception and has become almost identical with psychology. Of
course, for any one who thinks naturalistically (as the British
empiricists did in the beginning, like every unsophisticated mortal), psychology is the description of a very superficial and incidental complication in the animal kingdom: it treats of the curious sensibility and volatile thoughts awakened in the mind by
the growth and fortunes of the body. In noting these thoughts
and feelings, we can observe how far they constitute true
knowledge of the world in which they arise, how far they ignore it, and how far they play with it, by virtue of the poetry
and the syntax of discourse which they add out of their own exuberance; for fancy is a very fertile treacherous thing, as every
one finds when he dreams. But dreams run over into waking life,
and sometimes seem to permeate and to underlie it; and it was
just this suspicion that he might be dreaming awake, that dis-

course and tradition might be making a fool of him, that prompted the hard-headed Briton, even before the Reformation, to appeal from conventional beliefs to "experience." He was anxious to clear away those sophistries and impostures of which he was particularly apprehensive, in view of the somewhat foreign character of his culture and religion. Experience, he thought, would bear unimpeachable witness to the nature of things; for by experience he understood knowledge produced by direct contact with the object. Taken in this sense, experience is a method of discovery, an exercise of intelligence; it is the same observation of things, strict, cumulative, and analytic, which produces the natural sciences. It rests on naturalistic assumptions (since we know when and where we find our data) and could not fail to end in materialism. What prevented British empiricism from coming to this obvious conclusion was a peculiarity of the national temperament. The Englishman is not only distrustful of too much reasoning and too much theory (and science and materialism involve a good deal of both), but he is also fond of musing and of withdrawing into his inner man. Accordingly his empiricism took an introspective form; like Hamlet he stopped at the *how;* he began to think about thinking. His first care was now to arrest experience as he underwent it; though its presence could not be denied, it came in such a questionable shape that it could not be taken at its word. This mere presence of experience, this ghostly apparition to the inner man, was all that empirical philosophy could now profess to discover. Far from being an exercise of intelligence, it retracted all understanding, all interpretation, all instinctive faith; far from furnishing a sure record of the truths of nature, it furnished a set of pathological facts, the passive subject-matter of psychology. These now seemed the only facts admissible, and psychology, for the philosophers, became the only science. Experience could discover nothing, but all discoveries had to be retracted, so that they should revert to the fact of experience and terminate there. Evidently when the naturalistic background and meaning of experience have dropped out in this way, empiricism is a form of idealism, since whatever objects we can come upon will all be *a priori* and *a fortiori* and *sensu eminentiori* ideal in the mind. The irony of logic actually made English empiricism, understood in this psychological way, the starting-point for transcendentalism and for German philosophy.

Between these two senses of the word experience, meaning sometimes contact with things and at other times absolute feeling, the empirical school in England and America has been helplessly torn, without ever showing the courage or the self-knowledge to choose between them. I think we may say that on the whole their view has been this: that feelings or ideas were absolute atoms of existence, without any ground or source, so that the elements of their universe were all mental; but they conceived these psychical elements to be deployed in a physical time and even (since there were many simultaneous series of them) in some sort of space. These philosophers were accordingly idealists about substance but naturalists about the order and relations of existences; and experience on their lips meant feeling when they were thinking of particulars, but when they were thinking broadly, in matters of history or science, experience meant the universal nebula or cataract which these feelings composed—itself no object of experience, but one believed in and very imperfectly presented in imagination. These men believed in nature, and were materialists at heart and to all practical purposes; but they were shy intellectually, and seemed to think they ran less risk of error in holding a thing covertly than in openly professing it.

If any one, like Herbert Spencer, kept psychology in its place and in that respect remained a pure naturalist, he often forfeited this advantage by enveloping the positive information he derived from the sciences in a whirlwind of generalisations. The higher superstition, the notion that nature dances to the tune of some comprehensive formula or some magic rhyme, thus reappeared among those who claimed to speak for natural science. In their romantic sympathy with nature they attributed to her an excessive sympathy with themselves; they overlooked her infinite complications and continual irony, and candidly believed they could measure her with their thumb-rules. Why should philosophers drag a toy-net of words, fit to catch butterflies, through the sea of being, and expect to land all the fish in it? Why not take note simply of what the particular sciences can as yet tell us of the world? Certainly, when put together, they already yield a very wonderful, very true, and very sufficient picture of it. Are we impatient of knowing everything? But even if science was much enlarged it would have limits, both in penetration and in extent; and there would always remain, I will not say an infinity of unsolved problems (because "problems" are created by our impatience or our contradictions), but an infinity of undiscovered facts. Nature is like a beautiful woman that may be as delightfully and as truly known at a certain distance as upon a closer view; as to knowing her through and through, that is nonsense in both cases, and might not reward our pains. The love of all-inclusiveness is as dangerous in philosophy as in art. The savour of nature can be enjoyed by us only through our own senses and insight, and an outline map of the entire universe, even if it was not fabulously concocted, would not tell us much that was worth knowing about the outlying parts of it. Without suggesting for a moment that the proper study of mankind is man only—for it may be landscape or mathematics—we may safely say that their proper study is what lies within their range and is interesting to them. For this reason the moralists who consider principally human life and paint nature only as a background to their figures are apt to be better philosophers than the speculative naturalists. In human life we are at home, and our views on it, if one-sided, are for that very reason expressive of our character and fortunes. An unfortunate peculiarity of naturalistic philosophers is that usually they have but cursory and wretched notions of the inner life of the mind; they are dead to patriotism and to religion, they hate poetry and fancy and passion and even philosophy itself; and therefore (especially if their science too, as often happens, is borrowed and vague) we need not wonder if the academic and cultivated world despises them, and harks back to the mythology of Plato or Aristotle or Hegel, who at least were conversant with the spirit of man.

Philosophers are very severe towards other philosophers because they expect too much. Even under the most favourable circumstances no mortal can be asked to seize the truth in its wholeness or at its centre. As the senses open to us only partial perspectives, taken from one point of view, and report the facts in symbols which, far from being adequate to the full nature of what surrounds us, resemble the coloured signals of danger or of free way which a railway engine-driver peers at in the night, so our speculation, which is a sort of panoramic sense, approaches things peripherally and expresses them humanly. But how doubly dyed in this subjectivity must our thought be when an orthodoxy dominant for ages has twisted the universe into the service of moral interests, and when even the heretics are entangled in a scepticism so partial and arbitrary that it substitutes psychology, the most derivative and dubious of sciences, for the direct intelligent reading of experience! But this strain of subjectivity is not in all respects an evil; it is a warm purple dye. When a way of thinking is deeply rooted in the soil, and embodies the instincts or even the characteristic errors of a people, it has a value quite independent of its truth; it constitutes a phase of human life and can powerfully affect the intellectual drama in which it figures. It is a value of this sort that attaches to modern philosophy in general, and very particularly to the American thinkers I am about to discuss. There would be a sort of irrelevance and unfairness in measuring them by the standards of pure science or even of a classic sagacity, and reproaching them for not having reached perfect consistency or fundamental clearness. Men of intense feeling—and others will hardly count—are not mirrors but lights. If pure truth happened to be what they passionately desired, they would seek it single-mindedly, and in matters within their competence they would probably find it; but the desire for pure truth, like any other, must wait to be satisfied until its organ is ripe and the conditions are favourable. The nineteenth century was not a time and America was not a place where such an achievement could be expected. There the wisest felt themselves to be, as they were, questioners and apostles rather than serene philosophers. We should not pay them the doubtful compliment of attributing to them merits alien to their tradition and scope, as if the nobleness they actually possessed —their conscience, vigour, timeliness, and influence—were not enough.

❧ William James*

William James enjoyed in his youth what are called advantages: he lived among cultivated people, travelled, had teachers of various nationalities. His father was one of those somewhat obscure sages whom early America produced: mystics of independent mind, hermits in the desert of business, and heretics in the churches. They were intense individualists, full of veneration for the free souls of their children, and convinced that every one should paddle his own canoe, especially on the high seas. William James accordingly enjoyed a stimulating if slightly irregular education: he never acquired that reposeful mastery of particular authors and those safe ways of feeling and judging which are fostered in great schools and universities. In consequence he showed an almost physical horror of club sentiment and of the stifling atmosphere of all officialdom. He had a knack for drawing, and rather the temperament of the artist; but the unlovely secrets of nature and the troubles of man preoccupied him, and he chose medicine for his profession. Instead of practising, however, he turned to teaching physiology, and from that passed gradually to psychology and philosophy.

In his earlier years he retained some traces of polyglot student days at Paris, Bonn, Vienna, or Geneva; he slipped sometimes into foreign phrases, uttered in their full vernacular; and there was an occasional afterglow of Bohemia about him, in the

* Chapter III of *Character and Opinion in the United States.*

bright stripe of a shirt or the exuberance of a tie. On points of art or medicine he retained a professional touch and an unconscious ease which he hardly acquired in metaphysics. I suspect he had heartily admired some of his masters in those other subjects, but had never seen a philosopher whom he would have cared to resemble. Of course there was nothing of the artist in William James, as the artist is sometimes conceived in England, nothing of the æsthete, nothing affected or limp. In person he was short rather than tall, erect, brisk, bearded, intensely masculine. While he shone in expression and would have wished his style to be noble if it could also be strong, he preferred in the end to be spontaneous, and to leave it at that; he tolerated slang in himself rather than primness. The rough, homely, picturesque phrase, whatever was graphic and racy, recommended itself to him; and his conversation outdid his writing in this respect. He believed in improvisation, even in thought; his lectures were not minutely prepared. Know your subject thoroughly, he used to say, and trust to luck for the rest. There was a deep sense of insecurity in him, a mixture of humility with romanticism: we were likely to be more or less wrong anyhow, but we might be wholly sincere. One moment should respect the insight of another, without trying to establish too regimental a uniformity. If you corrected yourself tartly, how could you know that the correction was not the worse mistake? All our opinions were born free and equal, all children of the Lord, and if they were not consistent that was the Lord's business, not theirs. In reality, James was consistent enough, as even Emerson (more extreme in this sort of irresponsibility) was too. Inspiration has its limits, sometimes very narrow ones. But James was not consecutive, not insistent; he turned to a subject afresh, without egotism or pedantry; he dropped his old points, sometimes very good ones; and he modestly looked for light from others, who had less light than himself.

His excursions into philosophy were accordingly in the nature of raids, and it is easy for those who are attracted by one part of his work to ignore other parts, in themselves perhaps more valuable. I think that in fact his popularity does not rest on his best achievements. His popularity rests on three somewhat incidental books, *The Will to Believe*, *Pragmatism*, and *The Varie-*

ties of Religious Experience, whereas, as it seems to me, his best achievement is his *Principles of Psychology.* In this book he surveys, in a way which for him is very systematic, a subject made to his hand. In its ostensible outlook it is a treatise like any other, but what distinguishes it is the author's gift for evoking vividly the very life of the mind. This is a work of imagination; and the subject as he conceived it, which is the flux of immediate experience in men in general, requires imagination to read it at all. It is a literary subject, like autobiography or psychological fiction, and can be treated only poetically; and in this sense Shakespeare is a better psychologist than Locke or Kant. Yet this gift of imagination is not merely literary; it is not useless in divining the truths of science, and it is invaluable in throwing off prejudice and scientific shams. The fresh imagination and vitality of William James led him to break through many a false convention. He saw that experience, as we endure it, is not a mosaic of distinct sensations, nor the expression of separate hostile faculties, such as reason and the passions, or sense and the categories; it is rather a flow of mental discourse, like a dream, in which all divisions and units are vague and shifting, and the whole is continually merging together and drifting apart. It fades gradually in the rear, like the wake of a ship, and bites into the future, like the bow cutting the water. For the candid psychologist, carried bodily on this voyage of discovery, the past is but a questionable report, and the future wholly indeterminate; everything is simply what it is experienced as being.

At the same time, psychology is supposed to be a science, a claim which would tend to confine it to the natural history of man, or the study of behaviour, as is actually proposed by Auguste Comte and by some of James's own disciples, more jejune if more clear-headed than he. As matters now stand, however, psychology as a whole is not a science, but a branch of philosophy; it brings together the literary description of mental discourse and the scientific description of material life, in order to consider the relation between them, which is the nexus of human nature.

What was James's position on this crucial question? It is impossible to reply unequivocally. He approached philosophy as mankind originally approached it, without having a philosophy,

and he lent himself to various hypotheses in various directions.
He professed to begin his study on the assumptions of common
sense, that there is a material world which the animals that live
in it are able to perceive and to think about. He gave a congruous extension to this view in his theory that emotion is purely
bodily sensation, and also in his habit of conceiving the mind as
a total shifting sensibility. To pursue this path, however, would
have led him to admit that nature was automatic and mind simply
cognitive, conclusions from which every instinct in him recoiled.
He preferred to believe that mind and matter had independent
energies and could lend one another a hand, matter operating
by motion and mind by intention. This dramatic, amphibious
way of picturing causation is natural to common sense, and
might be defended if it were clearly defined; but James was insensibly carried away from it by a subtle implication of his
method. This implication was that experience or mental discourse not only constituted a set of substantive facts, but the
only substantive facts; all else, even that material world which
his psychology had postulated, could be nothing but a verbal
or fantastic symbol for sensations in their experienced order.
So that while nominally the door was kept open to any hypothesis regarding the conditions of the psychological flux, in truth
the question was prejudged. The hypotheses, which were parts
of this psychological flux, could have no object save other parts
of it. That flux itself, therefore, which he could picture so vividly,
was the fundamental existence. The *sense* of bounding over the
waves, the *sense* of being on an adventurous voyage, was the living fact; the rest was dead reckoning. Where one's gift is,
there will one's faith be also; and to this poet appearance was the
only reality.

   This sentiment, which always lay at the back of his mind,
reached something like formal expression in his latest writings,
where he sketched what he called radical empiricism. The word
experience is like a shrapnel shell, and bursts into a thousand
meanings. Here we must no longer think of its setting, its discoveries, or its march; to treat it radically we must abstract its
immediate objects and reduce it to pure data. It is obvious (and
the sequel has already proved) that experience so understood
would lose its romantic signification, as a personal adventure

or a response to the shocks of fortune. "Experience" would turn into a cosmic dance of absolute entities created and destroyed *in vacuo* according to universal laws, or perhaps by chance. No minds would gather this experience, and no material agencies would impose it; but the immediate objects present to any one would simply be parts of the universal fireworks, continuous with the rest, and all the parts, even if not present to anybody, would have the same status. Experience would then not at all resemble what Shakespeare reports or what James himself had described in his psychology. If it could be experienced as it flows in its entirety (which is fortunately impracticable), it would be a perpetual mathematical nightmare. Every whirling atom, every changing relation, and every incidental perspective would be a part of it. I am far from wishing to deny for a moment the scientific value of such a cosmic system, if it can be worked out; physics and mathematics seem to me to plunge far deeper than literary psychology into the groundwork of this world; but human experience is the stuff of literary psychology; we cannot reach the stuff of physics and mathematics except by arresting or even hypostatising some elements of appearance, and expanding them on an abstracted and hypothetical plane of their own. Experience, as memory and literature rehearse it, remains nearer to us than that: it is something dreamful, passionate, dramatic, and significative.

Certainly this personal human experience, expressible in literature and in talk, and no cosmic system however profound, was what James knew best and trusted most. Had he seen the developments of his radical empiricism, I cannot help thinking he would have marvelled that such logical mechanisms should have been hatched out of that egg. The principal problems and aspirations that haunted him all his life long would lose their meaning in that cosmic atmosphere. The pragmatic nature of truth, for instance, would never suggest itself in the presence of pure data; but a romantic mind soaked in agnosticism, conscious of its own habits and assuming an environment the exact structure of which can never be observed, may well convince itself that, for experience, truth is nothing but a happy use of signs—which is indeed the truth of literature. But if we once accept *any* system of the universe as literally true, the value of convenient signs to prepare us for such experience as is yet absent cannot be called truth: it is plainly nothing but a necessary inaccuracy. So, too, with the question of the survival of the human individual after death. For radical empiricism a human individual is simply a certain cycle or complex of terms, like any other natural fact; that some echoes of his mind should recur after the regular chimes have ceased, would have nothing paradoxical about it. A mathematical world is a good deal like music, with its repetitions and transpositions, and a little trill, which you might call a person, might well peep up here and there all over a vast composition. Something of that sort may be the truth of spiritualism; but it is not what the spiritualists imagine. Their whole interest lies not in the experiences they have, but in the interpretation they give to them, assigning them to troubled spirits in another world; but both another world and a spirit are notions repugnant to a radical empiricism.

I think it is important to remember, if we are not to misunderstand William James, that his radical empiricism and pragmatism were in his own mind only methods; his doctrine, if he may be said to have had one, was agnosticism. And just because he was an agnostic (feeling instinctively that beliefs and opinions, if they had any objective beyond themselves, could never be sure they had attained it), he seemed in one sense so favourable to credulity. He was not credulous himself, far from it; he was well aware that the trust he put in people or ideas might betray him. For that very reason he was respectful and pitiful to the trustfulness of others. Doubtless they were wrong, but who were we to say so? In his own person he was ready enough to face the mystery of things, and whatever the womb of time might bring forth; but until the curtain was rung down on the last act of the drama (and it might have no last act!) he wished the intellectual cripples and the moral hunchbacks not to be jeered at; perhaps they might turn out to be the heroes of the play. Who could tell what heavenly influences might not pierce to these sensitive half-flayed creatures, which are lost on the thick-skinned, the sane, and the duly goggled? We must not suppose, however, that James meant these contrite and romantic suggestions dogmatically. The agnostic, as well as the physician and neurologist in him, was never quite eclipsed. The hope that some new revelation might come from the lowly and weak could never mean to him what it meant to the early Christians. For him it was only a right conceded to them to experiment with their special faiths; he did not expect such faiths to be discoveries of absolute fact, which everybody else might be constrained to recognise. If any one had made such a claim, and had seemed to have some chance of imposing it universally, James would have been the first to turn against him; not, of course, on the ground that it was *impossible* that such an orthodoxy should be true, but with a profound conviction that it was to be feared and distrusted. No: the degree of authority and honour to be accorded to various human faiths was a moral question, not a theoretical one. All faiths were what they were experienced as being, in their capacity of faiths; these faiths, not their objects, were the hard facts we must respect. We cannot pass, except under the illusion of the moment, to anything firmer or on a deeper level. There was accordingly no sense of security, no joy, in James's apology for personal religion. He did not really believe; he merely believed in the right of believing that you might be right if you believed.

It is this underlying agnosticism that explains an incoherence which we might find in his popular works, where the story and the moral do not seem to hang together. Professedly they are works of psychological observation; but the tendency and suasion in them seems to run to disintegrating the idea of truth, recommending belief without reason, and encouraging superstition. A psychologist who was not an agnostic would have indicated, as far as possible, whether the beliefs and experiences he was describing were instances of delusion or of rare and fine perception, or in what measure they were a mixture of both. But James—and this is what gives such romantic warmth to these writings of his—disclaims all antecedent or superior knowledge, listens to the testimony of each witness in turn, and only by accident allows us to feel that he is swayed by the eloquence and vehemence of some of them rather than of others. This method is modest, generous, and impartial; but if James intended, as I think he did, to picture the *drama* of human belief, with its risks and triumphs, the method was inadequate. Dramatists never hesitate to assume, and to let the audience perceive, who is good and who bad, who wise and who foolish, in their pieces;

otherwise their work would be as impotent dramatically as
scientifically. The tragedy and comedy of life lie precisely in the
contrast between the illusions or passions of the characters and
their true condition and fate, hidden from them at first, but evident to the author and the public. If in our diffidence and scrupulous fairness we refuse to take this judicial attitude, we shall be
led to strange conclusions. The navigator, for instance, trusting
his "experience" (which here, as in the case of religious people,
means his imagination and his art), insists on believing that the
earth is spherical; he has sailed round it. That is to say, he has
seemed to himself to steer westward and westward, and has
seemed to get home again. But how should he know that home is
now where it was before, or that his past and present impressions of it come from the same, or from any, material object?
How should he know that space is as trim and tri-dimensional
as the discredited Euclidians used to say it was? If, on the contrary, my worthy aunt, trusting to her longer and less ambiguous
experience of her garden, insists that the earth is flat, and observes that the theory that it is round, which is only a theory, is
much less often tested and found useful than her own perception
of its flatness, and that moreover that theory is pedantic, intellec-
tualistic, and a product of academies, and a rash dogma to impose
on mankind for ever and ever, it might seem that on James's principle we ought to agree with her. But no; on James's real principles we need not agree with her, nor with the navigator either.
Radical empiricism, which is radical agnosticism, delivers us from
so benighted a choice. For the quarrel becomes unmeaning when
we remember that the earth is *both* flat and round, if it is experienced as being both. The substantive fact is not a single object
on which both the perception and the theory are expected to
converge; the substantive facts are the theory and the perception
themselves. And we may note in passing that empiricism, when it
ceases to value experience as a means of discovering external
things, can give up its ancient prejudice in favour of sense as
against imagination, for imagination and thought are immediate experiences as much as sensation is: they are therefore, for
absolute empiricism, no less actual ingredients of reality.

In *The Varieties of Religious Experience* we find the same
apologetic intention running through a vivid account of what

seems for the most part (as James acknowledged) religious disease. Normal religious experience is hardly described in it. Religious experience, for the great mass of mankind, consists in simple faith in the truth and benefit of their religious traditions. But to James something so conventional and rationalistic seemed hardly experience and hardly religious; he was thinking only of irruptive visions and feelings as interpreted by the mystics who had them. These interpretations he ostensibly presents, with more or less wistful sympathy, for what they were worth; but emotionally he wished to champion them. The religions that had sprung up in America spontaneously—communistic, hysterical, spiritistic, or medicinal—were despised by select and superior people. You might inquire into them, as you might go slumming, but they remained suspect and distasteful. This picking up of genteel skirts on the part of his acquaintance prompted William James to roll up his sleeves—not for a knock-out blow, but for a thorough clinical demonstration. He would tenderly vivisect the experiences in question, to show how living they were, though of course he could not guarantee, more than other surgeons do, that the patient would survive the operation. An operation that eventually kills may be technically successful, and the man may die cured; and so a description of religion that showed it to be madness might first show how real and how warm it was, so that if it perished, at least it would perish understood.

I never observed in William James any personal anxiety or enthusiasm for any of these dubious tenets. His conception even of such a thing as free-will, which he always ardently defended, remained vague; he avoided defining even what he conceived to be desirable in such matters. But he wished to protect the weak against the strong, and what he hated beyond everything was the *non possumus* of any constituted authority. Philosophy for him had a Polish constitution; so long as a single vote was cast against the majority, nothing could pass. The suspense of judgment which he had imposed on himself as a duty, became almost a necessity. I think it would have depressed him if he had had to confess that any important question was finally settled. He would still have hoped that something might turn up on the other side, and that just as the scientific hangman was about to despatch the

poor convicted prisoner, an unexpected witness would ride up
in hot haste, and prove him innocent. Experience seems to most
of us to lead to conclusions, but empiricism has sworn never to
draw them.

In the discourse on "The Energies of Men," certain physiological marvels are recorded, as if to suggest that the resources
of our minds and bodies are infinite, or can be infinitely enlarged by divine grace. Yet James would not, I am sure, have
accepted that inference. He would, under pressure, have drawn
in his mystical horns under his scientific shell; but he was not
naturalist enough to feel instinctively that the wonderful and
the natural are all of a piece, and that only our degree of habitu-
ation distinguishes them. A nucleus, which we may poetically
call the soul, certainly lies within us, by which our bodies and
minds are generated and controlled, like an army by a government. In this nucleus, since nature in a small compass has room
for anything, vast quantities of energy may well be stored up,
which may be tapped on occasion, or which may serve like an
electric spark to let loose energy previously existing in the grosser
parts. But the absolute autocracy of this central power, or its
success in imposing extraordinary trials on its subjects, is not an
obvious good. Perhaps, like a democratic government, the soul
is at its best when it merely collects and co-ordinates the impulses
coming from the senses. The inner man is at times a tyrant,
parasitical, wasteful, and voluptuous. At other times he is fanatical and mad. When he asks for and obtains violent exertions from
the body, the question often is, as with the exploits of conquerors
and conjurers, whether the impulse to do such prodigious things
was not gratuitous, and the things nugatory. Who would wish
to be a mystic? James himself, who by nature was a spirited
rather than a spiritual man, had no liking for sanctimonious transcendentalists, visionaries, or ascetics; he hated minds that run
thin. But he hastened to correct this manly impulse, lest it should
be unjust, and forced himself to overcome his repugnance. This
was made easier when the unearthly phenomenon had a healing
or saving function in the everyday material world; miracle
then re-established its ancient identity with medicine, and both
of them were humanised. Even when this union was not attained,
James was reconciled to the miracle-workers partly by his great

charity, and partly by his hunter's instinct to follow a scent, for he believed discoveries to be imminent. Besides, a philosopher who is a teacher of youth is more concerned to give people a right start than a right conclusion. James fell in with the hortatory tradition of college sages; he turned his psychology, whenever he could do so honestly, to purposes of edification; and his little sermons on habit, on will, on faith, and this on the latent capacities of men, were fine and stirring, and just the sermons to preach to the young Christian soldier. He was much less sceptical in morals than in science. He seems to have felt sure that certain thoughts and hopes—those familiar to a liberal Protestantism—were every man's true friends in life. This assumption would have been hard to defend if he or those he habitually addressed had ever questioned it; yet his whole argument for voluntarily cultivating these beliefs rests on this assumption, that they are beneficent. Since, whether we will or no, we cannot escape the risk of error, and must succumb to some human or pathological bias, at least we might do so gracefully and in the form that would profit us most, by clinging to those prejudices which help us to lead what we all feel is a good life. But what is a good life? Had William James, had the people about him, had modern philosophers anywhere, any notion of that? I cannot think so. They had much experience of personal goodness, and love of it; they had standards of character and right conduct; but as to what might render human existence good, excellent, beautiful, happy, and worth having as a whole, their notions were utterly thin and barbarous. They had forgotten the Greeks, or never known them.

This argument accordingly suffers from the same weakness as the similar argument of Pascal in favour of Catholic orthodoxy. You should force yourself to believe in it, he said, because if you do so and are right you win heaven, while if you are wrong you lose nothing. What would Protestants, Mohammedans, and Hindus say to that? Those alternatives of Pascal's are not the sole nor the true alternatives; such a wager—betting on the improbable because you are offered big odds—is an unworthy parody of the real choice between wisdom and folly. There is no heaven to be won in such a spirit, and if there was, a philosopher would despise it. So William James would have us bet on immortality, or bet on our power to succeed, because if we win the wager we can live to congratulate ourselves on our true instinct, while we lose nothing if we have made a mistake; for unless you have the satisfaction of finding that you have been right, the dignity of having been right is apparently nothing. Or if the argument is rather that these beliefs, whether true or false, make life better in this world, the thing is simply false. To be boosted by an illusion is not to live better than to live in harmony with the truth; it is not nearly so safe, not nearly so sweet, and not nearly so fruitful. These refusals to part with a decayed illusion are really an infection to the mind. Believe, certainly; we cannot help believing; but believe rationally, holding what seems certain for certain, what seems probable for probable, what seems desirable for desirable, and what seems false for false.

In this matter, as usual, James had a true psychological fact and a generous instinct behind his confused moral suggestions. It is a psychological fact that men are influenced in their beliefs by their will and desires; indeed, I think we can go further and say that in its essence belief is an expression of impulse, of readiness to act. It is only peripherally, as our action is gradually adjusted to things, and our impulses to our possible or necessary action, that our ideas begin to hug the facts, and to acquire a true, if still a symbolic, significance. We do not need a will to believe; we only need a will to study the object in which we are inevitably believing. But James was thinking less of belief in what we find than of belief in what we hope for: a belief which is not at all clear and not at all necessary in the life of mortals. Like most Americans, however, only more lyrically, James felt the call of the future and the assurance that it could be made far better, totally other, than the past. The pictures that religion had painted of heaven or the millennium were not what he prized, although his Swedenborgian connection might have made him tender to them, as perhaps it did to familiar spirits. It was the moral succour offered by religion, its open spaces, the possibility of miracles *in extremis*, that must be retained. If we recoiled at the thought of being dupes (which is perhaps what nature intended us to be), were we less likely to be dupes in disbelieving these sustaining truths than in believing them? Faith was needed to bring about the reform of faith itself, as well as all other reforms.

In some cases faith in success could nerve us to bring success about, and so justify itself by its own operation. This is a thought typical of James at his worst—a worst in which there is always a good side. Here again psychological observation is used with the best intentions to hearten oneself and other people; but the fact observed is not at all understood, and a moral twist is given to it which (besides being morally questionable) almost amounts to falsifying the fact itself. Why does belief that you can jump a ditch help you to jump it? Because it is a symptom of the fact that you *could* jump it, that your legs were fit and that the ditch was two yards wide and not twenty. A rapid and just appreciation of these facts has given you your confidence, or at least has made it reasonable, manly, and prophetic; otherwise you would have been a fool and got a ducking for it. Assurance is contemptible and fatal unless it is self-knowledge. If you had been rattled you might have failed, because that would have been a symptom of the fact that you were out of gear; you would have been afraid because you trembled, as James at his best proclaimed. You would never have quailed if your system had been reacting smoothly to its opportunities, any more than you would totter and see double if you were not intoxicated. Fear is a sensation of actual nervousness and disarray, and confidence a sensation of actual readiness; they are not disembodied feelings, existing for no reason, the devil Funk and the angel Courage, one or the other of whom may come down arbitrarily into your body, and revolutionise it. That is childish mythology, which survives innocently enough as a figure of speech, until a philosopher is found to take that figure of speech seriously. Nor is the moral suggestion here less unsound. What is good is not the presumption of power, but the possession of it: a clear head, aware of its resources, not a fuddled optimism, calling up spirits from the vasty deep. Courage is not a virtue, said Socrates, unless it is also wisdom. Could anything be truer both of courage in doing and of courage in believing? But it takes tenacity, it takes *reasonable* courage, to stick to scientific insights such as this of Socrates or that of James about the emotions; it is easier to lapse into the traditional manner, to search natural philosophy for miracles and moral lessons, and in morals proper, in the reasoned expression of preference, to splash about without a philosophy.

William James shared the passions of liberalism. He belonged to the left, which, as they say in Spain, is the side of the heart, as the right is that of the liver; at any rate there was much blood and no gall in his philosophy. He was one of those elder Americans still disquieted by the ghost of tyranny, social and ecclesiastical. Even the beauties of the past troubled him; he had a puritan feeling that they were tainted. They had been cruel and frivolous, and must have suppressed far better things. But what, we may ask, might these better things be? It may do for a revolutionary politician to say: "I may not know what I want—except office—but I know what I don't want"; it will never do for a philosopher. Aversions and fears imply principles of preference, goods acknowledged; and it is the philosopher's business to make these goods explicit. Liberty is not an art, liberty must be used to bring some natural art to fruition. Shall it be simply eating and drinking and wondering what will happen next? If there is some deep and settled need in the heart of man, to give direction to his efforts, what else should a philosopher do but discover and announce what that need is?

There is a sense in which James was not a philosopher at all. He once said to me: "What a curse philosophy would be if we couldn't forget all about it!" In other words, philosophy was not to him what it has been to so many, a consolation and sanctuary in a life which would have been unsatisfying without it. It would be incongruous, therefore, to expect of him that he should build a philosophy like an edifice to go and live in for good. Philosophy to him was rather like a maze in which he happened to find himself wandering, and what he was looking for was the way out. In the presence of theories of any sort he was attentive, puzzled, suspicious, with a certain inner prompting to disregard them. He lived all his life among them, as a child lives among grown-up people; what a relief to turn from those stolid giants, with their prohibitions and exactions and tiresome talk, to another real child or a nice animal! Of course grown-up people are useful, and so James considered that theories might be; but in themselves, to live with, they were rather in the way, and at bottom our natural enemies. It was well to challenge one or another of them when you got a chance; perhaps that challenge might break some spell, transform the strange landscape, and simplify life. A theory while you were creating or using it was like a story you were telling yourself or a game you were playing; it was a warm, self-justifying thing then; but when the glow of creation or expectation was over, a theory was a phantom, like a ghost, or like the minds of other people. To all other people, even to ghosts, William James was the soul of courtesy; and he was civil to most theories as well, as to more or less interesting strangers that invaded him. Nobody ever recognised more heartily the chance that others had of being right, and the right they had to be different. Yet when it came to understanding what they meant, whether they were theories or persons, his intuition outran his patience; he made some brilliant impressionistic sketch in his fancy and called it by their name. This sketch was as often flattered as distorted, and he was at times the dupe of his desire to be appreciative and give the devil his due; he was too impulsive for exact sympathy; too subjective, too romantic, to be just. Love is very penetrating, but it penetrates to possibilities rather than to facts. The logic of opinions, as well as the exact opinions themselves, were not things James saw easily, or traced with pleasure. He liked to take things one by one, rather than to put two and two together. He was a mystic, a mystic in love with life. He was comparable to Rousseau and to Walt Whitman; he expressed a generous and tender sensibility, rebelling against sophistication, and preferring daily sights and sounds, and a vague but indomitable faith in fortune, to any settled intellectual tradition calling itself science or philosophy.

A prophet is not without honour save in his own country; and until the return wave of James's reputation reached America from Europe, his pupils and friends were hardly aware that he was such a distinguished man. Everybody liked him, and delighted in him for his generous, gullible nature and brilliant sallies. He was a sort of Irishman among the Brahmins, and seemed hardly imposing enough for a great man. They laughed at his erratic views and his undisguised limitations. Of course a conscientious professor ought to know everything he professes to know, but then, they thought, a dignified professor ought to seem to know everything. The precise theologians and panoplied idealists, who exist even in America, shook their heads. What sound philosophy, said they to themselves, could be expected from an irresponsible doctor, who was not even a college graduate, a crude empiricist, and vivisector of frogs? On the other hand, the solid men of business were not entirely reassured concerning a teacher of youth who seemed to have no system in particular— the ignorant rather demand that the learned should have a system in store, to be applied at a pinch; and they could not quite swallow a private gentleman who dabbled in hypnotism, frequented mediums, didn't talk like a book, and didn't write like a book, except like one of his own. Even his pupils, attached as they invariably were to his person, felt some doubts about the profundity of one who was so very natural, and who after some interruption during a lecture—and he said life was a series of interruptions—would slap his forehead and ask the man in the front row "What *was* I talking about?" Perhaps in the first years of his teaching he felt a little in the professor's chair as a military man might feel when obliged to read the prayers at a funeral. He probably conceived what he said more deeply than a more scholastic mind might have conceived it; yet he would have been more comfortable if some one else had said it for him. He liked to open the window, and look out for a moment. I think he was glad when the bell rang, and he could be himself again until the next day. But in the midst of this routine of the class-room the spirit would sometimes come upon him, and, leaning his head on his hand, he would let fall golden words, picturesque, fresh from the heart, full of the knowledge of good and evil. Incidentally there would crop up some humourous characterisation, some candid confession of doubt or of instinctive preference, some pungent scrap of learning; radicalisms plunging sometimes into the sub-soil of all human philosophies; and, on occasion, thoughts of simple wisdom and wistful piety, the most unfeigned and manly that anybody ever had.

ɞ Josiah Royce*

Meantime the mantle of philosophical authority had fallen at Harvard upon other shoulders. A young Californian, Josiah Royce, had come back from Germany with a reputation for wisdom; and even without knowing that he had already produced a new proof of the existence of God, merely to look at him you would have felt that he was a philosopher; his great head seemed too heavy for his small body, and his portentous brow, crowned with thick red hair, seemed to crush the lower part of his face. "Royce," said William James of him, "has an indecent exposure of forehead." There was a suggestion about him of the benevolent ogre or the old child, in whom a preternatural sharpness of insight lurked beneath a grotesque mask. If you gave him any cue, or even without one, he could discourse broadly on any subject; you never caught him napping. Whatever the text-books and encyclopædias could tell him, he knew; and if the impression he left on your mind was vague, that was partly because, in spite of his comprehensiveness, he seemed to view everything in relation to something else that remained untold. His approach to anything was oblique; he began a long way off, perhaps with the American preface of a funny story; and when the point came in sight, it was at once enveloped again in a cloud of qualifications, in the parliamentary jargon of philosophy. The tap once turned on, out flowed the stream of systematic disquisition, one

* Chapter IV of *Character and Opinion in the United States.*

hour, two hours, three hours of it, according to demand or opportunity. The voice, too, was merciless and harsh. You felt the overworked, standardised, academic engine, creaking and thumping on at the call of duty or of habit, with no thought of sparing itself or any one else. Yet a sprightlier soul behind this performing soul seemed to watch and laugh at the process. Sometimes a merry light would twinkle in the little eyes, and a bashful smile would creep over the uncompromising mouth. A sense of the paradox, the irony, the inconclusiveness of the whole argument would pierce to the surface, like a white-cap bursting here and there on the heavy swell of the sea.

His procedure was first to gather and digest whatever the sciences or the devil might have to say. He had an evident sly pleasure in the degustation and savour of difficulties; biblical criticism, the struggle for life, the latest German theory of sexual insanity, had no terrors for him; it was all grist for the mill, and woe to any tender thing, any beauty or any illusion, that should get between that upper and that nether millstone! He seemed to say: If I were not Alexander how gladly would I be Diogenes, and if I had not a system to defend, how easily I might tell you the truth. But after the sceptic had ambled quizzically over the ground, the prophet would mount the pulpit to survey it. He would then prove that in spite of all those horrors and contradictions, or rather because of them, the universe was absolutely perfect. For behind that mocking soul in him there was yet another, a devout and heroic soul. Royce was heir to the Calvinistic tradition; piety, to his mind, consisted in trusting divine providence and justice, while emphasising the most terrifying truths about one's own depravity and the sinister holiness of God. He accordingly addressed himself, in his chief writings, to showing that all lives were parts of a single divine life in which all problems were solved and all evils justified.

It is characteristic of Royce that in his proof of something sublime, like the existence of God, his premise should be something sad and troublesome, the existence of error. Error exists, he tells us, and common sense will readily agree, although the fact is not unquestionable, and pure mystics and pure sensualists deny it. But if error exists, Royce continues, there must be a truth from which it differs; and the existence of truth (accord-

ing to the principle of idealism, that nothing can exist except
for a mind that knows it) implies that some one knows the truth;
but as to know the truth thoroughly, and supply the corrective
to every possible error, involves omniscience, we have proved
the existence of an omniscient mind or universal thought; and
this is almost, if not quite, equivalent to the existence of God.

What carried Royce over the evident chasms and assumptions
in this argument was his earnestness and passionate eloquence.
He passed for an eminent logician, because he was dialectical
and fearless in argument and delighted in the play of formal
relations; he was devoted to chess, music, and mathematics; but
all this show of logic was but a screen for his heart, and in his
heart there was no clearness. His reasoning was not pure logic
or pure observation; it was always secretly enthusiastic or ma-
licious, and the result it arrived at had been presupposed. Here,
for instance, no unprejudiced thinker, not to speak of a pure
logician, would have dreamt of using the existence of error to
found the being of truth upon. Error is a biological accident
which may any day cease to exist, say at the extinction of the human race; whereas the being of truth or fact is involved inde-
feasibly and eternally in the existence of anything whatever, past,
present, or future; every event of itself renders true or false any
proposition that refers to it. No one would conceive of such a
thing as error or suspect its presence, unless he had already
found or assumed many a truth; nor could anything be an error
actually unless the truth was definite and real. All this Royce of
course recognised, and it was in some sense the heart of what he
meant to assert and to prove; but it does not need proving and
hardly asserting. What needed proof was something else, of less
logical importance but far greater romantic interest, namely, that
the truth was hovering over us and about to descend into our
hearts; and this Royce was not disinclined to confuse with the
being of truth, so as to bring it within the range of logical argument. He was tormented by the suspicion that he might be himself in the toils of error, and fervently aspired to escape from it.
Error to him was no natural, and in itself harmless, incident of
finitude; it was a sort of sin, as finitude was too. It was a part of
the problem of evil; a terrible and urgent problem when your
first postulate or dogma is that moral distinctions and moral ex-

perience are the substance of the world, and not merely an incident in it. The mere being of truth, which is all a logician needs,
would not help him in this wrestling for personal salvation; as
he keenly felt and often said, the truth is like the stars, always
laughing at us. Nothing would help him but *possession* of the
truth, something eventual and terribly problematic. He longed
to believe that all his troubles and questions, some day and some-
where, must find their solution and quietus; if not in his own
mind, in some kindred spirit that he could, to that extent, identify with himself. There must be not only cold truth, not even
cold truth personified, but victorious *knowledge* of the truth,
breaking like a sunburst through the clouds of error. The nerve
of his argument was not logical at all; it was a confession of religious experience, in which the agonised consciousness of error
led to a strong imaginative conviction that the truth would be
found at last.

The truth, as here conceived, meant the whole truth about
everything; and certainly, if any plausible evidence for such a
conclusion could be adduced, it would be interesting to learn
that we are destined to become omniscient, or are secretly
omniscient already. Nevertheless, the aspiration of all religious
minds does not run that way. Aristotle tells us that there are
many things it is better not to know; and his sublime deity is
happily ignorant of our errors and of our very existence; more
emphatically so the even sublimer deities of Plotinus and the Indians. The omniscience which our religion attributes to God as
the searcher of hearts and the judge of conduct has a moral function rather than a logical one; it prevents us from hiding our sins
or being unrecognised in our merits; it is not conceived to be
requisite in order that it may be true that those sins or merits
have existed. Atheists admit the facts, but they are content or
perhaps relieved that they should pass unobserved. But here
again Royce slipped into a romantic equivocation which a strict
logician would not have tolerated. Knowledge of the truth, a
passing psychological possession, was substituted for the truth
known, and this at the cost of rather serious ultimate confusions.
It is the truth itself, the facts in their actual relations, that honest
opinion appeals to, not to another opinion or instance of knowledge; and if, in your dream of warm sympathy and public cor-

roboration, you lay up your treasure in some instance of knowledge, which time and doubt might corrupt, you have not laid up
your treasure in heaven. In striving to prove the being of truth,
the young Royce absurdly treated it as doubtful, setting a bad
example to the pragmatists; while in striving to lend a psychological quality to this truth and turning it into a problematical
instance of knowledge, he unwittingly deprived it of all authority and sublimity. To personify the truth is to care less for
truth than for the corroboration and sympathy which the truth,
become human, might bring to our opinions. It is to set up another thinker, ourself enlarged, to vindicate us; without considering that this second thinker would be shut up, like us, in his
own opinions, and would need to look to the truth beyond him as
much as we do.

To the old problem of evil Royce could only give an old answer, although he rediscovered and repeated it for himself in
many ways, since it was the core of his whole system. Good,
he said, is essentially the struggle with evil and the victory over
it; so that if evil did not exist, good would be impossible. I do
not think this answer set him at rest; he could hardly help feeling that all goods are not of that bellicose description, and that
not all evils produce a healthy reaction or are swallowed up in
victory; yet the fact that the most specious solution to this
problem of evil left it unsolved was in its way appropriate; for if
the problem had been really solved, the struggle to find a solution
and the faith that there was one would come to an end; yet perhaps this faith and this struggle are themselves the supreme good.
Accordingly the true solution of this problem, which we may all
accept, is that no solution can ever be found.

Here is an example of the difference between the being of
truth and the ultimate solution of all our problems. There is certainly a truth about evil, and in this case not an unknown truth;
yet it is no solution to the "problem" which laid the indomitable
Royce on the rack. If a younger son asks why he was not born
before his elder brother, that question may represent an intelligible state of his feelings; but there is no answer to it, because it
is a childish question. So the question why it is right that there
should be any evil is itself perverse and raised by false presumptions. To an unsophisticated mortal the existence of evil presents

a task, never a problem. Evil, like error, is an incident of animal
life, inevitable in a crowded and unsettled world, where one
spontaneous movement is likely to thwart another, and all to run
up against material impossibilities. While life lasts this task is recurrent, and every creature, in proportion to the vitality and integrity of his nature, strives to remove or abate those evils of
which he is sensible. When the case is urgent and he is helpless,
he will cry out for divine aid; and (if he does not perish first) he
will soon see this aid coming to him through some shift in the
circumstances that renders his situation endurable. Positive religion takes a naturalistic view of things, and requires it. It parts
company with a scientific naturalism only in accepting the authority of instinct or revelation in deciding certain questions of
fact, such as immortality or miracles. It rouses itself to crush evil,
without asking why evil exists. What could be more intelligible
than that a deity like Jehovah, a giant inhabitant of the natural
world, should be confronted with rivals, enemies, and rebellious
children? What could be more intelligible than that the inertia of
matter, or pure chance, or some contrary purpose, should mar
the expression of any platonic idea exercising its magic influence over the world? For the Greek as for the Jew the task of
morals is the same: to subdue nature as far as possible to the uses
of the soul, by whatever agencies material or spiritual may be at
hand; and when a limit is reached in that direction, to harden
and cauterise the heart in the face of inevitable evils, opening
it wide at the same time to every sweet influence that may descend to it from heaven. Never for a moment was positive religion entangled in a sophistical optimism. Never did it conceive
that the most complete final deliverance and triumph would *justify* the evils which they abolished. As William James put it, in
his picturesque manner, if at the last day all creation was shout-
ing hallelujah and there remained one cockroach with an unrequited love, *that* would spoil the universal harmony; it would
spoil it, he meant, in truth and for the tender philosopher, but
probably not for those excited saints. James was thinking chiefly
of the present and future, but the same scrupulous charity has its
application to the past. To remove an evil is not to remove the fact
that it has existed. The tears that have been shed were shed in
bitterness, even if a remorseful hand afterwards wipes them away.

To be patted on the back and given a sugar-plum does not reconcile even a child to a past injustice. And the case is much worse if we are expected to make our heaven out of the foolish and cruel pleasures of contrast, or out of the pathetic offuscation produced by a great relief. Such a heaven would be a lie, like the sardonic heavens of Calvin and Hegel. The existence of any evil anywhere at any time absolutely ruins a total optimism.

Nevertheless philosophers have always had a royal road to complete satisfaction. One of the purest of pleasures, which they cultivate above all others, is the pleasure of understanding. Now, as playwrights and novelists know, the intellect is no less readily or agreeably employed in understanding evil than in understanding good—more so, in fact, if in the intellectual man, besides his intelligence, there is a strain of coarseness, irony, or desire to belittle the good things others possess and he himself has missed. Sometimes the philosopher, even when above all meanness, becomes so devoted a naturalist that he is ashamed to remain a moralist, although this is what he probably was in the beginning; and where all is one vast cataract of events, he feels it would be impertinent of him to divide them censoriously into things that ought to be and things that ought not to be. He may even go one step farther. Awestruck and humbled before the universe, he may insensibly transform his understanding and admiration of it into the assertion that the existence of evil is no evil at all, but that the order of the universe is in every detail necessary and perfect, so that the mere mention of the word evil is blind and blasphemous.

This sentiment, which as much as any other deserves the name of pantheism, is often expressed incoherently and with a false afflatus; but when rationally conceived, as it was by Spinoza, it amounts to this: that good and evil are relations which things bear to the living beings they affect. In itself nothing— much less this whole mixed universe—can be either good or bad; but the universe wears the aspect of a good in so far as it feeds, delights, or otherwise fosters any creature within it. If we define the intellect as the power to see things as they are, it is clear that in so far as the philosopher is a pure intellect the universe will be a pure good to the philosopher; everything in it will give play to his exclusive passion. Wisdom counsels us therefore to become philosophers and to concentrate our lives as much as possible in pure intelligence, that we may be led by it into the ways of peace. Not that the universe will be proved thereby to be intrinsically good (although in the heat of their intellectual egotism philosophers are sometimes betrayed into saying so), but that it will have become in that measure a good to us, and we shall be better able to live happily and freely in it. If intelligibility appears in things, it does so like beauty or use, because the mind of man, in so far as it is adapted to them, finds its just exercise in their society.

This is an ancient, shrewd, and inexpugnable position. If Royce had been able to adhere to it consistently, he would have avoided his gratuitous problem of evil without, I think, doing violence to the sanest element in his natural piety, which was joy in the hard truth, with a touch of humour and scorn in respect to mortal illusions. There was an observant and docile side to him; and as a child likes to see things work, he liked to see processions of facts marching on ironically, whatever we might say about it. This was his sense of the power of God. It attached him at first to Spinoza and later to mathematical logic. No small part of his life-long allegiance to the Absolute responded to this sentiment.

The outlook, however, was complicated and half reversed for him by the transcendental theory of knowledge which he had adopted. This theory regards all objects, including the universe, as merely terms posited by the will of the thinker, according to a definite grammar of thought native to his mind. In order that his thoughts may be addressed to any particular object, he must first choose and create it of his own accord; otherwise his opinions, not being directed upon any object in particular within his ken, cannot be either true or false, whatever picture they may frame. What anything external may happen to be, when we do not mean to speak of it, is irrelevant to our discourse. If, for instance, the real Royce were not a denizen and product of my mind—of my deeper self—I could not so much as have a wrong idea of him. The need of this initial relevance in our judgments seems to the transcendentalist to drive all possible objects into the fold of his secret thoughts, so that he has two minds, one that seeks the facts and another that already possesses or rather constitutes them.

Pantheism, when this new philosophy of knowledge is adopted, seems at first to lose its foundations. There is no longer an external universe to which to bow; no little corner left for us in the infinite where, after making the great sacrifice, we may build a safe nest. The intellect to which we had proudly reduced ourselves has lost its pre-eminence; it can no longer be called the faculty of seeing things as they are. It has become what psychological critics of intellectualism, such as William James, understand by it: a mass of human propensities to abstraction, construction, belief, or inference, by which imaginary things and truths are posited in the service of life. It is therefore on the same plane exactly as passion, music, or æsthetic taste: a mental complication which may be an index to other psychological facts connected with it genetically, but which has no valid intent, no ideal transcendence, no assertive or cognitive function. Intelligence so conceived understands nothing: it is a buzzing labour in the fancy which, by some obscure causation, helps us to live on.

To discredit the intellect, to throw off the incubus of an external reality or truth, was one of the boons which transcendentalism in its beginnings brought to the romantic soul. But although at first the sense of relief (to Fichte, for instance) was most exhilarating, the freedom achieved soon proved illusory: the terrible Absolute had been simply transplanted into the self. You were your own master, and omnipotent; but you were no less dark, hostile, and inexorable to yourself than the gods of Calvin or of Spinoza had been before. Since every detail of this mock world was your secret work, you were not only wiser but also more criminal than you knew. You were stifled, even more than formerly, in the arms of nature, in the toils of your own unaccountable character, which made your destiny. Royce never recoiled from paradox or from bitter fact; and he used to say that a mouse, when tormented and torn to pieces by a cat, was realising his own deepest will, since he had sub-consciously chosen to be a mouse in a world that should have cats in it. The mouse really, in his deeper self, wanted to be terrified, clawed, and devoured. Royce was superficially a rationalist, with no tenderness for superstition in detail and not much sympathy with civilised religions; but we see here that in his heart he was loyal to the aboriginal principle of all superstition: reverence for what hurts. He said to himself that in so far as God was the devil—as daily experience and Hegelian logic proved was largely the case—devil-worship was true religion.

A protest, however, arose in his own mind against this doctrine. Strong early bonds attached him to moralism—to the opinion of the Stoics and of Kant that virtue is the only good. Yet if virtue were conceived after their manner, as a heroic and sublimated attitude of the will, of which the world hardly afforded any example, how should the whole whirligig of life be good also? How should moralism, that frowns on this wicked world, be reconciled with pantheism and optimism, that hug it to their bosom? By the ingenious if rather melodramatic notion that we should hug it with a bear's hug, that virtue consisted (as Royce often put it) in holding evil by the throat; so that the world was good because it was a good world to strangle, and if we only managed to do so, the more it deserved strangling the better world it was. But this Herculean feat must not be considered as something to accomplish once for all; the labours of Hercules must be not twelve but infinite, since his virtue consisted in performing them, and if he ever rested or was received into Olympus he would have left virtue—the only good—behind. The wickedness of the world was no reason for quitting it; on the contrary, it invited us to plunge into all its depths and live through every phase of it; virtue was severe but not squeamish. It lived by endless effort, turbid vitality, and *Sturm und Drang.* Moralism and an apology for evil could thus be reconciled and merged in the praises of tragic experience.

This had been the burden of Hegel's philosophy of life, which Royce admired and adopted. Hegel and his followers seem to be fond of imagining that they are moving in a tragedy. But because Æschylus and Sophocles were great poets, does it follow that life would be cheap if it did not resemble their fables? The life of tragic heroes is not good; it is misguided, unnecessary, and absurd. Yet that is what romantic philosophy would condemn us to; we must all strut and roar. We must lend ourselves to the partisan earnestness of persons and nations calling their rivals villains and themselves heroes; but this earnestness will be of the histrionic German sort, made to order and transferable at short notice from one object to another, since what truly matters is not that we should achieve our ostensible aim (which Hegel contemptuously called ideal) but that we should carry on perpetually, if possible with a *crescendo*, the strenuous experience of living in a gloriously bad world, and always working to reform it, with the comforting speculative assurance that we never can succeed. We never can succeed, I mean, in rendering reform less necessary or life happier; but of course in any specific reform we may succeed half the time, thereby sowing the seeds of new and higher evils, to keep the edge of virtue keen. And in reality we, or the Absolute in us, are succeeding all the time; the play is always going on, and the play's the thing.

It was inevitable that Royce should have been at home only in this circle of Protestant and German intuitions; a more refined existence would have seemed to him to elude moral experience. Although he was born in California he had never got used to the sunshine; he had never tasted peace. His spirit was that of courage and labour. He was tender in a bashful way, as if in tenderness there was something pathological, as indeed to his sense there was, since he conceived love and loyalty to be divine obsessions refusing to be rationalised; he saw their essence in the child who clings to an old battered doll rather than accept a new and better one. Following orthodox tradition in philosophy, he insisted on seeing reason at the bottom of things as well as at the top, so that he never could understand either the root or the flower of anything. He watched the movement of events as if they were mysterious music, and instead of their causes and potentialities he tried to divine their *motif*. On current affairs his judgments were highly seasoned and laboriously wise. If anything escaped him, it was only the simplicity of what is best. His reward was that he became a prophet to a whole class of earnest, troubled people who, having discarded doctrinal religion, wished to think their life worth living when, to look at what it contained, it might not have seemed so; it reassured them to learn that a strained and joyless existence was not their unlucky lot, or a consequence of their solemn folly, but was the necessary fate of all good men and angels. Royce had always experienced and seen about him a groping, burdened, mediocre life; he had observed how fortune is continually lying in ambush for us, in order to bring good out of evil and evil out of good. In his age and country all was change, preparation, hurry, material achievement; nothing was an old and sufficient possession; nowhere, or very much in the background, any leisure, simplicity, security, or harmony. The whole scene was filled with arts and virtues which were merely useful or remedial. The most pressing arts, like war and forced labour, presuppose evil, work immense havoc, and take the place of greater possible goods. The most indispensable virtues, like courage and industry, do likewise. But these seemed in Royce's world the only honourable things, and he took them to be typical of all art and virtue—a tremendous error. It is very true, however, that in the welter of material existence no concrete thing can be good or evil in every respect; and so long as our rough arts and virtues do more good than harm we give them honourable names, such as unselfishness, patriotism, or religion; and it remains a mark of good breeding among us to practise them instinctively. But an absolute love of such forced arts and impure virtues is itself a vice; it is, as the case may be, barbarous, vain, or fanatical. It mistakes something specific—some habit or emotion which may be or may have been good in some respect, or under some circumstances the lesser of two evils—for the very principle of excellence. But good and evil, like light and shade, are ethereal; all things, events, persons, and conventional virtues are in themselves utterly valueless, save as an immaterial harmony (of which mind is an expression) plays about them on occasion, when their natures meet propitiously, and bathes them in some tint of happiness or beauty. This immaterial harmony may be made more and more perfect; the difficulties in the way of perfection, either in man, in society, or in universal nature, are physical not logical. Worship of barbarous virtue is the blackest conservatism; it shuts the gate of heaven, and surrenders existence to perpetual follies and crimes. Moralism itself is a superstition. In its abstract form it is moral, too moral; it adores the conventional conscience, or perhaps a morbid one. In its romantic form, moralism becomes barbarous and actually immoral; it obstinately craves action and stress for their own sake, experience in the gross, and a good-and-bad way of living.

Royce sometimes conceded that there might be some pure goods, music, for instance, or mathematics; but the impure moral goods were better and could not be spared. Such a concession, however, if it had been taken to heart, would have ruined his whole moral philosophy. The romanticist must maintain that *only* what is painful can be noble and *only* what is lurid bright. A taste for turbid and contrasted values would soon seem perverse when once anything perfect had been seen and loved. Would it not have been better to leave out the worst of the crimes and plagues that have heightened the tragic value of the world? But if so, why stop before we had deleted them all? We should presently be horrified at the mere thought of passions that before had been found necessary by the barbarous tragedian to keep his audience awake; and the ear at the same time would become sensitive to a thousand harmonies that had been inaudible in the hurly-burly of romanticism. The romanticist thinks he has life by virtue of his confusion and torment, whereas in truth that torment and confusion are his incipient death, and it is only the modicum of harmony he has achieved in his separate faculties that keeps him alive at all. As Aristotle taught, unmixed harmony would be intensest life. The spheres might make a sweet and perpetual music, and a happy God is at least possible.

It was not in this direction, however, that Royce broke away on occasion from his Hegelian ethics; he did so in the direction of ethical dogmatism and downright sincerity. The deepest thing in him personally was conscience, firm recognition of duty, and the democratic and American spirit of service. He could not adopt a moral bias histrionically, after the manner of Hegel or Nietzsche. To those hardened professionals any rôle was acceptable, the more commanding the better; but the good Royce was like a sensitive amateur, refusing the rôle of villain, however brilliant and necessary to the play. In contempt of his own speculative insight, or in an obedience to it which forgot it for the time being, he lost himself in his part, and felt that it was infinitely important to be cast only for the most virtuous of characters. He retained inconsistently the Jewish allegiance to a God essentially the vindicator of only one of the combatants, not in this world often the victor; he could not stomach the providential scoundrels which the bad taste of Germany, and of Carlyle and Browning, was wont to glorify. The last notable act of his life was an illustration of this, when he uttered a ringing public de-

nunciation of the sinking of the *Lusitania*. Orthodox Hegelians
might well have urged that here, if anywhere, was a plain case
of the providential function of what, from a finite merely moral
point of view, was an evil in order to make a higher good possible—the virtue of German self-assertion and of American self-
assertion in antithesis to it, synthesised in the concrete good of
war and victory, or in the perhaps more blessed good of defeat.
What could be more unphilosophical and *gedankenlos* than the
intrusion of mere morality into the higher idea of world-devel-
opment? Was not the Universal Spirit compelled to bifurcate into
just such Germans and just such Americans, in order to attain
self-consciousness by hating, fighting against, and vanquishing
itself? Certainly it was American duty to be angry, as it was German duty to be ruthless. The Idea liked to see its fighting-cocks
at it in earnest, since that was what it had bred them for; but
both were good cocks. Villains, as Hegel had observed in describing Greek tragedy, were not less self-justified than heroes; they
were simply the heroes of a lower stage of culture. America and
England remained at the stage of individualism; Germany had advanced to the higher stage of organisation. Perhaps this necessary
war was destined, through the apparent defeat of Germany, to
bring England and America up to the German level. Of course;
and yet somehow, on this occasion, Royce passed over these profound considerations, which life-long habit must have brought
to his lips. A Socratic demon whispered No, No in his ear; it
would have been better for such things never to be. The murder
of those thousand passengers was not a providential act, requisite
to spread abroad a vitalising war; it was a crime to execrate altogether. It would have been better for Hegel, or whoever was responsible for it, if a millstone had been hanged about his neck
and he, and not those little ones, had been drowned at the bottom of the sea. Of this terrestrial cockpit Royce was willing to
accept the agony, but not the ignominy. The other cock was a
wicked bird.

This honest lapse from his logic was habitual with him at the
sight of sin, and sin in his eyes was a fearful reality. His conscience spoiled the pantheistic serenity of his system; and what
was worse (for he was perfectly aware of the contradiction) it
added a deep, almost remorseful unrest to his hard life. What

calm could there be in the double assurance that it was really
right that things should be wrong, but that it was really wrong
not to strive to right them? There was no conflict, he once observed, between science and religion, but the real conflict was
between religion and morality. There could indeed be no conflict in his mind between faith and science, because his faith
began by accepting all facts and all scientific probabilities in
order to face them religiously. But there was an invincible conflict between religion as he conceived it and morality, because
morality takes sides and regards one sort of motive and one kind
of result as better than another, whereas religion according to
him gloried in everything, even in the evil, as fulfilling the
will of God. Of course the practice of virtue was not excluded;
it was just as needful as evil was in the scheme of the whole; but
while the effort of morality was requisite, the judgments of morality were absurd. Now I think we may say that a man who finds
himself in such a position has a divided mind, and that while he
has wrestled with the deepest questions like a young giant, he
has not won the fight. I mean, he has not seen his way to any one
of the various possibilities about the nature of things, but has remained entangled, sincerely, nobly, and pathetically, in contrary
traditions stronger than himself. In the goodly company of philosophers he is an intrepid martyr.

In metaphysics as in morals Royce perpetually laboured the
same points, yet they never became clear; they covered a natural complexity in the facts which his idealism could not disentangle. There was a voluminous confusion in his thought; some
clear principles and ultimate possibilities turned up in it, now
presenting one face and now another, like chips carried down a
swollen stream; but the most powerful currents were below the
surface, and the whole movement was hard to trace. He had borrowed from Hegel a way of conceiving systems of philosophy,
and also the elements of his own thoughts, which did not tend
to clarify them. He did not think of correcting what incoherence
there might remain in any view, and then holding it in reserve,
as one of the possibilities, until facts should enable us to decide
whether it was true or not. Instead he clung to the incoherence
as if it had been the heart of the position, in order to be driven by
it to some other position altogether, so that while every view

seemed to be considered, criticised, and in a measure retained (since the argument continued on the same lines, however ill-chosen they might have been originally), yet justice was never done to it; it was never clarified, made consistent with itself, and then accepted or rejected in view of the evidence. Hence a vicious and perplexing suggestion that philosophies are bred out of philosophies, not out of men in the presence of things. Hence too a sophistical effort to find everything self-contradictory, and in some disquieting way both true and false, as if there were not an infinite number of perfectly consistent systems which the world might have illustrated.

Consider, for instance, his chief and most puzzling contention, that all minds are parts of one mind. It is easy, according to the meaning we give to the word mind, to render this assertion clear and true, or clear and false, or clear and doubtful (because touching unknown facts), or utterly absurd. It is obvious that all minds are parts of one flux or system of experiences, as all bodies are parts of one system of bodies. Again, if mind is identified with its objects, and people are said to be "of one mind" when they are thinking of the same thing, it is certain that many minds are often identical in part, and they would all be identical with portions of an omniscient mind that should perceive all that they severally experienced. The question becomes doubtful if what we mean by oneness of mind is unity of type; our information or plausible guesses cannot assure us how many sorts of experience may exist, or to what extent their development (when they develop) follows the same lines of evolution. The animals would have to be consulted, and the other planets, and the infinite recesses of time. The straitjacket which German idealism has provided is certainly far too narrow even for the varieties of human imagination. Finally, the assertion becomes absurd when it is understood to suggest that an actual instance of thinking, in which something, say the existence of America, is absent or denied, can be part of another actual instance of thinking in which it is present and asserted. But this whole method of treating the matter—and we might add anything that observation might warrant us in adding about multiple personalities—would leave out the problem that agitated Royce and that bewildered his readers. He wanted all minds to be one in some way which should be logically and morally necessary, and which yet, as he could not help feeling, was morally and logically impossible.

For pure transcendentalism, which was Royce's technical method, the question does not arise at all. Transcendentalism is an attitude or a point of view rather than a system. Its Absolute is thinking "as such," wherever thought may exert itself. The notion that there are separate instances of thought is excluded, because space, time, and number belong to the visionary world posited by thought, not to the function of thinking; individuals are figments of constructive fancy, as are material objects. The stress of moral being is the same wherever it may fall, and there are no finite selves, or relations between thinkers; also no infinite self, because on this principle the Absolute is not an existent being, a psychological monster, but a station or office; its essence is a task. Actual thinking is therefore never a part of the Absolute, but always the Absolute itself. Thinkers, finite or infinite, would be existing persons or masses of feelings; such things are dreamt of only. *Any* system of existences, *any* truth or matter of fact waiting to be recognised, contradicts the transcendental insight and stultifies it. The all-inclusive mind is my mind as I think, mind in its living function, and beyond that philosophy cannot go.

Royce, however, while often reasoning on this principle, was incapable of not going beyond it, or of always remembering it. He could not help believing that constructive fancy not only feigns individuals and instances of thought, but is actually seated in them. The Absolute, for instance, must be not merely the abstract subject or transcendental self in all of us (although it was that too), but an actual synthetic universal mind, the God of Aristotle and of Christian theology. Nor was it easy for Royce, a sincere soul and a friend of William James, not to be a social realist; I mean, not to admit that there are many collateral human minds, in temporal existential relations to one another, any of which may influence another, but never supplant it nor materially include it. Finite experience was not a mere element in infinite experience; it was a tragic totality in itself. I was not God looking at myself, I was myself looking for God. Yet this strain was utterly incompatible with the principles of transcendentalism; it turned philosophy into a simple anticipation of science, if not into an indulgence in literary psychology. Knowledge would then have been only faith leaping across the chasm of coexistence and guessing the presence and nature of what surrounds us by some hint of material influence or brotherly affinity. Both the credulity and the finality which such naturalism implies were offensive to Royce, and contrary to his sceptical and mystical instincts. Was there some middle course?

The audience in a theatre stand in a transcendental relation to the persons and events in the play. The performance may take place to-day and last one hour, while the fable transports us to some heroic epoch or to an age that never existed, and stretches through days and perhaps years of fancied time. Just so transcendental thinking, while actually timeless and not distributed among persons, might survey infinite time and rehearse the passions and thoughts of a thousand characters. Thought, after all, needs objects, however fictitious and ideal they may be; it could not think if it thought nothing. This indispensable world of appearance is far more interesting than the reality that evokes it; the qualities and divisions found in the appearance diversify the monotonous function of pure thinking and render it concrete. Instances of thought and particular minds may thus be introduced consistently into a transcendental system, provided they are distinguished not by their own times and places, but only by their themes. The transcendental mind would be a pure poet, with no earthly life, but living only in his works, and in the times and persons of his fable. This view, firmly and consistently held, would deserve the name of absolute idealism, which Royce liked to give to his own system. But he struggled to fuse it with social realism, with which it is radically incompatible. Particular minds and the whole process of time, for absolute idealism, are *ideas* only; they are thought of and surveyed, they never think or lapse actually. For this reason genuine idealists can speak so glibly of the mind of a nation or an age. It is just as real and unreal to them as the mind of an individual; for within the human individual they can trace unities that run through and beyond him, so that parts of him, identical with parts of other people, form units as living as himself; for it is all a web of themes, not a concourse of existences. This is the very essence and pride of idealism, that knowledge is not knowledge of the world but is the world itself, and that the units of discourse, which are inter-woven and crossed units, are the only individuals in being. You may call them persons, because "person" means a mask; but you cannot call them souls. They are knots in the web of history. They are words in their context, and the only spirit in them is the sense they have for me.

Royce, however, in saying all this, also wished not to say it, and his two thick volumes on *The World and the Individual* leave their subject wrapped in utter obscurity. Perceiving the fact when he had finished, he very characteristically added a "Supplementary Essay" of a hundred more pages, in finer print, in which to come to the point. Imagine, he said, an absolutely exhaustive map of England spread out upon English soil. The map would be a part of England, yet would reproduce every feature of England, including itself; so that the map would reap-pear on a smaller scale within itself an infinite number of times, like a mirror reflected in a mirror. In this way we might be indi-viduals within a larger individual, and no less actual and com-plete than he. Does this solve the problem? If we take the illustra-tion as it stands, there is still only one individual in existence, the material England, all the maps being parts of its single surface; nor will it at all resemble the maps, since it will be washed by the sea and surrounded by foreign nations, and not, like the maps, by other Englands enveloping it. If, on the contrary, we equalise the status of all the members of the series, by making it infinite in both directions, then there would be no England at all, but only map within map of England. There would be no absolute mind inclusive but not included, and the Absolute would be the series as a whole, utterly different from any of its members. It would be a series while they were maps, a truth while they were minds; and if the Absolute from the beginning had been regarded as a truth only, there never would have been any diffi-culty in the existence of individuals under it. Moreover, if the in-dividuals are all exactly alike, does not their exact similarity de-feat the whole purpose of the speculation, which was to vin-dicate the equal reality of the whole and of its *limited* parts? And if each of us, living through infinite time, goes through precisely the same experiences as every one else, why this vain repetition? Is it not enough for this insatiable world to live its life once?

Why not admit solipsism and be true to the transcendental method? Because of conscience and good sense? But then the infinite series of maps is useless, England is herself again, and the prospect opens before us of an infinite number of supplementary essays.

Royce sometimes felt that he might have turned his hand to other things than philosophy. He once wrote a novel, and its want of success was a silent disappointment to him. Perhaps he might have been a great musician. Complexity, repetitions, vagueness, endlessness are hardly virtues in writing or thinking, but in music they might have swelled and swelled into a real sublimity, all the more that he was patient, had a voluminous meandering memory, and loved technical devices. But rather than a musician—for he was no artist—he resembled some great-hearted mediæval peasant visited by mystical promptings, whom the monks should have adopted and allowed to browse among their theological folios; a Duns Scotus earnest and studious to a fault, not having the lightness of soul to despise those elaborate sophistries, yet minded to ferret out their secret for himself and walk by his inward light. His was a Gothic and scholastic spirit, intent on devising and solving puzzles, and honouring God in systematic works, like the coral insect or the spider; eventually creating a fabric that in its homely intricacy and fulness arrested and moved the heart, the web of it was so vast, and so full of mystery and yearning.

❧ Dewey's Naturalistic Metaphysics*

Here is a remarkable rereading of things with a new and difficult kind of sincerity, a near-sighted sincerity comparable in philosophy to that of contemporary painters in their painful studies. The intellect here, like the fancy there, arrests its dogmatic vision and stops short at some relational term which was invisible because it is only a vehicle in natural seeing. No wonder that these near elements, abstracted and focussed in themselves, have a queer look. For my part, I am entirely persuaded of the genuineness and depth of Dewey's views, within the limits of his method and taken as he means them. He is, fortunately, not without an active band of followers who will be able to interpret and elaborate them in his own spirit. I am hardly in their case, and all I can hope to accomplish is to fix the place and character of this doctrine in relation to the points of view which I instinctively take or which seem to me, on reflection, to be most comprehensive. And I will append such conclusions as I may provisionally reach on this subject to a phrase by which Dewey himself characterises his system: *Naturalistic Metaphysics.* In what sense is this system naturalistic? In what sense is it metaphysical? How comes it that these two characters (which to me seem contradictory) can be united in this philosophy?

Naturalism is a primary system, or rather it is not a special

* From *Obiter Scripta* (New York: Charles Scribner's Sons, 1936). Originally a review of John Dewey's *Experience and Nature.*

system at all, but the spontaneous and inevitable body of beliefs
involved in animal life, beliefs of which the various philosophical systems are either extensions (a supernatural environment,
itself natural in its own way, being added to nature) or interpretations (as in Aristotle and Spinoza) or denials (as in idealism).
Children are interested in their bodies, with which they identify
themselves; they are interested in animals, adequate playmates
for them, to be bullied with a pleasing risk and a touch of wonder. They are interested later in mechanical contrivances and
in physical feats and adventures. This boyish universe is indefinitely extensible on its own plane; it may have heaven around it
and fairyland in its interstices; it covers the whole field of possible material action to its uttermost reaches. It is the world of naturalism. On this material framework it is easy to hang all the immaterial objects, such as words, feelings, and ideas, which may be
eventually distinguished in human experience. We are not compelled in naturalism, or even in materialism, to ignore immaterial
things; the point is that any immaterial things which are recognised shall be regarded as names, aspects, functions, or concomitant products of those physical things among which action goes
on. A naturalist may distinguish his own person or self, provided
he identifies himself with his body and does not assign to his soul
any fortunes, powers, or actions save those of which his body is
the seat and organ. He may recognise other spirits, human, animal, or divine, provided they are all proper to natural organisms
figuring in the world of action, and are the natural moral transcript, like his own feelings, of physical life in that region. Naturalism may, accordingly, find room for every sort of psychology,
poetry, logic, and theology, if only they are content with their
natural places. Naturalism will break down, however, so soon as
words, ideas, or spirits are taken to be substantial on their own
account, and powers at work prior to the existence of their organs, or independent of them. Now it is precisely such disembodied powers and immaterial functions prior to matter that are
called metaphysical. Transcendentalism is not metaphysical if it
remains a mere method, because then it might express the natural
fact that any animal mind is its own centre and must awake in
order to know anything: it becomes metaphysical when this
mind is said to be absolute, single, and without material condi-

tions. To admit anything metaphysical in this sense is evidently to abandon naturalism.

It would be hard to find a philosopher in whom naturalism, so conceived, was more inveterate than in Dewey. He is very severe against the imagination, and even the intellect, of mankind for having created figments which usurp the place and authority of the mundane sphere in which daily action goes on. The typical philosopher's fallacy, in his eyes, has been the habit of hypostatising the conclusions to which reflection may lead, and deputing them to be prior realities—the fallacy of dogmatism. These conclusions are in reality nothing but suggestions or, as Dewey calls them, "meanings" surrounding the passing experience in which, at some juncture, a person is immersed. They may be excellent in an instrumental capacity, if by their help instinctive action can be enlarged or adjusted more accurately to absent facts; but it would be sheer idolatry to regard them as realities or powers deeper than obvious objects, producing these objects and afterwards somehow revealing themselves, just as they are, to the thoughts of metaphysicians. Here is a rude blow dealt at dogma of every sort: God, matter, Platonic ideas, active spirits, and creative logics all seem to totter on their thrones; and if the blow could be effective, the endless battle of metaphysics would have to end for lack of combatants.

Meantime there is another motive that drives Dewey to naturalism: he is the devoted spokesman of the spirit of enterprise, of experiment, of modern industry. To him, rather than to William James, might be applied the saying of the French pragmatist, Georges Sorel, that his philosophy is calculated to justify all the assumptions of American society. William James was a psychologist of the individual, preoccupied with the varieties of the human imagination and with the possible destinies of the spirit in other worlds. He was too spontaneous and rare a person to be a good mirror of any broad general movement; his Americanism, like that of Emerson, was his own and within him, and perhaps more representative of America in the past than in the future. In Dewey, on the contrary, as in current science and ethics, there is a pervasive quasi-Hegelian tendency to dissolve the individual into his social functions, as well as everything substantial or actual into something relative or transitional. For him events, situations, and histories hold all facts and all persons in solution. The master-burden of his philosophy, which lends it its national character, is a profound sympathy with the enterprise of life in all lay directions, in its technical and moral complexity, and especially in its American form, where individual initiative, although still demanded and prized, is quickly subjected to overwhelming democratic control. This, if I am not mistaken, is the heart of Dewey's pragmatism, that it is the pragmatism of the people, dumb and instinctive in them, and struggling in him to a laboured but radical expression. His pragmatism is not inspired by any wish to supply a new argument to support some old speculative dogma. Nor is he interested, like Nietzsche and Vaihinger, in a heroic pessimism, desperately living as if postulates were true which it knows to be false. He is not interested in speculation at all, balks at it, and would avoid it if he could; his inspiration is sheer fidelity to the task in hand and sympathy with the movement afoot: a deliberate and happy participation in the attitude of the American people, with its omnivorous human interests and its simplicity of purpose.

Now the philosophy by which Americans live, in contrast to the philosophies which they profess, is naturalistic. In profession they may be Fundamentalists, Catholics, or idealists, because American opinion is largely pre-American; but in their hearts and lives they are all pragmatists, and they prove it even by the spirit in which they maintain those other traditional allegiances, not out of rapt speculative sympathy, but because such allegiance seems an insurance against moral dissolution, guaranteeing social cohesion and practical success. Their real philosophy is the philosophy of enterprise. Now enterprise moves in the infinitely extensible boyish world of feats and discoveries—in the world of naturalism. The practical arts, as Dewey says, assume a mechanical unity and constancy established in the universe. Otherwise discoveries made to-day would not count to-morrow, inventions could not be patented, the best-laid plans might go astray, all work might be wasted, and the methods of experts could not be adjusted more and more accurately to their tasks. This postulated mechanical system must evidently include the hands and brain of the worker, which are intertwined inextricably with the work done. It must also include his mind, if his mind is to be of any practical account and to make any difference in his work. Hence the implicit American philosophy, which it is Dewey's privilege to make explicit, involves behaviourism. This doctrine is new and amazing if taken to deny the existence of thought; but on its positive side, in so far as it puts all efficient processes on one level, it has been an implication of naturalism from time immemorial. For a naturalist nothing can be substantial or efficacious in thought except its organs and instruments, such as brains, training, words, and books. Actual thought, being invisible and imponderable, eludes this sort of chase. It has always been rather ignored by materialists; but it remained for American optimists to turn their scorn of useless thought into a glad denial of its existence. This negative implication of behaviourism follows also from the common-sense view that mind and body act upon each other alternately; for when this view is carried out with empirical rigour, it corrects the speculative confusion which first suggested it. What it called mind turns out never to have been anything but a habit in matter, a way people have of acting, speaking, and writing. The actuality of spirit, mystically momentary, does not fall within the purview of this empirical inventory any more than the realm of truth, invisibly eternal. Men of affairs, who can easily tell a clever man from a fool, are behaviourists by instinct; but they may scout their own conviction when it is proposed to them by philosophers in paradoxical language. The business intellect, by the time it comes to theorising, is a little tired. It will either trust a first impression, and bluff it out, or else it will allow comfortable traditional assurances in these hazy regions to relieve it of responsibility.

Is Dewey a behaviourist? On the positive side of the theory, he certainly is; and it is only when we interpret what he says about ideas, meanings, knowledge, or truth behaviouristically, that the sense and the force of it begin to appear. Often, indeed, he seems to jump the barrier, and to become a behaviourist in the negative sense also, denying the existence of thought: because it would be to deny its existence if we reduced it to its material manifestations. At least at one point, however, the existence of thought in its actuality and spiritual concentration is admitted plainly. Not, indeed, on the ground which to most philosophers would seem obvious and final, namely, that people some-

times do actually feel and think. This consideration might seem
to Dewey irrelevant, because actual feeling and thinking are ac-
counted for initially, on his view, by the absolute existence of
the specious or conventional world: they do not need to be introduced again among its details. An impersonal transcendental spectator, though never mentioned, is always assumed; and the spectacle of nature unrolled before him may be, and strictly speaking must be, wholly observable and material. There cannot be
any actual mind in experience except the experience itself. The
consideration which nevertheless leads Dewey to graft something
consciously actual and spiritual upon the natural world is of
quite another sort. Essentially, I suspect, it flows from his choice
of "events" to be his metaphysical elements (of which more presently); incidentally it is attached to the sympathetic study which
he has made of Aristotle. Events, he thinks, have natural "end-
ings," "culminations," or "consummations." They are not arbitrary sections made in the flux of nature, as if by geometrical
planes passed across the current of a river. They are natural
waves, pulsations of being, each of which, without any interruption in its material inheritance and fertility, forms a unit of a
higher order. These units (if I may express the matter in my own
language) fall sometimes into the realm of truth, when they are
simply observable patterns or rhythms, and sometimes into the
realm of spirit, as in animal perception or intent, when the complex tensions of bodily or social life generate a single sound, an
actual pang, or a vivid idea. Mind at such moments possesses a
hypostatic spiritual existence, over and above the whole behaviourist or pragmatic ground-work of mind: it has become conscious, or as Aristotle would say, has reached its second entelechy
and become intellect in act. This hypostatic spiritual existence
Dewey seems to recognise at least in æsthetic contemplation; but
evidently every actual feeling or idea, however engrossed in action or however abstractly intellectual, is in the same case.

Such an admission, if taken to heart, would have leavened this
whole philosophy; but Dewey makes it grudgingly, and hastens
to cover it up. For instance, when he comes upon the phrase
"knowledge of acquaintance," he says that acquaintance implies
recognition and recognition familiarity; on the ground, I suppose,
that people are called "acquaintances" when they bow to one

another: and we are left with an uncomfortable suspicion that it is impossible to inspect anything for the first time. In another place we are told that consummations are themselves fruitful and ends are also means. Yes, but in what sense? Of course, no earthly flame is so pure as to leave no ashes, and the highest wave sinks presently into the trough of the sea; but this is true only of the substance engaged, which, having reached a culmination here, continues in its course; and the habit which it then acquired may, within limits, repeat the happy achievement, and propagate the light. One torch by material contact may kindle another torch; and if the torches are similar and the wind steady, the flames, too, may be similar and even continuous; but if any one says that the visible splendour of one moment helps to produce that of another, he does not seem ever to have seen the light. It will therefore be safer to proceed as if the realm of actual spirit had not been broached at this point, and as if the culminations recognised were only runs or nodes discoverable in nature, as in the cycle of reproduction or in sentences in discourse. The behaviourist landscape will then not be split by any spiritual lightning, and naturalism will seem to be established in its most unqualified form. Yet in this case how comes it that Dewey has a metaphysics of his own, that cosmology is absent from his system, and that every natural fact becomes in his hands so strangely unseizable and perplexing?

This question, which is the crux of the whole system, may be answered, I think, in a single phrase: *the dominance of the foreground*. In nature there is no foreground or background, no here, no now, no moral cathedra, no centre so really central as to reduce all other things to mere margins and mere perspectives. A foreground is by definition relative to some chosen point of view, to the station assumed in the midst of nature by some creature tethered by fortune to a particular time and place. If such a foreground becomes dominant in a philosophy naturalism is abandoned. Some local perspective or some casual interest is set up in the place of universal nature or behind it, or before it, so that all the rest of nature is reputed to be intrinsically remote or dubious or merely ideal. This dominance of the foreground has always been the source of metaphysics; and the metaphysics has varied according as the foreground has been occupied by lan-

guage or fancy or logic or sceptical self-consciousness or religious rapture or moral ambition. Now the dominance of the foreground is in all Dewey's traditions: it is the soul of transcendentalism and also of empiricism; it is the soul of moralism and of that
kind of religion which summons the universe to vindicate human
notions of justice or to subserve the interests of mankind or of
some special nation or civilisation. In America the dominance of
the foreground is further emphasised by the prevalent absorption in business life and in home affections, and by a general feeling that anything ancient, foreign, or theoretical cannot be of
much consequence.[1] Pragmatism may be regarded as a synthesis
of all these ways of making the foreground dominant: the most
close-reefed of philosophical craft, most tightly hugging appearance, use, and relevance to practice today and here, least drawn
by the lure of speculative distances. Nor would Dewey, I am
sure, or any other pragmatist, ever be a naturalist instinctively or
on the wings of speculative insight, like the old Ionians or the
Stoics or Spinoza, or like those many mystics, Indian, Jewish, or
Mohammedan, who, heartily despising the foreground, have
fallen in love with the greatness of nature and have sunk speech-
less before the infinite. The pragmatist becomes, or seems to become, a naturalist only by accident, when as in the present age
and in America the dominant foreground is monopolised by material activity; because material activity, as we have seen, involves
naturalistic assumptions, and has been the teacher and the proof
of naturalism since the beginning of time. But elsewhere and at
other periods experience is free to offer different perspectives
into which the faithful pragmatist will be drawn with equal zeal;
and then pragmatic metaphysics would cease to be naturalistic
and become, perhaps, theological. Naturalism in Dewey is accordingly an assumption imposed by the character of the prevalent arts; and as he is aware that he is a naturalist only to that extent and on that ground, his naturalism is half-hearted and short-

---

[1] I can imagine the spontaneous pragmatism of some president of a State
University, if obliged to defend the study of Sanskrit before a committee of
senators. "You have been told," he would say, "that Sanskrit is a dead language. Not at all: Sanskrit is Professor Smith's department, and growing.
The cost is trifling, and several of our sister universities are making it a
fresh requirement for the Ph.D. in classics. That, gentlemen, is what Sanskrit *is.*"

winded. It is the specious kind of naturalism possible also to such idealists as Emerson, Schelling, or any Hegelian of the Left, who may scrupulously limit their survey, in its range of objects, to nature and to recorded history, and yet in their attitude may remain romantic, transcendental, piously receiving as absolute the inspiration dominating moral life in their day and country. The idealists, being self-conscious, regarded this natural scene as a landscape painted by spirit; Dewey, to whom self-consciousness is anathema, regards it as a landscape that paints itself; but it is still something phenomenal, all above board. Immediacy, which was an epistemological category, has become a physical one: natural events are conceived to be compounded of such qualities as appear to human observers, as if the character and emergence of these qualities had nothing to do with the existence, position, and organs of those observers. Nature is accordingly simply experience deployed, thoroughly specious and pictorial in texture. Its parts are not (what they are in practice and for living animal faith) substances presenting accidental appearances. They are appearances integrally woven into a panorama entirely relative to human discourse. Naturalism could not be more romantic: nature here is not a world but a story.

We have seen that the foreground, by its dominance, determines whether the empirical philosopher shall be provisionally a naturalist or shall try being something else. What now, looked at more narrowly, is the character of this foreground? Its name is Experience; but lest we should misunderstand this ambiguous word, it is necessary to keep in mind that in this system experience is impersonal. It is not, as a literary psychologist might suppose, a man's feelings and ideas forming a life-long soliloquy, his impressions of travel in this world. Nor is it, as a biologist might expect, such contact of sensitive animals with their environment as adapts them to it and teaches them to remember it. No: experience is here taken in a transcendental, or rather in a moral, sense, as something romantically absolute and practically coercive. There exists a social medium, the notorious scene of all happenings and discoveries, the sum of those current adventures in which anybody might participate. Experience is deputed to include everything to which experience might testify: it is the locus of public facts. It is therefore identical with nature, to the extent

and in the aspects in which nature is disclosed to man. Death, for
instance, should be set down as a fact of experience. This would
not be possible if experience were something personal, unless
indeed death were only a transition to another life. For so long
as a man's sensations and thoughts continue, he is not dead, and
when dead he has no more thoughts or sensations. But is such
actual death, we may ask, the death that Dewey can have in
mind? The only death open to experience is the death of others
(here is a neat proof of immortality for those who like it); and
death, for the pragmatist, simply *is* burial. To suppose that a
train of thoughts and feelings going on in a man invisibly might
at last come to an end, would be to place the fact of death in a
sphere which Dewey does not recognise, namely, in the realm
of truth; for it would simply be true that the man's thoughts had
ceased, although neither he nor anybody else could find that
fact in experience. For other people it would remain a fact assumed and credited, for him it would be a destiny that overtook
him. Yet Experience, as Dewey understands it, must include
such undiscoverable objects of common belief, and such a real,
though unobserved, order of events. The dominant foreground
which he calls Experience is accordingly filled and bounded not
so much by experience as by convention. It is the social world.

How conventional this foreground is will appear even more
clearly if we note the elements which are said to compose it.
These are events, histories, situations, affairs. The words "affairs" and "situations," in their intentional vagueness, express
very well the ethical nerve of this philosophy; for it is essentially a moral attitude or a lay religion. Life is a practical predica-
ment; both necessity and duty compel us to do something about
it, and also to think something about it, so as to know what to
do. This is the categorical imperative of existence; and according
to the Protestant tradition (diametrically opposed to the Indian)
the spirit, in heeding its intrinsic vocation, is not alienated from
earthly affairs, but on the contrary pledges itself anew to prose-
cute them with fidelity. Conscience and nature here exercise
their suasion concurrently, since conscience merely repeats the
summons to enter a field of responsibility—nature—formed by
the deposit of its past labours. The most homely business, like the
widest policies, may be thus transfused with a direct metaphysi-

cal inspiration; and although Dewey avoids all inflated eloquence on this theme, it is clear that his philosophy of Experience is a transcendental moralism. The other two terms, however, "events" and "histories," point to the flux of matter, although this is still gathered up and subdivided under units of discourse. "Event" is now a favourite word among philosophers who are addressed to the study of nature, but bring with them an empirical logic; and it well expresses that conjunction. An event does not involve a spectator, and does involve an environment on the same plane as the event: so far events belong directly to the flux of nature. At the same time an event is a change, and all the dialectic of change applies to the conception. Are events the crises between existence characterised in one way and existence characterised in another way? Or are events the intervals between such crises? But if these intervals, each having a somewhat different quality, were taken separately, they would not lodge in a common space or time; there would be no crises between them, no change, and (as I think would appear in the end) they themselves would have no existence. If events are to be successive, and fragments of the flux of nature, they must be changes in an abiding medium. In other words, an event, in its natural being, is a mode of substance, the transit of an essence. Moreover, natural events would have to be microscopic, because intervals containing no internal crisis, however long or even eternal they might seem sentimentally, could not be measured and would count as instants. This corollary is well fitted to remind us that nature laughs at our dialectic and goes on living in her own way. Her flux, like the flow of a river, is far more substantial than volatile, all sleepy continuity, derivation, persistence, and monotony. The most ordinary form of change in her—perhaps the only fundamental form—is motion; and it would be highly artificial to call the parts of a motion events where there are no crises and no intervals. Even night and day, unless we choose a particular point on the earth's surface for our station, are not events, since both are perpetual. It is apparently only on higher levels, genetically secondary, that nature produces events, where movement becomes rhythmical, and a culmination is followed by a breakdown and a repetition, as in animal birth and death. These secondary rhythms naturally attract the attention of a human observer, whose units of perception are all impressionistic and pictorial; he selects events from the vast continuities of nature because they go with rhythms in his own organism, with which his intuitions—the only vital culminations—are conjoined. Hence the empirical impression that nature is a series of events, although if they were mere events they could not be parts of nature, but only essences succeeding one another before vacant attention or in discourse; in other words, we should be in the mock world of psychologism.

The superficial level proper to empirical events becomes even more obvious if instead of calling them events we call them histories. The parts of nature seem events when we ignore their substance and their essence and consider only their position; anything actual is an event only, so to speak, at its margins, where it ceases to be itself. But before the parts of nature can seem to be histories, we must impose on them dramatic unities fetched from a far more derivative sphere. Histories are moral units, framed by tracing the thread of some special interest through the maze of things, units impossible to discriminate before the existence of passions and language. As there is a literary psychology which represents the mind as a mass of nameable pictures and describable sentiments, so there is a romantic metaphysics which hypostatises history and puts it in the place of nature. "Histories" bring us back into the moral foreground where we found "situations" and "affairs." The same predicaments of daily life are viewed now in a temporal perspective, rather than as they beset us at any one moment.

That the foreground of human life is necessarily moral and practical (it is so even for artists) and that a philosophy which limits itself to clarifying moral perspectives may be a very great philosophy, has been known to the judicious since the days of Socrates. Why could not Dewey have worked out his shrewd moral and intellectual economy within the frame of naturalism, which he knows is postulated by practice, and so have brought clearness and space into the picture, without interposing any metaphysics? Because it is an axiom with him that nothing but the immediate is real. This axiom, far from being self-evident, is not even clear: for everything is "real" in some sense, and there is much doubt as to what sort of being is immediate. At first the axiom produced psychological idealism, because the proudly discoursing minds of philosophers took for granted that the immediate for each man could be only his own thoughts. Later it has been urged (and, I think, truly) that the immediate is rather any object—whether sensible or intelligible makes no difference —found lying in its own specious medium; so that immediatism is not so much subjective as closely attentive and mystically objective. Be it noted, however, that this admitted objectivity of natural things remains internal to the immediate sphere: they must never be supposed to possess an alleged substantial existence beyond experience. This experience is no longer subjective, but it is still transcendental, absolute, and groundless; indeed it has ceased to seem subjective only because it seems unconditioned; and in order to get to the bottom and to the substance of anything, we must still ask with Emerson, What is this *to me?* or with William James, What is this *experienced as?* As Dewey puts it, these facts of experience simply *are* or *are had*, and there is nothing more to say about them. Such evidence flooding immediate experience I just now called mystical, using the epithet advisedly; because in this direct possession of being there is no division of subject and object, but rapt identification of some term, intuition of some essence. Such is sheer pleasure or pain, when no source or object is assigned to it; such is æsthetic contemplation; such is pure thinking, the flash of intellectual light. This mystical paradise is indefinitely extensible, like life, and far be it from me to speak evil of it; it is there only that the innocent spirit is at home. But how should pragmatism, which is nothing if not prehensile, take root in this Eden? I am afraid pragmatism is the serpent; for there is a forbidden tree in the midst, the tree of Belief in the Eventual, the fruit of which is Care; and it is evident that our first parents must have partaken of it copiously; perhaps they fed on nothing else. Now when immediate experience is crossed by Care it suffers the most terrible illusion, for it supposes that the eventual about which it is troubled is controllable by the immediate, as by wishes, omens, or high thoughts; in other words, that the essences given in the immediate exist, generate their own presence, and may persist and rearrange themselves and so generate the future. But this is sheer superstition and trust in magic; the philosophy not of experience but of inexperience. The immediate, whether a paradise or a hell, is al-

ways specious; it is peopled by spectres which, if taken for existing and working things, are illusions; and although they are real
enough, in that they have definite character and actual presence,
as a dream or a pain has, their reality ends there; they are unsub-
stantial, volatile, leaving no ashes, and their existence, even when
they appear, is imputed to them by a hidden agency, the demon
of Care, and lies wholly in being perceived.

Thus immediate experience of things, far from being fundamental in nature, is only the dream which accompanies our
action, as the other dreams accompany our sleep; and every
naturalist knows that this waking dream is dependent for its
existence, quality, intensity, and duration on obscure processes in the living body, in its interplay with its environment;
processes which go back, through seeds, to the first beginnings of
life on earth. Immediate experience is a consummation; and this
not in æsthetic contemplation alone, but just as much in birth-
pangs or the excitement of battle. All its episodes, intermittent
and wildly modulated, like the sound of wind in a forest, are
bound together and rendered relevant to one another only by
their material causes and instruments. So tenuous is immediate
experience that the behaviourist can ignore it altogether without
inconvenience, substituting everywhere objects of conventional
belief in their infinite material plane. The immediate is, indeed,
recognised and prized only by mystics, and Dewey himself is assured of possessing it only by virtue of his social and ethical
mysticism, by which the whole complex theatre of contemporary
action seems to him to be given immediately: whereas to others of
us (who are perhaps mystical at other points) this world of practice seems foreign, absent from our better moments, approach-
able even at the time of action only by animal faith and blind
presumption, and compacted, when we consider its normal
texture, out of human conventions, many of them variable and
foolish. A pragmatist who was not an ethical or social mystic,
might explore that world scientifically, as a physician, politician,
or engineer, and remain throughout a pure behaviourist or materialist, without noticing immediate experience at all, or once
distinguishing what was given from what was assumed or asserted. But to the mystic, if he is interested in that world, it all
comes forward into the immediate; it becomes indubitable, but

at the same time vague. Actual experience sucks in the world in
which conventional experience, if left to dogmatise, would have
supposed it was going on; and a luminous cloud of immediacy
envelops everything and arrests the eye, in every direction, on a
painted perspective; for if any object becomes immediate, whatever it may be, it becomes visionary. That same spiritual actuality
which Dewey, in passing, scarcely recognised at the top of animal life, he now comes upon from within, and without observing its natural locus, lays at the basis of the universe. The universe, in his system, thereby appears inverted, the accidental order of discovery being everywhere substituted for the natural
order of genesis; and this with grave consequences, since it is
not so easy for the universe as for an individual to stand on its
head.[1]

Consider, for instance, the empirical status of the past. The
only past that ever *is* or *is had* is a specious past, the fading survival of it in the present. Now the form which things wear in
the foreground, according to this philosophy, is their *real* form;
and the meaning which such immediate facts may assume hangs
on their use in executing some living purpose. What follows in
regard to past time? That the survival or memory of it comprises
all its reality, and that all the meaning of it lies in its possible relevance to actual interests. A memory may serve as a model or condition in shaping some further enterprise, or may be identified
with a habit acquired by training, as when we have learned a
foreign language and are ready to speak it. Past experience is

[1] A curious reversal of the terms "natural" and "ideal" comes about as we
assume that the immediate is substantial or that it is visionary. Suppose I say
that "everything ideal emanates from something natural." Dewey agrees,
understanding that everything remote emanates from something immediate.
But what I meant was that everything immediate—sensation, for instance,
or love—emanates from something biological. Not, however (and this is
another verbal snare), from the concepts of biological science, essences immediately present to the thoughts of biologists, but from the largely unknown or humanly unknowable process of animal life. I suppose we should
not call some of our ideas scientific if they did not trace the movement of
nature more accurately and reliably than do our random sensations or dramatic myths; they are therefore presumably truer in regard to those distribu-
tive aspects of nature which they select. But science is a part of human
discourse, and necessarily poetical, like language. If literal truth were necessary (which is not the case in practice in respect to nature) it would be
found only, perhaps, in literature—in the reproduction of discourse by discourse.

accordingly real only by virtue of its vital inclusion in some present undertaking, and yesterday is *really* but a term perhaps useful
in the preparation of to-morrow. The past, too, must work if it
would live, and we may speak without irony of "the futurity of
yesterday" in so far as yesterday has any pragmatic reality.

This result is consistent with the general principle of empirical criticism by which we are forbidden to regard God, truth, or
the material cosmos as anything but home vistas. When this principle is applied to such overwhelming outer realities, it lightens
the burden of those who hate external compulsions or supports;
they can henceforth believe they are living in a moral universe
that changes as they change, with no sky lowering over them
save a portable canopy which they carry with them on their travels. But now this pleasant principle threatens the march of experience itself: for if my ancestors have no past existence save by
working in me now, what becomes of my present being, if ever I
cease to work in my descendants? Does experience to-day draw
its whole existence from their future memories? Evidently this
cannot be the doctrine proposed; and yet if it be once admitted
that all the events in time are equally real and equally central,
then at every point there is a by-gone past, intrinsically perfectly
substantial and self-existent; a past which such memories or con-
tinuations as may be integral to life at this later moment need
continue only very partially, or need recover only schemati-
cally, if at all. In that case, if I ever find it convenient to forget
my ancestors, or if my descendants find it advantageous to forget me, this fact might somewhat dash their vanity or mine if we
should hear of it, but cannot touch our substantial existence or
the truth of our lives. Grant this, and at once the whole universe
is on its feet again; and all that strange pragmatic reduction of
yesterday to to-morrow, of Sanskrit to the study of Sanskrit, of
truth to the value of discovering some truth, and of matter to
some human notion of matter, turns out to have been a needless
equivocation, by which the perspectives of life, avowedly relative, have been treated as absolute, and the dominance of the
foreground has been turned from a biological accident into a
metaphysical principle. And this quite wantonly: because practice, far from suggesting such a reduction, precludes it, and requires every honest workman to admit the democratic equality

of the past and the future with the present, and to regard the inner processes of matter with respect and not with transcendental arrogance. The living convictions of the pragmatist himself are those involved in action, and therefore naturalistic in the dogmatic sense; action involves belief, belief judgment, and judgment dogma; so that the transcendental metaphysics and the practical naturalism of the pragmatist are in sharp contradiction, both in logic and in spirit. The one expresses his speculative egotism, the other his animal faith.

Of course, it is not Dewey nor the pragmatic school that is to blame for this equivocation; it is a general heirloom, and has infected all that criticism of scholastic dogma on which modern philosophy is founded. By expressing this critical principle more thoroughly, the pragmatists have hoped to clear the air, and perhaps ultimately may help to do so. Although I am myself a dogmatic naturalist, I think that the station assumed by Dewey, like the transcendental station generally, is always legitimate. Just as the spirit has a right to soliloquise, and to regard existence as a strange dream, so any society or nation or living interest has a right to treat the world as its field of action, and to recast the human mind, as far as possible, so as to adapt it exclusively to that public function. That is what all great religions have tried to do, and what Sparta and Carthage would have done if they had produced philosophers. Why should not America attempt it? Reason is free to change its logic, as language to change its grammar; and the critic of the life of reason may then distinguish, as far as his penetration goes, how much in any such logic or grammar is expressive of material circumstances, how much is exuberant rhetoric, how much local, and how much human. Of course, at every step such criticism rests on naturalistic dogmas; we could not understand any phase of human imagination, or even discover it, unless we found it growing in the common world of geography and commerce. In this world fiction arises, and to this world it refers. In so far as criticism can trace back the most fantastic ideas—mythology, for instance—to their natural origin, it should enlighten our sympathies, since we should all have lived in the society of those images, if we had had the same surroundings and passions; and if in their turn the ideas prevalent in our own day can be traced back to the material conditions that bred them, our judgment should be enlightened also. Controversy, when naturalism is granted, can yield to interpretation, reconciling the critical mind to convention, justifying moral diversity, and carrying the sap of life to every topmost intellectual flower. All positive transcendental insights, whether empirical, national, or moral, can thus be honoured (and disinfected) by the baldest naturalism, remaining itself international, Bohemian, and animal. The luminous fog of immediacy has a place in nature; it is a meteorological and optical effect, and often a blessing. But why should immediacy be thought to be absolute or a criterion of reality? The great error of dogmatists, in hypostatising their conclusions into alleged pre-existent facts, did not lie in believing that facts of some kind pre-existed; the error lay only in framing an inadequate view of those facts and regarding it as adequate. God and matter are not any or all the definitions which philosophers may give of them: they are the realities confronted in action, the mysterious but momentous background, which philosophers and other men mean to describe by their definitions or myths or sensible images. To hypostatise these human symbols, and identify them with matter or with God, is idolatry: but the remedy for idolatry is not iconoclasm, because the senses, too, or the heart or the pragmatic intellect, can breed only symbols. The remedy is rather to employ the symbols pragmatically, with detachment and humour, trusting in the steady dispensations of the substance beyond.

❧ The Genteel
Tradition at Bay*

I. Analysis of Modernity

Twenty years ago the genteel tradition in America seemed ready
to melt gracefully into the active mind of the country. There
were few misgivings about the perfect health and the all-embrac-
ing genius of the nation: only go full speed ahead and everything
worth doing would ultimately get done. The churches and universities might have some pre-American stock-in-trade, but there
was nothing stubborn or recalcitrant about them; they were
happy to bask in the golden sunshine of plutocracy; and there
was a feeling abroad—which I think reasonable—that wherever
the organisation of a living thing is materially perfected, there an
appropriate moral and intellectual life will arise spontaneously.
But the gestation of a native culture is necessarily long, and the
new birth may seem ugly to an eye accustomed to some other
form of excellence. Will the new life ever be as beautiful as the
old? Certain too tender or too learned minds may refuse to credit
it. Old Harvard men will remember the sweet sadness of Professor Norton. He would tell his classes, shaking his head with
a slight sigh, that the Greeks did not play football. In America
there had been no French cathedrals, no Venetian school of painting, no Shakespeare, and even no gentlemen, but only gentle-
manly citizens. The classes laughed, because that recital of home

* New York: Charles Scribner's Sons, 1931.

truths seemed to miss the humour of them. It was jolly to have
changed all that; and the heartiness of the contrary current of
life in everybody rendered those murmurs useless and a little
ridiculous. In them the genteel tradition seemed to be breathing
its last. Now, however, the worm has turned. We see it raising
its head more admonishingly than ever, darting murderous
glances at its enemies, and protesting that it is not genteel or an-
tiquated at all, but orthodox and immortal. Its principles, it declares, are classical, and its true name is Humanism.

The humanists of the Renaissance were lovers of Greek and
of good Latin, scornful of all that was crabbed, technical, or
fanatical: they were pleasantly learned men, free from any kind
of austerity, who, without quarrelling with Christian dogma,
treated it humanly, and partly by tolerance and partly by ridicule
hoped to neutralise all its metaphysical and moral rigour. Even
when orthodoxy was reaffirmed in the seventeenth century and
established all our genteel traditions, some humanistic leaven
was mixed in: among Protestants there remained a learned unrest and the rationalistic criticism of tradition: among Catholics
a classical eloquence draping everything in large and seemly
folds, so that nothing trivial, barbaric, or ugly should offend the
cultivated eye. But apart from such influences cast upon orthodoxy, the humanists continued their own labours. Their sympathy with mankind was not really universal, since it stopped
short at enthusiasm, at sacrifice, at all high passion or belief; but
they loved the more physical and comic aspects of life everywhere and all curious knowledge, especially when it could be
turned against prevalent prejudices or abuses. They believed in
the sufficient natural goodness of mankind, a goodness humanised by frank sensuality and a wink at all amiable vices; their truly
ardent morality was all negative, and flashed out in their hatred
of cruelty and oppression and in their scorn of imposture. This
is still the temper of revolutionaries everywhere, and of philosophers of the extreme Left. These, I should say, are more truly
heirs to the humanists than the merely academic people who still
read, or pretend to read, the classics, and who would like to go on
thrashing little boys into writing Latin verses. Greek and Roman
studies were called the humanities because they abstracted from
Christian divinity; and it was for this paganising or humanising

value that they were loved; much as Platonism is espoused by some theologians, because it enables them to preserve a metaphysical moralism independent of that historic religious faith of which they are secretly ashamed. The humanist would not deserve his name if he were not in sympathy with the suppressed sides of human nature (sometimes, as to-day perhaps, the highest sides of it); and he must change his aversions as the ruling convention changes its idols. Thus hatred of exact logic, of asceticism, and of Gothic earnestness, with praise of the misjudged pleasures of a young body and a free mind, could supply the humanist with a sufficient inspiration so long as Christian orthodoxy remained dominant; but when the strongholds of superstition and morose tyranny (as he called them) were in ruins, and tenanted only by a few owls or a bevy of cooing pigeons, his angry occupation was gone. The great courts and the great court preachers were humanistic enough. Nothing therefore remained for him but to turn wit, or savant, or polite poet, and to spread his philanthropic sympathies thinner and thinner over all human things. Eastern civilisations claimed a place in his affections side by side with the ancients: he must make room even for savage arts and savage virtues—they were so human—nor could he exclude for ever that wonderful mediæval art and philosophy which, in the flush of the Renaissance, he had derided and deposed. Thus humanism ended at last in a pensive agnosticism and a charmed culture, as in the person of Matthew Arnold.

It is against this natural consequence of the old humanism that the new American humanists, in a great measure, seem to be protesting. They feel the lameness of that conclusion: and indeed a universal culture always tolerant, always fluid, smiling on everything exotic and on everything new, sins against the principle of life itself. We exist by distinction, by integration round a specific nucleus according to a particular pattern. Life demands a great insensibility, as well as a great sensibility. If the humanist could really live up to his ancient maxim, *humani nil a me alienum puto*, he would sink into moral anarchy and artistic impotence —the very things from which our liberal, romantic world is so greatly suffering. The three R's of modern history, the Renaissance, the Reformation, and the Revolution, have left the public mind without any vestige of discipline. The old humanism it-

self is impotent and scattered; no man of the world any longer
remembers his Latin. Indeed, those three R's were inwardly at
war with one another. The Renaissance, if it had had full swing,
would never have become, even locally or by mistake, either
Protestant or revolutionary: what can a pure poet or humanist
have in common with religious faction, or with a sentimental
faith in liberty and democracy? Such a free mind might really
have understood the ancients, and might have passed grandly
with them into a complete naturalism, universal and impartial on
its intellectual side (since the intellect is by right all-seeing)
but in politics and morals fiercely determinate, with an animal
and patriotic intensity of will, like Carthage and Sparta, and like
the Soviets and the Fascists of to-day. Such political naturalism
was clearly conceived by Bacon and Machiavelli, and by many
princes and nobles who took the Protestant side, not in the least
for religious reasons, but because they were supermen wishing
to be free from all trammels, with a clergy to serve them, and all
wealth and initiative in their own hands. Those princes and
nobles had their day, but the same motives work to this hour in
the nations or classes that have taken their place.

I think that in each of the three R's we may distinguish an
efficacious hidden current of change in the unconscious world
from the veneer of words and sentiments that may have served to
justify that change, or to mask it in the popular mind, and often
in the mind of the leaders. The Renaissance really tended to
emancipate the passions and to exploit nature for fanciful and for
practical human uses: it simply continued all that was vivacious
and ornate in the Middle Ages. It called those ages barbarous,
partly for writing dog Latin and partly for being hard, penitential, warlike, and migratory; one might almost say, for being
religious. The mind of the Renaissance was not a pilgrim mind,
but a sedentary city mind, like that of the ancients: in this respect
and in its general positivism, the Renaissance was truly a revival
of antiquity. If merchants and princelings travelled or fought,
it was in order to enrich themselves at home, and not because of
an inward unrest or an unreturning mission, such as life itself is
for a pure soul. If here or there some explorer by vocation or
some great philosopher had still existed (and I know of none)
he would have been a continuator of the crusaders or the scho-

lastics. A genius typical of the Renaissance, such as Leonardo or Shakespeare, could not be of that consecrated kind. In his omnivorous intelligence and zest, in his multiform contacts and observations, in so many lights kindled inconclusively, such a genius, except for the intensity of his apprehension, would not have been a master or a poet at all. He would have been, like Bacon and Machiavelli, a prophet of Big Business. There might still be passion and richness in the accents, but the tidings were mean. The Renaissance, for all its poetry, scholarship, and splendour, was a great surrender of the spirit to the flesh, of the essence for the miscellany of human power.

The Reformation in like manner had a mental façade which completely hid the forces that really moved it, and the direction in which its permanent achievements would lie. It gave out that it was a religious reform and revival, and it easily enlisted in its cause all the shocked consciences, restless intellects, and fanatical hearts of the day; but in its very sincerity it substituted religious experience for religious tradition, and that, if the goal had been really religious, would have been suicide: for in religious experience, taken as its own criterion, there is nothing to distinguish religion from moral sentiment or from sheer madness. Kant and other German philosophers have actually reduced religion to false postulates or dramatic metaphors necessary to the heroic practice of morality. But why practise folly heroically and call it duty? Because conscience bids. And why does conscience bid that? *Because society and empire require it.* Meantime, in popular quarters, we see religion, or the last shreds of it, identified with occult science or sympathetic medicine. The fact is, I think, that the Reformation from the beginning lived on impatience of religion and appealed to lay interests: to the love of independence, national and personal; to free thought; to local pride; to the lure of plunder and enterprise; to the sanctity of thrift. Many a writer (Macaulay, for instance) demonstrates the superiority of Protestantism by pointing to its social fruits: better roads, neater villages, less begging and cheating, more schools, more commerce, greater scientific advance and philosophic originality. Admirable things, except perhaps the last: and we learn that religion is to be regarded as an instrument for producing a liberal well-being. But when this is secured, and we have creature comforts, a re-

spectable exterior, and complete intellectual liberty, what in turn
are the spiritual fruits? None: for the spirit, in this system, is
only an instrument, and its function is fulfilled if those earthly
advantages are realised. It was so, at bottom, with the ancient
Jews: and the intensity of religious emotions in the prophet or
the revivalist must not blind us to the tragic materialism at his
heart. I think we might say of Protestantism something like what
Goethe said of Hamlet. Nature had carelessly dropped an acorn
into the ancient vase of religion, and the young oak, growing
within, shattered the precious vessel.

In the Revolution (which is not yet finished) the same doubleness is perhaps less patent: liberty, fraternity, and equality have
been actually achieved in some measure, even if they lack that
Arcadian purity and nobleness which the revolutionary prophets expected. Their cry had been for limpid virtue, antique
heroism, and the radical destruction of unreason: the event has
brought industrialism, populousness, comfort, and the dominance of the average man, if not of the average woman.

The whole matter is complicated by the presence of yet another R, Romance, which lies in an entirely different category
from the Renaissance, the Reformation, and the Revolution. Romance is not, like these, inspired by any modern sense of out-
rage or by any moral or political theory. It is neither hortatory
nor contemptuous; not a rebellion against anything. I don't know
whether its springs should be called Celtic or Norse or simply
primitive and human, or whether any subtle currents from Alex-
andria or Arabia, or from beyond, swelled the flood in the dark
ages. Suffice it that Romance is something very old, and supplies
that large element which is neither classical nor Christian in mediæval and modern feeling. It lies deeper, I think, in most of us
than any conventional belief or allegiance. It involves a certain
sense of homelessness in a chaotic world, and at the same time a
sense of meaning and beauty there. To Romance we owe the
spirit of adventure; the code of honour, both masculine and feminine; chivalry and heraldry; feudal loyalty; hereditary nobility;
courtesy, politeness, and pity; the love of nature; rhyme and
perhaps lyric melody; imaginative love and fidelity; sentimentality; humour. Romance was a great luminous mist blowing from
the country into the ancient town; in the wide land of Romance

everything was vaguely placed and man migratory; the knight, the troubadour, or the palmer carried all his permanent possessions on his back, or in his bosom. So did the wandering student and the court fool. There was much play with the picturesque and the miraculous; perhaps the cockiness of changing fashions has the same source. Fancy has freer play when men are not deeply respectful to custom or reason, but feel the magic of strangeness and distance, and the profound absurdity of things. Even the intellect in the romantic world became subject to moods: attention was arrested at the subjective. "Experience"— the story-teller's substance—began to seem more interesting and sure than the causes of experience or the objects of knowledge. The pensive mind learned to trace the Gothic intricacies of music and mathematics, and to sympathise too much with madness any longer to laugh at it. The abnormal might be heroic; and there could be nothing more sure and real than the intense and the immediate. In this direction, Romance developed into British and German philosophy, in which some psychological phantasm, sensuous or logical, interposes itself in front of the physical world, covers and absorbs it. Mixed with revolutionary passions, Romance also produced the philosophy of Rousseau; and mixed with learning and archæology, the classical revival of Goethe and his time; finally, by a sort of reduplication or reversion of romantic interest upon Romance itself, there followed the literary and architectural romanticism of the nineteenth century.

Romance is evidently a potent ingredient in the ethos of the modern world; and I confess that I can hardly imagine in the near future any poetry, morality, or religion not deeply romantic. Something wistful, a consciousness of imperfection, the thought of all the other beauties destroyed or renounced in achieving anything, seems inseparable from breadth in sympathy and knowledge; and such breadth is the essence of modern enlightenment. But is not this intelligent humility itself a good? Is it not a prerequisite to a sane happiness? The accident of birth, with all its consequences, offers us the first and palmary occasion for renunciation, measure, and reason. Why not frankly rejoice in the benefits, so new and extraordinary, which our state of society affords? We may not possess those admirable things which Professor Norton pined for, but at least (besides football) haven't

we Einstein and Freud, Proust and Paul Valéry, Lenin and Mus-
solini? For my part, though a lover of antiquity, I should certainly congratulate myself on living among the moderns, if the
moderns were only modern enough, and dared to face nature
with an unprejudiced mind and a clear purpose. Never before
was the mental landscape so vast. What if the prospect, when the
spirit explores it, seems rather a quagmire, as it were the Marshes
of Glynn, rich only in weak reeds and rank grasses? Has not the
spirit always loved the wilderness? Does not the wide morass
open out here and there into a quiet pool, with water-lilies, and
is not the sky, with all its wonders, often reflected there? Do not
the screeching wild-fowl cleave this air with avidity? I think that
the simple lover of the beautiful may well be content to take his
turn and have his day almost anywhere in the pageant of human
history. Wherever he might be born, or wherever banished, he
could never be separated from his inner mind or from a fundamental kinship with his fellow-creatures. Even if his feet were
without foothold in the dreary bog, his spirit need not be
starved or impatient. Amid weeds and rushes, if he would only
watch them, and breathing deep the very freedom of emptiness,
he might forget the oaks and roses of terra firma, even for five
hundred or a thousand years.

So far, then, the gist of modern history would seem to be this:
a many-sided insurrection of the unregenerate natural man,
with all his physical powers and affinities, against the regimen of
Christendom. He has convinced himself that his physical life is
not as his ghostly mentors asserted, a life of sin; and why should
it be a life of misery? Society has gradually become a rather
glorious, if troubled, organisation of matter, and of man for material achievements. Even our greatest troubles, such as the late
war, seem only to accelerate the scientific bridling of matter:
troubles do not cease, but surgery and aviation make remarkable
progress. Big Business itself is not without its grave worries:
wasted production, turbulent labour, rival bosses, and an inherited form of government, by organised parties and elections,
which was based on revolutionary maxims, and has become irrelevant to the true work of the modern world if not disastrous
for it. Spiritual distress, too, cannot be banished by spiritual anarchy; in obscure privacy and in the sordid tragedies of doubt and

of love, it is perhaps more desperate than ever. We live in an age of suicides. Yet this spiritual distress may be disregarded, like bad dreams, so long as it remains isolated and does not organise any industrial revolt or any fresh total discouragement and mystic withdrawal, such as ushered in the triumph of Christianity. For the present, Big Business continues to generate the sort of intelligence and loyalty which it requires: it favours the most startling triumphs of mind in abstract science and mechanical art, without any philosophic commitments regarding their ultimate truth or value. Indeed, mechanical art and abstract science are other forms of Big Business, and congruous parts of it. They, too, are instinctive undertakings, in which ambition, co-operation, and rivalry keep the snowball rolling and getting bigger and bigger. Some day attention will be attracted elsewhere, and the whole vain thing will melt away unheeded. But while the game lasts and absorbs all a man's faculties, its rules become the guides of his life. In the long run, obedience to them is incompatible with anarchy, even in the single mind. Either the private anarchy will ruin public order, or the public order will cure private anarchy.

The latter, on the whole, has happened in the United States, and may be expected to become more and more characteristic of the nation. There, according to one of the new humanists, "The accepted vision of a good life is to make a lot of money by fair means; to spend it generously; to be friendly; to move fast; to die with one's boots on." This sturdy ideal has come to prevail naturally, despite the preachers and professors of sundry finer moralities; it includes virtue and it includes happiness, at least in the ancient and virile sense of these words. We are invited to share an industrious, cordial, sporting existence, self-imposed and self-rewarding. There is plenty of room, in the margin and in the pauses of such a life, for the intellectual tastes which any one may choose to cultivate; people may associate in doing so; there will be clubs, churches, and colleges by the thousand; and the adaptable spirit of Protestantism may be relied upon to lend a pious and philosophical sanction to any instinct that may deeply move the national mind. Why should any one be dissatisfied? Is it not enough that millionaires splendidly endow libraries and museums, that the democracy loves them, and that even the Bolsheviks prize the relics of Christian civilisation

when laid out in that funereal documentary form? Is it not
enough that the field lies open for any young professor in love
with his subject to pursue it hopefully and ecstatically, until perhaps it begins to grow stale, the face of it all cracked and wrinkled
with little acrid controversies and perverse problems? And when
not pressed so far, is it not enough that the same studies should
supply a pleasant postscript to business, a congenial hobby or
night-cap for ripe rich elderly people? May not the ardent humanist still cry (and not in the wilderness): Let us be well-bal-
anced, let us be cultivated, let us be high-minded; let us control
ourselves, as if we were wild; let us chasten ourselves, as if we had
passions; let us learn the names and dates of all famous persons;
let us travel and see all the pictures that are starred in Baedeker;
let us establish still more complete museums at home, and sometimes visit them in order to show them to strangers; let us build
still more immense libraries, containing all known books, good,
bad, and indifferent, and let us occasionally write reviews of some
of them, so that the public, at least by hearsay, may learn which
are which.

Why be dissatisfied? I am sure that the true heirs to the three
R's would not ask for more. Even Romance gets its due; what
could be more romantic than the modern world, like a many-
decked towering liner, a triumph of mechanism, a hive of varied
activities, sailing for sailing's sake? Big Business is an amiable
monster, far kindlier and more innocent than anything Machiavelli could have anticipated, and no less lavish in its patronage of
experiment, invention, and finery than Bacon could have desired.
The discontent of the American humanists would be unintelligible if they were really humanists in the old sense; if they represented in some measure the soul of that young oak, bursting
the limits of Christendom. Can it be that they represent rather
the shattered urn, or some one of its fragments? The leaders, indeed, though hardly their followers, might pass for rather censorious minds, designed by nature to be the pillars of some
priestly orthodoxy; and their effort, not as yet very successful,
seems to be to place their judgments upon a philosophical basis.
After all, we may actually be witnessing the demise of the genteel tradition, though by a death more noble and glorious than
some of us had looked for. Instead of expiring of fatigue, or evap-

orating into a faint odour of learning and sentiment hanging about Big Business, this tradition, in dying, may be mounting again to its divine source. In its origin it was a severe and explicit philosophy, Calvinism; not essentially humanistic at all, but theocratic. Theocracy is what all the enemies of the three R's, and more, the enemies of Romance, must endeavour to restore, if they understand their own position. Wealth, learning, sport, and beneficence, even on a grand scale, must leave them cold, or positively alarm them, if these fine things are not tightly controlled and meted out according to some revealed absolute standard. Culture won't do, they must say, unless it be the one right culture: learning won't do, unless it fills out the one true philosophy. No more sentimentality, then, or intellectual snobbery; away with the sunset glow and the organ peals overheard in a churchyard. Let us have honest bold dogmas supported by definite arguments: let us re-establish our moral sentiments on foundations more solid than tradition or gentility. Boundless liberal opportunity, such as Big Business offers, is a futile romantic lure. Even the most favourable turn of the fashion in education, criticism, and literature would not last for ever. The opposite schools would continue to advertise their wares; and only the unpredictable shifts of human moods and customs could here or there decide the issue. The best fruits of time, in any case, are unexpected. If our edifice is to be safe, we must lay the foundations in eternity.

Is this really the meaning of the American humanists, which they have hardly ventured to propose, even to themselves? If so, the summons is bold and the programme radical: nothing less than to brush away the four R's from the education and the sentiment of the modern world, and to reinstate a settled belief in a supernatural human soul and in a precise divine revelation. These, as they say in Spain, are major words, and we shall have to proceed with caution.

II. The Appeal to the Supernatural

Almost all nations and religions, and especially the liberal party in them, think themselves the salt of the earth. They believe that only their special institutions are normal or just, and hope to see them everywhere adopted. They declare that only the scrip-

tures handed down by their own clergy are divinely inspired;
that only their native language is clear, convenient, deeply beautiful, and ultimately destined to become universal; that only the
logic of their home philosophers is essentially cogent; and that
the universal rule of morals, if not contained in tablets preserved
in their temple, is concentrated in an insoluble pellet of moral
prejudice, like the categorical imperative of Kant, lodged in
their breast. Not being content, or not being able, to cultivate
their local virtues in peace at home, they fiercely desire to sweep
everything foreign from the face of the earth. Is this madness?
No: I should say it was only hasty, transporting a vital necessity
into absurd metaphysical terms. Moral absolutism is the shadow
of moral integrity.

Now moral integrity and its shadow, moral absolutism, were
always a chief part of the genteel tradition in America. They
were perhaps its essence; and we need not wonder that the heirs
to this tradition, in order to reaffirm the integrity of soul which
they feel to be slipping away from them, clutch at its shadow,
ethical absolutism, which perhaps they think is its principle.
But such principles are verbal; they are not sources; and absolutism, even if reinstated philosophically, would never actually re-
establish integrity in a dissolute mind or in a chaotic society.
The natural order of derivation and growth is the opposite, and
nature must first produce a somewhat integrated soul before that
soul can discover or pursue the ideal of integrity.

Nevertheless, merely to reinstate absolutism philosophically
would be a great feat, and would prove the hopeless perversity of
relaxing integrity in any degree whatever. If, for instance, the
human soul were supernatural and had its proper life and perfection in another world, then indeed all the variety of human
tastes, temperaments, and customs would be variety only in self-
ignorance and error. There would be an eternal criterion, apart
from all places, persons, and times, by which everything should
be judged, namely: Does this conduce to the salvation of the
soul? Salvation would mean self-recovery, emergence from distraction, life beginning anew, not romantically, in some arbitrary
fresh adventure in an exotic landscape, but inwardly, by the pure
exercise of those functions which are truly native and sufficient
to the spirit. The supernatural constitution and affinities of the

soul would supply a criterion for all human affairs; not one absurdly imposed by one earthly creature upon another, as I was just now protesting, but one imposed by the visiting spirit upon the whole natural world. For however admirable and innocent the whole life of nature might be in itself, it would probably be in some directions sympathetic and in others poisonous and horrible to the native of a different sphere.

What, then, would a supernatural world be if it existed? I don't mean to ask what such a world would contain: it might evidently contain anything. I am only asking what relation any occult world must bear to nature, as we know nature, if that other world is to deserve the titles of existent and of supernatural. If it is to be existent, and not like the realms of poetry or mathematics merely conceived, it must, I think, be in dynamic relations with ourselves and with our world. Miracles, reports, incarnations, and ascensions, or at least migrations of the soul, must connect the two worlds, and make them, in reality, parts of one and the same universe. The supra-mundane and the mundane taken together would compose the total reality with which human knowledge, morality, and sentiment must reckon if they would not be ultimately stultified by the facts.

Supernaturalism, in its own eyes, is accordingly simply a completed naturalism, a naturalism into which certain ulterior facts and forces, hidden from our near-sighted and imperfect science, have been duly admitted. The morality inspired by supernaturalism will also be a naturalistic morality in principle: only that the soul will then be confronted by other opportunities and other dangers than her earthly life contains. Reason will have to take longer views, and the passions will be arrested, excited, or transformed by a larger prospect.

On the other hand, if this possible other world is to be called supernatural in any significant sense, it must not be confused with the chaotic, the groundlessly miraculous, the *infra*-natural. I am far from wishing to deny that the infra-natural exists; that below the superficial order which our senses and science find in the world, or impose upon it, there may not be an intractable region of incalculable accidents, chance novelties, or inexplicable collapses. Perhaps what we call the order of nature may be only a cuticle imperfectly formed round a liquid chaos. This speculative possibility is worth entertaining in the interests of scientific modesty and spiritual detachment; and it positively fascinates some ultra-romantic minds, that detest to be caged even in an infinite world, if there is any order in it. Indetermination seems to them liberty; they feel that idiocy and accident are far more deeply rooted than method in their own being, and they think it must be so also in the world at large: and perhaps they are right. All this underlying chaos, however, if it exists, has nothing to do with that supernatural sphere—a sphere and not a medley—to which morality and religion may be tempted to appeal. As the Indian, Platonic, and Christian imagination has conceived it, the supernatural has an eternal nature and a sublime order of its own. It forms an elder cosmos surrounding our nether world and destined to survive it. In that cosmos a hierarchy of spirits continually descends and ascends all the steps of moral decline and exaltation; and there the inexplicable burdens and tantalising glories of this life find their origin and their fulfilment.

There is nothing impossible, therefore, in the existence of the supernatural: its existence seems to me decidedly probable; there is infinite room for it on every side. But, then, this almost tangible supernatural world is only the rest of nature, nature in her true depths and in her true infinity, which is presumably a rich and unmapped infinity of actual being, not the cheap ideal infinity of the geometers. The question is only what evidences we may have of the existence of this hidden reality, and of its character; whether, for instance, it is likely that the outlying parts of the universe should be more sympathetic to our moral nature than this particular part to which we are native, and which our science describes because this is the part which we have to reckon with in action.

Now to this question the Platonic and Christian tradition replies, among other things, that the soul herself is a sufficient witness to her own supernatural origin, faculties, and destiny, inasmuch as she knows herself to be a pure spirit, synthetic and intelligent, endowed with free will, and immortal. We are not really native to this world, except in respect to our bodies; our souls are native to a spiritual world, from which we fetch our standards of truth and beauty, and in which alone we can be happy. Such is the thesis: and we must never let this ancient citadel of absolutism fall into the enemy's hands if we expect safely to hold the outworks and to claim for ourselves a universal jurisdiction in taste, politics, and morals. Moreover, this citadel encloses a sanctuary: our philosophical supernaturalism would be uselessly vague without a positive revelation.

If we were not especially informed concerning the nature and destiny of all human souls, how could we legislate for them universally? How could we assert that all types of virtue, except our one official type, are either rudimentary or corrupt, and that although biologically various types radiate from a centre and diverge more and more the nearer they come to perfection, morally this is not so, but all human souls, in spite of what they may think, can be saved only by marching compulsorily in single file, after the same kind of happiness? We must possess a divine revelation to this effect, since without such a revelation our moral dogmatism would be avowedly only an expression of our particular temperament or local customs; and any romantic anarchist or dissolute epicurean might flout us, saying that his temperament and his customs were as good as our own or, to his feeling, better; and that he was innocent and happy in his way of life, and at peace with God—as indeed that loose, low creature, Walt Whitman, actually declared.

And the case would be particularly hopeless if the heretics, like us, were supernaturalists about the soul; because if they were mere naturalists we might rebuke them on medical grounds, as we warn a child munching too many sweets of the stomach-ache and the tooth-ache, lest he should be cloyed too late; or we might simply turn the cold shoulder of indifference and disgust upon the odious being, to signify his ostracism from our desirable society. But if he too was an immortal visitor from another world, he might well despise our earthly prudence and stupid persecutions, and he might assert against us his own unassailable vocation merely to will, or merely to laugh, or merely to understand. How, unless divinely illuminated, could we then pretend that we knew what was good for him better than he knew it himself? Nothing would be left for us except to thrash him: which at present we should be wisely disinclined to attempt; because in the arena of democratic jealousies and journalistic eloquence he would probably thrash us. No; we must boldly threaten him

with hell fire; he shall be thrashed in the other world, in the
world of spirit to which he appeals; and though the more picturesque forms of this threat may be out of date, and may raise
a smile, there are other forms of it terrible enough in themselves
and near to our daily experience. We have but to open the newspaper to read the last confidences of some suicide, and to learn
how the torments and the darkness of hell descend on the desperate rebel and the forlorn pleasure seeker. We must rely on the
horror which the facts of earthly life, when faced, inspire in the
innocent conscience. We must appeal to the profound doubt, the
profound unhappiness, the profound courage in the human soul,
so that she may accept our revelation as the key to the mystery
of her profound ignorance.

The alleged happiness of the epicurean or the romantic we
must assert to be a lie. In them, too, we must believe, a supernatural Christian soul is leading a painful and disgusted life;
for nothing can be more unnatural to her than naturalism.
Evil souls and ugly bodies are degenerate, not primitive; we are
all wretchedly fallen from an estate to which we secretly aspire
to return, although we may not clearly perceive our plight or understand the nature of that good which alone would render us
happy. We need to have the way of salvation preached to us,
whether it be salvation in this world or in another; and this
preaching we must receive on authority, if not on that of a special religion, at least that of the high philosophic tradition, Indian, Neo-Platonic, and Catholic, which represents the spiritual
wisdom of all ages. If we reject this authority and neglect to seek
the supernatural happiness which it prescribes, we shall be systematically sinning against ourselves, and literally losing our souls.

The same doctrine of a supernatural soul is indispensable if
we would justify another conviction dear to the absolute moralist; I mean, the consciousness of free will. A supernatural soul
would have a life and direction of her own: she would be an
efficacious member of an invisible cosmos, in which—since the
whole is the work of God—every being would have its appropriate gifts, functions, and destiny. The soul cannot create herself: she cannot determine the point of space and time at which
she will begin to show her colours: she cannot tell how long her
influence may be allowed to count in this world. But while her

union with the body endures, there will be a tug-of-war; and the issue will never be determined by either side taken alone. A man will therefore be no helpless slave of his body; his acts will not be predetermined physically without his soul's leave; they will be determined by the interplay of the physical with the spiritual forces in him: and on the spiritual side there will be two principal factors; his soul, with her native powers, affinities, and will, and the will and the grace of God, putting that soul in contact with particular circumstances and allowing her in that trial some measure of victory.

The soul, being an independent centre of force, would have come, on this hypothesis, into the body from without, and would continue to act upon it from within, until perhaps she escaped to pursue elsewhere her separate fortunes. This independent initiative of hers would be her free will: free in respect to material laws or solicitations, but of course conformable to her own instinct and native direction, as well as subject to the original dispositions and dynamic balance of the total universe, natural and supernatural. We must not confuse the dualism of origin in human acts, asserted by this theory of a supernatural soul, with any supposed absolute indetermination of either soul or body, or of their natural effects upon one another. Indeterminism, if it exists, belongs to the unintelligible foundations of things, to chaos, and to the subhuman: it is so far from vindicating the power of spirit over matter, that in this contest, as everywhere else, a real indeterminism would dislocate the normal relations of things and render them, to that extent, fortuitous.

The notion that absolute freedom might save many a critical situation, and that in general the intervention of groundless movements would tend towards a happy issue rests on a complete confusion. It is the gambler's fallacy. Empty possibility seems to him full of promise; but in fact sheer chance, throwing dice, would seldom throw sixes. The only force that really tends towards happy results is the innate force of the soul herself: for the soul, whether natural or supernatural, is an organising principle working, as in seeds, for a particular form of life which, if realised, would make her good and her perfection. If in this labour any groundless events occurred in her or in the circumstances, she would to that extent be the victim of chance. Energies dropped

into her and not exerted by herself would evidently do no
work of hers; they would not manifest her freedom, but only
her helplessness; they would be irruptions into her life of that
primitive contingency which is identical with fate. The result
would, to that extent, not be after her own mind, and she would
not be responsible for it. Sheer indeterminism like the danger of
earthquakes, if the healthy mind did not disregard it, would put
all human labour in jeopardy: it would dislocate all definite
hopes and calculations; in a sane life it would be the worst and
the most alien of agencies. Such a possibility is like the other face
of the moon, for ever turned away from human interests.

The kind of free will which concerns the moralist asserts
rather the autonomy of the soul, her power of manifesting herself, often surprisingly, in the realm of matter in ways which,
since they express her innate impulses, may have been already
vaguely prefigured and desired by her conscious mind. This freedom, or internal initiative, will be proper to the soul whether she
be natural or supernatural: in either case she will have a chosen
good to pursue, and a certain limited power of achieving it; but
if she is natural, her dispositions may change with the evolution
of animal life, and one of her forms will have no authority over
another; whereas, if she is supernatural, these material shifts will
change only the theatre of her activity or its instruments; her nature and her perfection will remain unchangeable.

If, then, the American humanists hope to maintain an absolute
criterion of taste and morals, I think they should hasten to embrace supernaturalism, in case they have not done so already.
The word supernatural has long been out of favour, partly because it denied to science an omniscience which, in theory,
science never claimed, and partly because it pointed to possible
realities far beyond that subjective sphere which is the only reality admitted by romantic idealism: but neither reason seems to
have any serious force. Supernaturalism, being an extension of
naturalism, is far sounder philosophically than subjectivism, and
morally at once humbler and more sublime. And that form of
supernaturalism which lies nearest at hand, Christian Platonism,
has the further advantage, in this case, of being remarkably humanistic. It deifies human morality and human intelligence.

Socrates and Plato, and some of the Fathers of the Church,

were excellent humanists. They had not, of course, that great rhetorical joy in all the passions which we find in the humanists of the Renaissance and, somewhat chastened, in Shakespeare. Platonism and Christianity, in their beginnings, were reactions against decadence, and necessarily somewhat disillusioned and ascetic. These philosophers were absorbed in preaching: I mean, in denouncing one-half of life and glorifying the other half; they were absolute moralists; and this dominance of ethical interests was confirmed by the Jewish and the Roman influences which permeated that age. Moreover a learned humanism was involved in the possession of Scriptures, demanding studies and eloquent expositions, which could not remain exclusively theological or legendary. In the Old Testament and even in the New, there were humanistic maxims, such as that the Sabbath was made for man, and not man for the Sabbath. Epicurus had crept into Ecclesiastes, and Plato into the Gospel of Saint John; and by a bolder stroke of humanism than any one had yet thought of, God himself had been made man. Man consequently might be superlatively important in his own eyes, without offence to the higher powers. He might proclaim his natural preferences even more vehemently and tenaciously than the heathen since round his conscience and his intellect he believed that the universe revolved, and had indeed been created expressly for his dubious and tragic glory.

This marked, and even absolute, humanism in Platonism and Christianity seems to some of us, who have no prejudice against supernaturalism in general, an argument against supernaturalism of that kind. There is a sort of acoustic illusion in it: the voice that reverberates from the heavens is too clearly a human voice. Is it not obvious that the reports contained in this revelation are not bits of sober information, not genuine reminiscences of a previous life, not messages literally conveyed from other worlds by translated prophets or visiting angels? Are they not clearly human postulates, made by ignorant mortals in sheer desperation or in poetic self-indulgence? Are they not ways of imagining a material vindication of lost causes, by a miraculous reversal, in the last instance, of every judgment of fate? Don Quixote, after twice mending and testing his ancestral helmet, and finding it fall apart at the first blow, mended it for the third time with a

green riband—green being the colour of hope—and, without
testing it this time, deputed it to be henceforth a trusty and a
perfect helmet. So when native zeal and integrity, either in nations or in persons, has given way to fatigue or contagion, a supernatural assurance needing no test may take possession of the
mind. Plato wrote his "Republic" after Athens had succumbed,
and his "Laws" after Syracuse had disappointed him; Neo-Plato-
nism and Christianity became persuasive when ancient civic life
had lost its savour. A wealth of wisdom survived, but little
manly courage; a dreamful courage of another sort, supernatural faith, transposed that wisdom into meekness; and sanctity
sprouted like the early crocus in the loam under the leafless
giants of antiquity.

Far be it from me to suggest that anybody ought to exchange his native religion or morality for a foreign one: he
would be merely blighting in himself the only life that was really
possible. But the travelling thoughts of the pure philosopher may
compare the minds and manners of various men; and considering
the supernatural world of Platonism and Christianity, he may
marvel to observe how very mundane that supernatural world is,
how moralistic and romantic, how royal, ecclesiastical, legal,
and dramatic an apotheosis of national or pious ambitions. At
best, as in Plotinus, it lifts to cosmic dimensions the story of spiritual experience. But how shall any detached philosopher believe
that the whole universe, which may be infinite, is nothing but
an enlarged edition, or an expurgated edition, of human life?
This is only a daylight religion; the heavens in its view are near,
and pleasantly habitable by the Olympians; the spheres fit the
earth like a glove; the sky is a tent spread protectingly or shaken
punitively over the human nest.

In the East, the philosopher will remember, there are, as it
were, night religions, simpler perhaps than ours but more metaphysical, inspired by the stars or the full moon. Taken as information, their account of the other world is no better than ours,
but their imagination is more disinterested and their ontology
bolder. They are less afraid that the truth might be disconcerting.
Is the colour which those inhuman religions lend to morality
less suitable to mankind? I am sure that a Hindu, a Moslem, or a
Buddhist is amply sustained in his home virtues by his tradi-

tional precepts and rites; he does not need to transpose these virtues out of their human sphere; the universe can sanction in man
the virtues proper to man without needing to imitate them on its
own immeasurable scale.

That was a confused and insolent ambition in Milton to justify
the ways of God to man. Impartial reflection upon ultimate
things tends to purify, without condemning, all the natural
passions, because being natural, they are inevitable and inherently
innocent, while being *only* natural, they are all relative and, in
a sense, vain. Platonism and Christianity, on the contrary, except
in a few natural mystics and speculative saints, seem to sacrifice
ruthlessly one set of passions merely in order to intensify another set. Ultimate insights cannot change human nature; but
they may remove that obfuscation which accompanies any passion, and a virtuous passion especially, when its relativity is not
understood. Human nature includes intelligence, and cannot
therefore be perfected without such an illumination, and the
equipoise which it brings: and this would seem to be a better
fruit of meditation upon the supernatural than any particular
regimen to be forced upon mankind in the name of heaven. Not
that the particular regimen sanctified by Platonic and Christian
moralists is at all inacceptable; but they did not require any supernatural assistance to draw it up. They simply received back
from revelation the humanism which they had put into it.

III. Moral Adequacy of Naturalism

Suppose we discount as fabulous every projection of human
morality into the supernatural: need we thereby relapse into
moral anarchy? In one sense, and from the point of view of the
absolute or monocular moralist, we must; because the whole
moral sphere then relapses into the bosom of nature, and nature, though not anarchical, is not governed by morality. But for
a philosopher with two eyes, the natural status of morality in the
animal world does not exclude the greatest vigour in those moral
judgments and moral passions which belong to his nature. On the
contrary, I think that it is only when he can see the natural origin and limits of the moral sphere that a moralist can be morally
sane and just. Blindness to the biological truth about morality is
not favourable to purity of moral feeling: it removes all sense of

proportion and relativity; it kills charity, humility, and humour; and it shuts the door against that ultimate light which comes to the spirit from the spheres above morality.

The Greeks—if I may speak like Professor Norton—the early Greeks, who as yet had little experience of philosophers, sometimes invited their philosophers to legislate for them. Their problem was not so unlike that which confronts us today: in the midst of increasing bustle and numbers, the preponderance of towns, the conflict of classes, close and dangerous foreign relations, freer manners, new ideas in science and art. How did those early sages set to work? In one way, they didn't mince matters: the rule of life which each of them proposed for his city covered the whole life of the citizen, military, political, intellectual, ceremonial, and athletic: but on the other hand, for each city the rule proposed was different: severe and unchangeable at Sparta, liberal and variable at Athens; while the idealistic brotherhood of the Pythagoreans prescribed astronomy and sweet numbers for Magna Græcia. It was in quite other circumstances that Socrates and Plato, Moses and President Wilson came forward to legislate unasked, and for the universe.

I am afraid that even some of those earlier sages were not perfect naturalists. They did not merely consider the extant organism for which they were asked to prescribe, or endeavour to disentangle, in its own interests, the diseases or dangers which might beset it. A legislating naturalist would be like a physician or horticulturalist or breeder of animals: he would remove obstructions and cut out barren deformities; he would have a keen eye for those variations which are spontaneous and fertile, gladly giving them free play; and he would know by experience those other variations into which nature may be coaxed by grafting and watering. In all his measures he would be guided by the avowed needs and budding potentialities of his client. Perhaps some of those Greek lawgivers, the Pythagoreans, for instance, had something of the missionary about them, and while full of adoration for the harmonies of nature as they conceived them, conceived these harmonies idealistically, and felt called upon to correct nature by the authority of a private oracle. In this their philosophy, apart from some cosmological errors, may have

proved its depth, and may have been prophetic of the revolution that was destined to undermine ancient society.

The only natural unit in morals is the individual man, because
no other natural unit is synthesised by nature herself into a living spirit. The state is only a necessary cradle for the body of the
individual, and nursery for his mind; and he can never really renounce his prescriptive right to shatter the state or to reform it,
according to his physical and spiritual necessities. Even when his
spontaneous fidelity causes him to forget or to deny this right,
the force of fidelity is at that very moment exercising that right
within him. Yet it was an intermediate and somewhat artificial
unit, the ancient city, that was asking those early philosophers
for counsel; and that counsel could not be good, or honestly
given, unless it considered the life of the individual within the
walls, and the life of the world outside, only as they might contribute to the perfection of the city.

Morality—by which I mean the principle of all choices in
taste, faith, and allegiance—has a simple natural ground. The living organism is not infinitely elastic; if you stretch it too much, it
will snap; and it justifiably cries out against you somewhat before
the limit is reached. This animal obstinacy is the backbone of all
virtue, though intelligence, convention, and sympathy may very
much extend and soften its expression. As the brute unconditionally wills to live, so the man, especially the strong masterful man,
unconditionally wills to live after a certain fashion. To be pli-
ant, to be indefinite, seems to him ignominious.

Very likely, in his horror of dissipating his strength or deviat-
ing from his purpose, he will give opprobrious names to every
opposite quality. His hot mind may not be able to conceive as
virtues in others any traits which would not be virtues in himself.
Yet this moral egotism, though common or even usual, is not
universal in virtuous people. On the contrary, precisely those
who are most perfect escape it: they do not need the support of
the majority, or of the universal voice, in order to fortify them
in some shaky allegiance. They know what they want and what
they love: the evident beauty of the beautiful is not enhanced
or removed by agreement. In its victorious actuality a man's
work must be local and temporary; it satisfies his impulse in his

day, and he is not forbidden to feel that in some secret sense the glory of it is eternal.

In this way aristocratic people, who are sure of their own taste and manners, are indifferent, except for a general curiosity, to the disputes of critics and pedants, and perhaps to the maxims of preachers; such things are imposing only to those who are inwardly wondering what they ought to do, and how they ought to feel. A truly enlightened mind is all the simpler for being enlightened and thinks, not without a modest sort of irony, that art and life exist to be enjoyed and not to be estimated. Why should different estimations annoy any one who is not a snob, when, if they are sincere, they express different enjoyments?

Even in politics, the masters who are most determined and intelligent, like those diverse Greek lawgivers, or like the Fascists of our day, do not dream of imposing their chosen polity on all nations. They are proud, with a local and schoolboy pride, of their special customs. Or perhaps the perfect aristocrat gets beyond that; he is too amiable, too well-informed, to feel the glow of a real pre-eminence, but smiles at his own ways as he might at the ways of the natives anywhere. He seems to himself only an odd native of an odd world; but perhaps the chief advantage which his good breeding bestows upon him is that he can afford to regard the other odd natives without hatred or envy.

Accordingly, a reasonable physician of the soul would leave his patients to prescribe for themselves, though not before subjecting them to a Socratic or even Freudian inquisition, or searching of heart, in order to awaken in them a radical self-knowledge, such as amid conventions and verbal illusions they probably do not possess. Evidently a regimen determined in this way has no validity for any other being, save in the measure in which, as a matter of fact, that other being partakes in the same nature and would find his sincere happiness in the same things. This is seldom or never exactly the case. Nothing is more multiform than perfection. No interest, no harmony, shuts out the legitimacy or the beauty of any other. It shuts out from itself only those qualities which are incompatible with perfection of that kind, there: as the perfect diamond shuts out the ruby, and the perfect ruby rejects the lovely colour of the emerald. But from nature, in her indefinite plasticity, nothing is shut out *a priori;* and no sort of virtue need be excluded by a rational moralist from the place where that virtue is native, and may be perfect.

Perfection is the most natural form of existence, simply carrying out the organic impulse by which any living creature arises at all; nor can that impulse ever find its quietus and satisfaction short of perfection; and nevertheless perfection is rare and seems wonderful, because division or weakness within the organism, or contrariety without, usually nips perfection in the bud. These biological troubles have their echo in the conscience. The alternation between pride and cowardice, between lust and shame, becomes a horrible torment to the spirit; and the issue in any case is unhappy, because a divided soul cannot be perfected. This distress, grown permanent, probably infects the imagination. Mysterious half-external forces—demons and duties—are seen looming behind these contrary natural promptings; and fantastic sanctions, heaven and hell, are invented for the future, enormously exaggerating the terrors of the choice. Thus while on the whole morality which men impose on themselves is rational, the reasons which they give for it are apt to be insane.

What is reason? There is a certain plasticity in some organisms which enables them to profit by experience. Instead of pushing for ever against a stone wall, they learn to go round it or over it. This plasticity, even when not under pressure, may take to play and experiment; toys are made which may become instruments; and the use of sounds as signals may enable the talking animal to recall absent things and to anticipate the future. Moreover, many animals mimic what they see; they transpose themselves dramatically into the objects surrounding them, especially into other animals of the same species. This transposition gives a moral reality, in their own spirit, to all their instinctive coaxing, deceiving, or threatening of one another. Their mind begins to conceive and to compare mere possibilities; it turns to story-telling and games; life becomes a tangle of eager plans and ambitions; and in quiet moments the order of merely imaginary things grows interesting for its own sake. There is a pleasure in embracing several ideas in a single act of intuition so as to see how far they are identical or akin or irrelevant.

Such a power of intellectual synthesis is evidently the mental counterpart of the power of acting with reference to changing or eventual circumstances: whether in practice or in speculation, it is the faculty of putting two and two together, and this faculty is what we call reason. It is what the idiot lacks, the fool neglects, and the madman contradicts. But in no case is reason a code, an oracle, or an external censor condemning the perceptions of sense or suppressing animal impulses. On the contrary, in the moral life, reason is a harmony of the passions, a harmony which perceptions and impulses may compose in so far as they grow sensitive to one another, and begin to move with mutual deference and a total grace.

Such at least was the life of reason which the humanists of the Renaissance thought they discovered, as it were embalmed, in Greek philosophy, poetry, and sculpture. Socrates had expressed this principle paradoxically when he taught that virtue is knowledge—self-knowledge taken to heart and applied prudently in action. Not that spontaneous preferences, character, and will could be dispensed with: these were presupposed; but it was reason that alone could mould those animal components of human nature into a noble and modest happiness.

But is there anything compulsory in reason? Is there not still liberty for fools? Can reason reasonably forbid them to exist? Certainly not, if they like to be fools: I should be sorry to see reason so uselessly kicking against the pricks. But a naturally synthetic mind (and all mind is naturally synthetic) hates waste and confusion; it hates action and speech at cross purposes; and these instinctive aversions implicitly pledge all mind to the ideal of a perfect rationality. Nobody is forbidden to be mindless; but in the mindful person the passions have spontaneously acquired a sense of responsibility to one another; or if they still allow themselves to make merry separately—because liveliness in the parts is a good without which the whole would be lifeless —yet the whole possesses, or aspires to possess, a unity of direction, in which all the parts may conspire, even if unwittingly.

So far, reason might be said to be prescriptive, and to impose a method on all moral life. Yet even where this method is exemplified in action, and life has become to that extent rational, nothing is prescribed concerning the elements which shall enter into that harmony. The materials for the synthesis are such at each point as nature and accident have made them; even in the same man or in the same nation they will be shifting perpetually, so that equally rational beings may have utterly disconnected interests, or interests hopelessly opposed. This diversity will be acceptable, so long as the parties are isolated, like China before the age of discoverers and missionaries; but where there is physical contact and contagion, the appeal must be to war, or to some other form of continued material pressure, such as industrial development or compulsory education: and in such a conflict both sides are apt to lose their original virtues, while the unthought-of virtues of the compound arise in their place.

In another direction the criterion of reason leaves the texture of life undetermined: the degree of unison requisite for harmony may differ in different rational systems. It is perhaps a classical prejudice that all happiness should be architectural. It might be simple and, like disillusioned Christian charity, alms for the moment. The finality of the incidental is more certain, and may be no less perfect, than the finality of great totals, like a life or a civilisation. A good verse is much more unmistakably good than a good epic. Organisation is everywhere presupposed, otherwise there could be no bodily life and no moral intuition: but where the level of intuition is reached, which is the supreme or spiritual level, the dead mass of the pyramid beneath that apex becomes indifferent. Reason cannot prescribe the girth of a man, or his stature; it can only reveal to his imperfect self his possible perfection. On this account I am not sure that the romantic temperament or art can be condemned off-hand for not being organic enough. Why be so pervasively organic? A flood of details and an alteration of humours may possibly bring the human heart as near as it can come to the heart of things, which I suspect is very fluid; and perhaps the human spirit is not at its best in the spider-like task of construction. Contemplation is freer and may be contemplation of anything.

Why is naturalism supposed to be favourable to the lower sides of human nature? Are not the higher sides just as natural? If anything, the naturalist, being a philosopher, might be expected to move most congenially and habitually on the higher levels. Perhaps the prejudice comes from the accident that when one element of human nature is reinforced by a supernatural sanction, and falsely assigned to a specially divine influence, the unsanctioned remainder alone retains the name of the natural. So Zola can come to be regarded as more naturalistic than Shakespeare, because more sordid in his naturalism, and less adequate; and Shakespeare can be regarded as more naturalistic than Virgil, although Virgil's feeling for things rural as well as for the cosmos at large was more naturalistic than Shakespeare's. Virgil is less romantic, playful, and vague: for the ancients poetised the actual surroundings and destiny of man, rather than the travesty of these facts in human fancy, and the consequent dramas within the spirit.

I think that pure reason in the naturalist may attain, without subterfuge, all the spiritual insights which supernaturalism goes so far out of the way to inspire. Spirituality is only a sort of return to innocence, birdlike and childlike. Experience of the world may have complicated the picture without clouding the vision. In looking before and after, and learning to take another man's point of view, ordinary intelligence has already transcended a brutal animality; it has learned to conceive things as they are, disinterestedly, contemplatively. Although intellect arises quite naturally, in the animal act of dominating events in the interests of survival, yet essentially intellect disengages itself from that servile office (which is that of its organ only) and from the beginning is speculative and impartial in its own outlook, and thinks it not robbery to take the point of view of God, of the truth, and of eternity.

In this congenital spiritual life of his, man regards himself as one creature among a thousand others deserving to be subordinated and kept in its place in his own estimation: a spiritual life not all at war with animal interests, which it presupposes, but detached from them in allegiance, withdrawn into the absolute, and reverting to them only with a charitable and qualified sympathy, such as the sane man can have for the madman, or the soul in general for inanimate things: and of course, it is not only others that the spiritual man regards in this way, but primarily himself. Yet this gift of transcending humanity in sympathy with the truth is a part, and the most distinctive part, of human nature. Reason vindicates insights and judgments which, though overruling those of the world, overrule them within the human heart, with its full consent and to its profound peace and satisfaction. The disillusioned philosopher is (at least in his own opinion) happier than the fool: the saint is at least as human as the man in the street, and far more steadfast and unrepining in his type of humanity.

That the fruition of happiness is intellectual (or as perhaps we should now call it, æsthetic) follows from the comprehensive scope of that intuition in which happiness is realised, a scope which distinguishes happiness from carnal pleasures; for although happiness, like everything else, can be experienced only in particular moments, it is found in conceiving the total issue and ultimate fruits of life; and no passing sensation or emotion could be enjoyed with a free mind, unless the blessing of reason and of a sustained happiness were felt to hang over it. All experience can of course never be synthesised in act, because life is a passage and has many centres; yet such a synthesis is adumbrated everywhere; and when it is partially attained, in some reflective or far-seeing moment, it raises the mind to a contemplation which is very far from cold, being in fact ecstatic; yet this ecstasy remains intellectual in that it holds together the burden of many successive and disparate things, which in blind experience would exclude one another: somewhat as a retentive ear, in a silence following upon music, may gather up the mounting strains of it in a quiet rapture. In raising truth to intuition of truth, in surveying the forms and places of many things at once and conceiving their movement, the intellect performs the most vital of possible acts, locks flying existence, as it were, in its arms, and stands, all eyes and breathless, at the top of life.

Reason may thus lend itself to sublimation into a sort of virtual omniscience or divine ecstasy: yet even then reason remains a harmony of material functions spiritually realised, as in Aristotle the life of God realises spiritually the harmonious revolutions of the heavens. So it is with reason in morals. It is essential to the validity of a moral maxim that it should be framed in the interest of natural impulses: otherwise that maxim would be a whim or an impertinence. The human impulses to be harmonised should not be without a certain persistence and strength; they should be honest, self-renewing, and self-rewarding, so as not to prove treacherous factors in the method of life to be adopted; and this method in its turn, becoming a custom and an institution, should be a gracious thing, beautiful and naturally glorious, as are love, patriotism, and religion; else the passion for living in political and religious union, beyond the limits of utility, would be sheer folly. But there are fusions, transmutations, and self-surrenders in which a naturally social animal finds an ultimate joy. True reason restrains only to liberate; it checks only in order that all currents, mingling in that moment's pause, may take a united course.

As to conscience and the sense of imposed duty, we may suppose them to be the voice of reason conveyed by tradition, in words that have grown mysterious and archaic, and at the same time solemn and loud. In so far as conscience is not this, but really a personal and groundless sentiment, it may be left to cancel its own oracles. Those who have lived in Boston—and who else should know?—are aware how earnestly the reformed New England conscience now disapproves of its disapprovals. Positive blushes and an awkward silence fall on a worthy family of my acquaintance at the least mention of one of their ancestors, who once wrote a terrifying poem about the Day of Doom. Conscience is an index to integrity of character, and under varying circumstances may retain an iron rigidity, like the staff and arrow of a weather-vane; but if directed by sentiment only, and not by a solid science of human nature, conscience will always be pointing in a different direction.

And in what direction exactly, we may ask, does conscience point so impressively in the American humanists, that they feel constrained to invoke a supernatural sanction for their maxims and to go forth and preach them to the whole world? I am at a loss to reply; because I can find little in their recommendations except a cautious allegiance to the genteel tradition. But can the way of Matthew Arnold and of Professor Norton be the way of life for all men for ever? If there be really a single supernatural vocation latent in all souls, I can imagine it revealed to some supreme sage in a tremendous vision, like that which came to Buddha under the Bo-Tree, or to Socrates when he heard, or dreamt that he heard, the Sibyl of Mantinæa discoursing on mortal and immortal love. There is much in any man's experience, if he reflects, to persuade him that the circumstances of this life are a strange accident to him, and that he belongs by nature to a different world. If all the American humanists had become Catholics like Newman, or even like Mr. T. S. Eliot, I should understand the reason.

But can it be that all Latins and Slavs, all Arabs, Chinamen, and Indians, if they were not benighted in mind and degenerate in body, would be model Anglo-Americans? That is what British and American politicians and missionaries seem to believe: all nations are expected gladly to exchange their religion and their customs for the Protestant genteel tradition. I am myself an ardent admirer of the Anglo-American character. I almost share that "extraordinary faith in the moral efficacy of cold baths and dumb-bells" which Mr. Bertrand Russell attributes to the Y. M. C. A. Sport, companionship, reading-rooms, with an occasional whiff of religious sentiment to stop foul mouths and turn aside hard questions—all this composes a saving tonic for the simple masculine soul habitually in the service of Big Business; while for the more fastidious, or the more fashionable, I can see the value of the English public school and the Anglican Church, which Mr. Russell thinks mere instruments of oppression. To me—seeing them, I confess, at a more romantic distance—they seem instruments rather of a beautiful integration: none of those fierce darts of intellectual sincerity which Mr. Russell would like, but something voluminous, comfortable, and sane, on a political, conventional, and sporting level.

The senses, which we use successfully in action, distort the objects on which we act, yet do so harmlessly and poetically, because our bodies are quick to understand those perceptions before our minds have had time to consider them narrowly. In the same way understanding relieves a truly intelligent man from fussiness about social institutions and conventions: they are absurd, yet absurdity is not incompatible with their natural function, which may be indispensable. But in philosophy, when ultimately the spirit comes face to face with the truth, convention and absurdity are out of place; so is humanism and so is the genteel tradition; so is morality itself.

The commandment *Thou shalt not kill*, for instance, is given out on divine authority, and infinite sanctions are supposed to

confirm it in the other world. Yet the basis of this commandment is not cosmic or supernatural, but narrowly human. It expresses the natural affection of kindred for one another, an affection surviving and woefully rebuking any rash murder; and it
expresses also the social and political need of living, within a certain territory, in safety and mutual trust. In its human atmosphere, the thunder of that precept is therefore not hollow; the
sharp bolts of remorse and ruin follow closely upon it. But in the
cosmos at large, is killing forbidden? If so, the fabric of creation
must be monstrous and sinful indeed. The moving equilibrium of
things, so blind and inexorable, yet often so magnificent, becomes
a riddle to be deciphered, a labyrinth of punishments and favours,
the work of some devil, or at least a work of God so contami-
nated with evil as to be a caricature of the divine intentions. And
not in human life only: the ferocity and agony of the jungle and
the strange gropings of life in the depths of the sea, become perverse and scandalous; existence seems a disease, and the world a
garden of poisons, through which a man must pick his way with
fear and trembling, girded high, and dreading to touch the
earth with his bare foot, or a fellow-creature with his hand. Had
it been the Creator who said *Thou shalt not kill*, and said it to the
universe, existence would have been arrested.

When therefore a tender conscience extends its maxims beyond their natural basis, it not only ceases to be rational in its
deliverances, and becomes fanatical, but it casts the livid colours of its own insanity upon nature at large. A strained holiness, never without its seamy side, ousts honourable virtue,
and the fear of so many enemies becomes the greatest enemy
of the soul. No true appreciation of anything is possible without a sense of its *naturalness*, of the innocent necessity by which
it has assumed its special and perhaps extraordinary form. In a
word, the principle of morality is naturalistic. Call it humanism
or not, only a morality frankly relative to man's nature is
worthy of man, being at once vital and rational, martial and
generous; whereas absolutism smells of fustiness as well as of
faggots.

III

The American Will

ᐓ English Liberty in America*

The straits of Dover, which one may sometimes see across, have sufficed so to isolate England that it has never moved quite in step with the rest of Europe in politics, morals, or art. No wonder that the Atlantic Ocean, although it has favoured a mixed emigration and cheap intercourse, should have cut off America so effectually that all the people there, even those of Latin origin, have become curiously different from any kind of European. In vain are they reputed to have the same religions or to speak the same languages as their cousins in the old world; everything has changed its accent, spirit, and value. Flora and fauna have been intoxicated by that untouched soil and fresh tonic air, and by those vast spaces; in spite of their hereditary differences of species they have all acquired the same crude savour and defiant aspect. In comparison with their European prototypes they seem tough, meagre, bold, and ugly. In the United States, apart from the fact that most of the early colonists belonged to an exceptional type of Englishman, the scale and speed of life have made every-strangely un-English. There is cheeriness instead of dogged-ness, confidence instead of circumspection; there is a desire to quizz and to dazzle rather than a fear of being mistaken or of being shocked; there is a pervasive cordiality, exaggeration, and farcical humour; and in the presence of the Englishman, when by chance he turns up or is thought of, there is an invincible impa-

* Chapter VII of *Character and Opinion in the United States.*

tience and irritation that his point of view should be so fixed, his mind so literal, and the freight he carries so excessive (when you are sailing in ballast yourself), and that he should seem to take so little notice of changes in the wind to which you are nervously sensitive.

Nevertheless there is one gift or habit, native to England, that has not only been preserved in America unchanged, but has found there a more favourable atmosphere in which to manifest its true nature—I mean the spirit of free co-operation. The root of it is free individuality, which is deeply seated in the English inner man; there is an indomitable instinct or mind in him which he perpetually consults and reveres, slow and embarrassed as his expression of it may be. But this free individuality in the Englishman is crossed and biassed by a large residue of social servitude. The church and the aristocracy, entanglement in custom and privilege, mistrust and bitterness about particular grievances, warp the inner man and enlist him against his interests in alien causes; the straits of Dover were too narrow, the shadow of a hostile continent was too oppressive, the English sod was soaked with too many dews and cut by too many hedges, for each individual, being quite master of himself, to confront every other individual without fear or prejudice, and to unite with him in the free pursuit of whatever aims they might find that they had in common. Yet this slow co-operation of free men, this liberty in democracy—the only sort that America possesses or believes in —is wholly English in its personal basis, its reserve, its tenacity, its empiricism, its public spirit, and its assurance of its own rightness; and it deserves to be called English always, to whatever countries it may spread.

The omnipresence in America of this spirit of co-operation, responsibility, and growth is very remarkable. Far from being neutralised by American dash and bravura, or lost in the opposite instincts of so many alien races, it seems to be adopted at once in the most mixed circles and in the most novel predicaments. In America social servitude is reduced to a minimum; in fact we may almost say that it is reduced to subjecting children to their mothers and to a common public education, agencies that are absolutely indispensable to produce the individual and enable him to exercise his personal initiative effectually; for after all, whatever metaphysical egotism may say, one cannot vote to be created. But once created, weaned, and taught to read and write, the young American can easily shoulder his knapsack and choose his own way in the world. He is as yet very little trammelled by want of opportunity, and he has no roots to speak of in place, class, or religion. Where individuality is so free, co-operation, when it is justified, can be all the more quick and hearty. Everywhere co-operation is taken for granted, as something that no one would be so mean or so short-sighted as to refuse. Together with the will to work and to prosper, it is of the essence of Americanism, and is accepted as such by all the unkempt polyglot peoples that turn to the new world with the pathetic but manly purpose of beginning life on a new principle. Every political body, every public meeting, every club, or college, or athletic team, is full of it. Out it comes whenever there is an accident in the street or a division in a church, or a great unexpected emergency like the late war. The general instinct is to run and help, to assume direction, to pull through somehow by mutual adaptation, and by seizing on the readiest practical measures and working compromises. Each man joins in and gives a helping hand, without a preconceived plan or a prior motive. Even the leader, when he is a natural leader and not a professional, has nothing up his sleeve to force on the rest, in their obvious good-will and mental blankness. All meet in a genuine spirit of consultation, eager to persuade but ready to be persuaded, with a cheery confidence in their average ability, when a point comes up and is clearly put before them, to decide it for the time being, and to move on. It is implicitly agreed, in every case, that disputed questions shall be put to a vote, and that the minority will loyally acquiesce in the decision of the majority and build henceforth upon it, without a thought of ever retracting it.

Such a way of proceeding seems in America a matter of course, because it is bred in the bone, or imposed by that permeating social contagion which is so irresistible in a natural democracy. But if we consider human nature at large and the practice of most nations, we shall see that it is a very rare, wonderful, and unstable convention. It implies a rather unimaginative optimistic assumption that at bottom all men's interests are similar and compatible, and a rather heroic public spirit—such that no spe-

cial interest, in so far as it has to be overruled, shall rebel and
try to maintain itself absolutely. In America hitherto these conditions happen to have been actually fulfilled in an unusual measure. Interests have been very similar—to exploit business opportunities and organise public services useful to all; and these similar
interests have been also compatible and harmonious. A neighbour,
even a competitor, where the field is so large and so little pre-
empted, has more often proved a resource than a danger. The
rich have helped the public more than they have fleeced it, and
they have been emulated more than hated or served by the enterprising poor. To abolish millionaires would have been to dash
one's own hopes. The most opposite systems of religion and education could look smilingly upon one another's prosperity, because the country could afford these superficial luxuries, having a
constitutional religion and education of its own, which everybody drank in unconsciously and which assured the moral cohesion of the people. Impulses of reason and kindness, which are
potential in all men, under such circumstances can become effective; people can help one another with no great sacrifice to themselves, and minorities can dismiss their special plans without sorrow, and cheerfully follow the crowd down another road. It was
because life in America was naturally more co-operative and more
plastic than in England that the spirit of English liberty, which
demands co-operation and plasticity, could appear there more
boldly and universally than it ever did at home.

English liberty is a method, not a goal. It is related to the
value of human life very much as the police are related to public
morals or commerce to wealth; and it is no accident that the
Anglo-Saxon race excels in commerce and in the commercial as
distinguished from the artistic side of industry, and that having
policed itself successfully it is beginning to police the world at
large. It is all an eminence in temper, good-will, reliability, accommodation. Probably some other races, such as the Jews and
Arabs, make individually better merchants, more shrewd, patient,
and loving of their art. Englishmen and Americans often seem to
miss or force opportunities, to play for quick returns, or to settle down into ponderous corporations; for successful men they
are not particularly observant, constant, or economical. But the
superiority of the Oriental is confined to his private craft; he has

not the spirit of partnership. In English civilisation the individual is neutralised; it does not matter so much even in high places if he is rather stupid or rather cheap; public spirit sustains him, and he becomes its instrument all the more readily, perhaps, for not being very distinguished or clear-headed in himself. The community prospers; comfort and science, good manners and generous feelings are diffused among the people, without the aid of that foresight and cunning direction which sometimes give a temporary advantage to a rival system like the German. In the end, adaptation to the world at large, where so much is hidden and unintelligible, is only possible piecemeal, by groping with a genuine indetermination in one's aims. Its very looseness gives the English method its lien on the future. To dominate the world co-operation is better than policy, and empiricism safer than inspiration. Anglo-Saxon imperialism is unintended; military conquests are incidental to it and often not maintained; it subsists by a mechanical equilibrium of habits and interests, in which every colony, province, or protectorate has a different status. It has a commercial and missionary quality, and is essentially an invitation to pull together—an invitation which many nations may be incapable of accepting or even of understanding, or which they may deeply scorn, because it involves a surrender of absolute liberty on their part; but whether accepted or rejected, it is an offer of co-operation, a project for a limited partnership, not a complete plan of life to be imposed on anybody.

It is a wise instinct, in dealing with foreigners or with material things (which are foreigners to the mind), to limit oneself in this way to establishing external relations, partial mutual adjustments, with a great residuum of independence and reserve; if you attempt more you will achieve less; your interpretations will become chimerical and your regimen odious. So deep-seated is this prudent instinct in the English nature that it appears even at home; most of the concrete things which English genius has produced are expedients. Its spiritual treasures are hardly possessions, except as character is a possession; they are rather a standard of life, a promise, an insurance. English poetry and fiction form an exception; the very incoherence and artlessness which they share with so much else that is English lend them an absolute value as an expression. They are the mirror and prattle of the inner man—a boyish spirit astray in the green earth it loves, rich in wonder, perplexity, valour, and faith, given to opinionated little prejudices, but withal sensitive and candid, and often laden, as in *Hamlet*, with exquisite music, tender humour, and tragic self-knowledge. But apart from the literature that simply utters the inner man, no one considering the English language, the English church, or English philosophy, or considering the common law and parliamentary government, would take them for perfect realisations of art or truth or an ideal polity. Institutions so jumbled and limping could never have been planned; they can never be transferred to another setting, or adopted bodily; but special circumstances and contrary currents have given them birth, and they are accepted and prized, where they are native, for keeping the door open to a great volume and variety of goods, at a moderate cost of danger and absurdity.

Of course no product of mind is *merely* an expedient; all are concomitantly expressions of temperament; there is something in their manner of being practical which is poetical and catches the rhythm of the heart. In this way anything foreign—and almost all the elements of civilisation in England and America are foreign—when it is adopted and acclimatised, takes on a native accent, especially on English lips; like the Latin words in the language, it becomes thoroughly English in texture. The English Bible, again, with its archaic homeliness and majesty, sets the mind brooding, not less than the old ballad most redolent of the native past and the native imagination; it fills the memory with solemn and pungent phrases; and this incidental spirit of poetry in which it comes to be clothed is a self-revelation perhaps more pertinent and welcome to the people than the alien revelations it professes to transmit. English law and parliaments, too, would be very unjustly judged if judged as practical contrivances only; they satisfy at the same time the moral interest people have in uttering and enforcing their feelings. These institutions are ceremonious, almost sacramental; they are instinct with a dramatic spirit deeper and more vital than their utility. Englishmen and Americans love debate; they love sitting round a table as if in consultation, even when the chairman has pulled the wires and settled everything beforehand, and when each of the participants listens only to his own remarks and votes according to his party.

They love committees and commissions; they love public dinners with after-dinner speeches, those stammering compounds
of facetiousness, platitude, and business. How distressing such
speeches usually are, and how helplessly prolonged, does not escape anybody; yet every one demands them notwithstanding, because in pumping them up or sitting through them he feels he is
leading the political life. A public man must show himself in
public, even if not to advantage. The moral expressiveness of
such institutions also helps to redeem their clumsy procedure;
they would not be useful, nor work at all as they should, if people did not smack their lips over them and feel a profound
pleasure in carrying them out. Without the English spirit, without the faculty of making themselves believe in public what they
never feel in private, without the habit of clubbing together and
facing facts, and feeling duty in a cautious, consultative, experimental way, English liberties forfeit their practical value; as we
see when they are extended to a volatile histrionic people like
the Irish, or when a jury in France, instead of pronouncing simply on matters of fact and the credibility of witnesses, rushes in
the heat of its patriotism to carry out, by its verdict, some political policy.

The practice of English liberty presupposes two things: that
all concerned are fundamentally unanimous, and that each has a
plastic nature, which he is willing to modify. If fundamental
unanimity is lacking and all are not making in the same general
direction, there can be no honest co-operation, no satisfying
compromise. Every concession, under such circumstances, would
be a temporary one, to be retracted at the first favourable moment; it would amount to a mutilation of one's essential nature,
a partial surrender of life, liberty, and happiness, tolerable for a
time, perhaps, as the lesser of two evils, but involving a perpetual
sullen opposition and hatred. To put things to a vote, and to accept unreservedly the decision of the majority, are points essential to the English system; but they would be absurd if fundamental agreement were not presupposed. Every decision that the
majority could conceivably arrive at must leave it still possible
for the minority to live and prosper, even if not exactly in the
way they wished. Were this not the case, a decision by vote would
be as alien a fatality to any minority as the decree of a foreign

tyrant, and at every election the right of rebellion would come into play. In a hearty and sound democracy all questions at issue must be minor matters; fundamentals must have been silently agreed upon and taken for granted when the democracy arose. To leave a decision to the majority is like leaving it to chance— a fatal procedure unless one is willing to have it either way. You must be able to risk losing the toss; and if you do you will acquiesce all the more readily in the result, because, unless the winners cheated at the game, they had no more influence on it than yourself—namely none, or very little. You acquiesce in democracy on the same conditions and for the same reasons, and perhaps a little more cheerfully, because there is an infinitesimally better chance of winning on the average; but even then the enormity of the risk involved would be intolerable if anything of vital importance was at stake. It is therefore actually required that juries, whose decisions may really be of moment, should be unanimous; and parliaments and elections are never more satisfactory than when a wave of national feeling runs through them and there is no longer any minority nor any need of voting.

Free government works well in proportion as government is superfluous. That most parliamentary measures should be trivial or technical, and really devised and debated only in government offices, and that government in America should so long have been carried on in the shade, by persons of no name or dignity, is no anomaly. On the contrary, like the good fortune of those who never hear of the police, it is all a sign that co-operative liberty is working well and rendering overt government unnecessary. Sometimes kinship and opportunity carry a whole nation before the wind; but this happy unison belongs rather to the dawn of national life, when similar tasks absorb all individual energies. If it is to be maintained after lines of moral cleavage appear, and is to be compatible with variety and distinction of character, all further developments must be democratically controlled and must remain, as it were, in a state of fusion. Variety and distinction must not become arbitrary and irresponsible. They must take directions that will not mar the general harmony, and no interest must be carried so far as to lose sight of the rest. Science and art, in such a vital democracy, should remain popular, helpful, bracing; religion should be broadly national and in the spirit of the times. The variety and distinction allowed must be only variety and distinction of service. If they ever became a real distinction and variety of life, if they arrogated to themselves an absolute liberty, they would shatter the unity of the democratic spirit and destroy its moral authority.

The levelling tendency of English liberty (inevitable if plastic natures are to co-operate and to make permanent concessions to one another's instincts) comes out more clearly in America than in England itself. In England there are still castles and rural retreats, there are still social islands within the Island, where special classes may nurse particular allegiances. America is all one prairie, swept by a universal tornado. Although it has always thought itself in an eminent sense the land of freedom, even when it was covered with slaves, there is no country in which people live under more overpowering compulsions. The prohibitions, although important and growing, are not yet, perhaps, so many or so blatant as in some other countries; but prohibitions are less galling than compulsions. What can be forbidden specifically—bigamy, for instance, or heresy—may be avoided by a prudent man without renouncing the whole movement of life and mind which, if carried beyond a certain point, would end in those trespasses against convention. He can indulge in hypothesis or gallantry without falling foul of the positive law, which indeed may even stimulate his interest and ingenuity by suggesting some indirect means of satisfaction. On the other hand, what is exacted cuts deeper; it creates habits which overlay nature, and every faculty is atrophied that does not conform with them. If, for instance, I am compelled to be in an office (and up to business, too) from early morning to late afternoon, with long journeys in thundering and sweltering trains before and after and a flying shot at a quick lunch between, I am caught and held both in soul and body; and except for the freedom to work and to rise by that work—which may be very interesting in itself—I am not suffered to exist morally at all. My evenings will be drowsy, my Sundays tedious, and after a few days' holiday I shall be wishing to get back to business. Here is as narrow a path left open to freedom as is left open in a monastic establishment, where bell and book keep your attention fixed at all hours upon the hard work of salvation—an infinite vista, certainly, if

your soul was not made to look another way. Those, too, who
may escape this crushing routine—the invalids, the ladies, the fops
—are none the less prevented by it from doing anything else
with success or with a good conscience; the bubbles also must
swim with the stream. Even what is best in American life is compulsory—the idealism, the zeal, the beautiful happy unison of its
great moments. You must wave, you must cheer, you must push
with the irresistible crowd; otherwise you will feel like a traitor,
a soulless outcast, a deserted ship high and dry on the shore. In
America there is but one way of being saved, though it is not
peculiar to any of the official religions, which themselves must silently conform to the national orthodoxy, or else become impotent and merely ornamental. This national faith and morality are
vague in idea, but inexorable in spirit; they are the gospel of work
and the belief in progress. By them, in a country where all men
are free, every man finds that what most matters has been settled
for him beforehand.

Nevertheless, American life *is* free as a whole, because it is
mobile, because every atom that swims in it has a momentum
of its own which is felt and respected throughout the mass, like
the weight of an atom in the solar system, even if the deflection
it may cause is infinitesimal. In temper America is docile and
not at all tyrannical; it has not predetermined its career, and its
merciless momentum is a passive resultant. Like some Mississippi
or Niagara, it rolls its myriad drops gently onward, being but the
suction and pressure which they exercise on one another. Any
tremulous thought or playful experiment anywhere may be a
first symptom of great changes, and may seem to precipitate
the cataract in a new direction. Any snowflake in a boy's sky may
become the centre for his *boule de neige,* his prodigious fortune;
but the monster will melt as easily as it grew, and leaves nobody
poorer for having existed. In America there is duty everywhere,
but everywhere also there is light. I do not mean superior understanding or even moderately wide knowledge, but openness to
light, an evident joy in seeing things clearly and doing them
briskly, which would amount to a veritable triumph of art and
reason if the affairs in which it came into play were central and
important. The American may give an exorbitant value to subsidiary things, but his error comes of haste in praising what he

possesses, and trusting the first praises he hears. He can detect sharp practices, because he is capable of them, but vanity or wickedness in the ultimate aims of a man, including himself, he cannot detect, because he is ingenuous in that sphere. He thinks life splendid and blameless, without stopping to consider how far folly and malice may be inherent in it. He feels that he himself has nothing to dread, nothing to hide or apologise for; and if he is arrogant in his ignorance, there is often a twinkle in his eye when he is most boastful. Perhaps he suspects that he is making a fool of himself, and he challenges the world to prove it; and his innocence is quickly gone when he is once convinced that it exists. Accordingly the American orthodoxy, though imperious, is not unyielding. It has a keener sense for destiny than for policy. It is confident of a happy and triumphant future, which it would be shameful in any man to refuse to work for and to share; but it cannot prefigure what that bright future is to be. While it works feverishly in outward matters, inwardly it only watches and waits; and it feels tenderly towards the unexpressed impulses in its bosom, like a mother towards her unborn young.

There is a mystical conviction, expressed in Anglo-Saxon life and philosophy, that our labours, even when they end in failure, contribute to some ulterior achievement in which it is well they should be submerged. This Anglo-Saxon piety, in the form of trust and adaptability, reaches somewhat the same insight that more speculative religions have reached through asceticism, the insight that we must renounce our wills and deny ourselves. But to have a will remains essential to animals, and having a will we must kick against the pricks, even if philosophy thinks it foolish of us. The spirit in which parties and nations beyond the pale of English liberty confront one another is not motherly nor brotherly nor Christian. Their valorousness and morality consist in their indomitable egotism. The liberty they want is absolute liberty, a desire which is quite primitive. It may be identified with the love of life which animates all creation, or with the pursuit of happiness which all men would be engaged in if they were rational. Indeed, it might even be identified with the first law of motion, that all bodies, if left free, persevere in that state of rest, or of motion in a straight line, in which they happen to find themselves. The enemies of this primitive freedom are all such exter-

nal forces as make it deviate from the course it is in the habit of
taking or is inclined to take; and when people begin to reflect
upon their condition, they protest against this alien tyranny, and
contrast in fancy what they would do if they were free with
what under duress they are actually doing. All human struggles
are inspired by what, in this sense, is the love of freedom. Even
craving for power and possessions may be regarded as the love
of a free life on a larger scale, for which more instruments and
resources are needed. The apologists of absolute will are not slow,
for instance, to tell us that Germany in her laborious ambitions
has been pursuing the highest form of freedom, which can be attained only by organising all the resources of the world, and the
souls of all subsidiary nations, around one luminous centre of
direction and self-consciousness, such as the Prussian government was eminently fitted to furnish. Freedom to exercise absolute will methodically seems to them much better than English
liberty, because it knows what it wants, pursues it intelligently,
and does not rely for success on some measure of goodness in
mankind at large. English liberty is so trustful! It moves by a series of checks, mutual concessions, and limited satisfactions; it
counts on chivalry, sportsmanship, brotherly love, and on that
rarest and least lucrative of virtues, fair-mindedness: it is a broad-
based, stupid, blind adventure, groping towards an unknown
goal. Who but an Englishman would think of such a thing! A
fanatic, a poet, a doctrinaire, a dilettante—any one who has a
fixed aim and clear passions—will not relish English liberty. It
will seem bitter irony to him to give the name of liberty to something so muffled, exacting, and oppressive. In fact English liberty is a positive infringement and surrender of the freedom most
fought for and most praised in the past. It makes impossible the
sort of liberty for which the Spartans died at Thermopylæ, or
the Christian martyrs in the arena, or the Protestant reformers at
the stake; for these people all died because they would not co-
operate, because they were not plastic and would never consent
to lead the life dear or at least customary to other men. They insisted on being utterly different and independent and inflexible
in their chosen systems, and aspired either to destroy the society
round them or at least to insulate themselves in the midst of it,
and live a jealous, private, unstained life of their own within their

city walls or mystical conclaves. Any one who passionately loves
his particular country or passionately believes in his particular
religion cannot be content with less liberty or more democracy
than that; he must be free to live absolutely according to his ideal,
and no hostile votes, no alien interests, must call on him to deviate
from it by one iota. Such was the claim to religious liberty which
has played so large a part in the revolutions and divisions of the
western world. Every new heresy professed to be orthodoxy itself, purified and restored; and woe to all backsliders from the
reformed faith! Even the popes, without thinking to be ironical,
have often raised a wail for liberty. Such too was the aspiration
of those mediæval cities and barons who fought for their liberties
and rights. Such was the aspiration even of the American declaration of independence and the American constitution: cast-iron
documents, if only the spirit of co-operative English liberty had
not been there to expand, embosom, soften, or transform them.
So the French revolution and the Russian one of to-day have
aimed at establishing society once for all on some eternally just
principle, and at abolishing all traditions, interests, faiths, and
even words that did not belong to their system. Liberty, for all
these pensive or rabid apostles of liberty, meant liberty for themselves to be just so, and to remain just so for ever, together with
the most vehement defiance of anybody who might ask them,
for the sake of harmony, to be a little different. They summoned
every man to become free in exactly their own fashion, or have
his head cut off.

Of course, to many an individual, life even in any such free city
or free church, fiercely jealous of its political independence and
moral purity, would prove to be a grievous servitude; and there
has always been a sprinkling of rebels and martyrs and scornful
philosophers protesting and fuming against their ultra-independ-
ent and nothing-if-not-protesting sects. To co-operate with any
body seems to these *esprits forts* contamination, so sensitive are
they to any deviation from the true north which their compass
might suffer through the neighbourhood of any human magnet.
If it is a weakness to be subject to influence, it is an imprudence
to expose oneself to it; and to be subject to influence seems ignominious to any one whose inward monitor is perfectly articulate
and determined. A certain vagueness of soul, together with a great

gregariousness and tendency to be moulded by example and by prevalent opinion, is requisite for feeling free under English liberty. You must find the majority right enough to live with; you must give up lost causes; you must be willing to put your favourite notions to sleep in the family cradle of convention. Enthusiasts for democracy, peace, and a league of nations should not deceive themselves; they are not everybody's friends; they are the enemies of what is deepest and most primitive in everybody. They inspire undying hatred in every untamable people and every absolute soul.

It is in the nature of wild animal life to be ferocious or patient, and in either case heroic and uncompromising. It is inevitable, in the beginning, that each person or faction should come into the lists to serve some express interest, which in itself may be perfectly noble and generous. But these interests are posited alone and in all their ultimate consequences. The parties meet, however diplomatic their procedure, as buyers and sellers bargain in primitive markets. Each has a fixed programme or, as he perhaps calls it, an ideal; and when he has got as much as he can get to-day, he will return to the charge to-morrow, with absolutely unchanged purpose. All opposed parties he regards as sheer enemies to be beaten down, driven off, and ultimately converted or destroyed. Meantime he practises political craft, of which the climax is war; a craft not confined to priests, though they are good at it, but common to every missionary, agitator, and philosophical politician who operates in view of some vested interest or inflexible plan, in the very un-English spirit of intrigue, cajolery, eloquence, and dissimulation. His art is to worm his way forward, using people's passions to further his own ends, carrying them off their feet in a wave of enthusiasm, when that is feasible, and when it is not, recommending his cause by insidious half-measures, flattery of private interests, confidence-tricks, and amiable suggestions, until he has put his entangled victims in his pocket; or when he feels strong enough, brow-beating and intimidating them into silence. Such is the inevitable practice of every prophet who heralds an absolute system, political or religious, and who pursues the unqualified domination of principles which he thinks right in themselves and of a will which is self-justified and irresponsible.

Why, we may ask, are people so ready to set up absolute claims, when their resources are obviously so limited that permanent success is impossible, and their will itself, in reality, is so fragile that it abandons each of its dreams even before it learns that it cannot be realised? The reason is that the feebler, more ignorant, and more childlike an impulse is, the less it can restrain itself or surrender a part of its desire in order the better to attain the rest. In most nations and most philosophies the intellect is rushed; it is swept forward and enamoured by the first glimpses it gets of anything good. The dogmas thus precipitated seem to relieve the will of all risks and to guarantee its enterprises; whereas in fact they are rendering every peril tragic by blinding us to it, and every vain hope incorrigible. A happy shyness in the English mind, a certain torpor and lateness in its utterance, have largely saved it from this calamity, and just because it is not brilliant it is safe. Being reticent, it remains fertile; being vague in its destination, it can turn at each corner down the most inviting road. In this race the intellect has chosen the part of prudence, leaving courage to the will, where courage is indispensable. How much more becoming and fortunate is this balance of faculties for an earthly being than an intellect that scales the heavens, refuting and proving everything, while the will dares to attempt and to reform nothing, but fritters itself away in sloth, petty malice, and irony! In the English character modesty and boldness appear in the right places and in a just measure. Manliness ventures to act without pretending to be sure of the issue; it does not cry that all is sure, in order to cover up the mortal perils of finitude; and manliness has its reward in the joys of exploration and comradeship.

It is this massive malleable character, this vigorous moral youth, that renders co-operation possible and progressive. When interests are fully articulate and fixed, co-operation is a sort of mathematical problem; up to a certain precise limit, people can obviously help one another by summoning their efforts, like sailors pulling at a rope, or by a division of labour; they can obviously help one another when thereby they are helping themselves. But beyond that, there can be nothing but mutual indifference or eternal hostility. This is the old way of the world. Most of the lower animals, although they run through surprising transformations during their growth, seem to reach maturity by a predetermined method and in a predetermined form. Nature does everything for them and experience nothing, and they live or die, as the case may be, true to their innate character. Mankind, on the contrary, and especially the English races, seem to reach physical maturity still morally immature; they need to be finished by education, experience, external influences. What so often spoils other creatures improves them. If left to themselves and untrained, they remain all their lives stupid and coarse, with no natural joy but drunkenness; but nurseries and schools and churches and social conventions can turn them into the most refined and exquisite of men, and admirably intelligent too, in a cautious and special fashion. They may never become, for all their pains, so agile, graceful, and sure as many an animal or *a priori* man is without trouble, but they acquire more representative minds and a greater range of material knowledge. Such completion, in the open air, of characters only half-formed in the womb may go on in some chance direction, or it may go on in the direction of a greater social harmony, that is, in whatever direction is suggested to each man by the suasion of his neighbours. Society is a second mother to these souls; and the instinct of many animals would remain inchoate if the great instinct of imitation did not intervene and enable them to learn by example. Development in this case involves assimilation; characters are moulded by contagion and educated by democracy. The sphere of unanimity tends to grow larger, and to reduce the margin of diversity to insignificance. The result is an ever-increasing moral unison, which is the simplest form of moral harmony and emotionally the most coercive.

Democracy is often mentioned in the same breath with liberty, as if they meant the same thing; and both are sometimes identified with the sort of elective government that prevails in Great Britain and the United States. But just as English liberty seems servitude to some people because it requires them to cooperate, to submit to the majority, and to grow like them, so English democracy seems tyranny to the wayward masses, because it is constitutional, historical, and sacred, narrowing down the power of any group of people at any time to voting for one of two or three candidates for office, or to saying yes or no to some specific proposal—both the proposals and the candidates being set before them by an invisible agency; and fate was never more inexorable or blinder than is the grinding of this ponderous political mill, where routine, nepotism, pique, and swagger, with love of office and money, turn all the wheels. And the worst of it is that the revolutionary parties that oppose this historical machine repeat all its abuses, or even aggravate them. It would be well if people in England and America woke up to the fact that it is in the name of natural liberty and direct democracy that enemies both within and without are already rising up against their democracy and their liberty. Just as the Papacy once threatened English liberties, because it would maintain one inflexible international religion over all men, so now an international democracy of the disinherited many, led by the disinherited few, threatens English liberties again, since it would abolish those private interests which are the factors in any co-operation, and would reduce everybody to forced membership and forced service in one universal flock, without property, family, country, or religion. That life under such a system might have its comforts, its arts, and its atomic liberties, is certain, just as under the Catholic system it had its virtues and consolations; but both systems presuppose the universality of a type of human nature which is not English, and perhaps not human.

The great advantage of English liberty is that it is in harmony with the nature of things; and when living beings have managed to adapt their habits to the nature of things, they have entered the path of health and wisdom. No doubt the living will is essentially absolute, both at the top and at the bottom, in the ferocious animal and in the rapt spirit; but it is absolute even then only in its deliverance, in what it asserts or demands; nothing can be less absolute or more precarious than the living will in its existence. A living will is the flexible voice of a thousand submerged impulses, of which now one and now another comes to the surface; it is responsive, without knowing it, to a complex forgotten past and a changing, unexplored environment. The will is a mass of passions; when it sets up absolute claims it is both tragic and ridiculous. It may be ready to be a martyr, but it will have to be one. Martyrs are heroic; but unless they have the nature of things on their side and their cause can be victorious, their heroism is

like that of criminals and madmen, interesting dramatically but
morally detestable. Madmen and criminals, like other martyrs,
appeal to the popular imagination, because in each of us there is
a little absolute will, or a colony of little absolute wills, aching to
be criminal, mad, and heroic. Yet the equilibrium by which we
exist if we are sane, and which we call reason, keeps these rebellious dreams under; if they run wild, we are lost. Reason is a harmony; and it has been reputed by egotistical philosophers to
rule the world (in which unreason of every sort is fundamental
and rampant), because when harmony between men and nature
supervenes at any place or in any measure, the world becomes
intelligible and safe, and philosophers are able to live in it. The
passions, even in a rational society, remain the elements of life,
but under mutual control, and the life of reason, like English
liberty, is a perpetual compromise. Absolute liberty, on the contrary, is impracticable; it is a foolish challenge thrown by a new-
born insect buzzing against the universe; it is incompatible with
more than one pulse of life. All the declarations of independence
in the world will not render anybody really independent. You
may disregard your environment, you cannot escape it; and your
disregard of it will bring you moral impoverishment and some
day unpleasant surprises. Even Robinson Crusoe—whom of-
fended America once tried to imitate—lived on what he had
saved from the wreck, on footprints and distant hopes. Liberty
to be left alone, not interfered with and not helped, is not English liberty. It is the primeval desire of every wild animal or barbarous tribe or jealous city or religion, claiming to live and to
tramp through the world in its own sweet way. These combative
organisms, however, have only such strength as the opposite principle of co-operation lends them inwardly; and the more liberty
they assume in foreign affairs the less liberty their members can
enjoy at home. At home they must then have organisation at all
costs, like ancient Sparta and modern Germany; and even if the
restraints so imposed are not irksome and there is spontaneous
unison and enthusiasm in the people, the basis of such a local
harmony will soon prove too narrow. Nations and religions will
run up against one another, against change, against science,
against all the realities they had never reckoned with; and more
or less painfully they will dissolve. And it will not be a normal

and fruitful dissolution, like that of a man who leaves children and heirs. It will be the end of that evolution, the choking of that ideal in the sand.

This collapse of fierce liberty is no ordinary mutation, such as time brings sooner or later to everything that exists, when the circumstances that sustained it in being no longer prevail. It is a deep tragedy, because the narrower passions and swifter harmonies are more beautiful and perfect than the chaos or the dull broad equilibrium that may take their place. Co-operative life is reasonable and long-winded; but it always remains imperfect itself, while it somewhat smothers the impulses that enter into it. Absolute liberty created these elements; inspiration, free intelligence, uncompromising conviction, a particular home and breeding-ground, were requisite to give them birth. Nothing good could arise for co-operation to diffuse or to qualify unless first there had been complete liberty for the artist and an uncontaminated perfection in his work. Reason and the principle of English liberty have no creative afflatus; they presuppose spontaneity and yet they half stifle it; and they can rest in no form of perfection, because they must remain plastic and continually invite amendments, in order to continue broadly adjusted to an infinite moving world. Their work is accordingly like those cathedrals at which many successive ages have laboured, each in its own style. We may regret, sometimes, that some one design could not have been carried out in its purity, and yet all these secular accretions have a wonderful eloquence; a common piety and love of beauty have inspired them; age has fused them and softened their incongruities; and an inexpressible magic seems to hang about the composite pile, as if God and man breathed deeply within it. It is a harmony woven out of accidents, like every work of time and nature, and all the more profound and fertile because no mind could ever have designed it. Some such natural structure, formed and reformed by circumstances, is the requisite matrix and home for every moral being.

Accordingly there seem to have been sober sense and even severe thought behind the rant of Webster when he cried, "Liberty *and* Union, now and for ever, one and inseparable!" because if for the sake of liberty you abandon union and resist a mutual adaptation of purposes which might cripple each of them, your liberty loses its massiveness, its plasticity, its power to survive change; it ceases to be tentative and human in order to become animal and absolute. Nature must always produce little irresponsible passions that will try to rule her, but she can never crown any one of them with more than a theatrical success; the wrecks of absolute empires, communisms, and religions are there to prove it. But English liberty, because it is co-operative, because it calls only for a partial and shifting unanimity among living men, may last indefinitely, and can enlist every reasonable man and nation in its service. This is the best heritage of America, richer than its virgin continents, which it draws from the temperate and manly spirit of England. Certainly absolute freedom would be more beautiful if we were birds or poets; but co-operation and a loving sacrifice of a part of ourselves—or even of the whole, save the love in us—are beautiful too, if we are men living together. Absolute liberty and English liberty are incompatible, and mankind must make a painful and a brave choice between them. The necessity of rejecting and destroying some things that are beautiful is the deepest curse of existence.

A Letter to Logan Pearsall Smith*

Rome, Dec. 2. 1921

Dear Smith

. . . This taste of mine for living in the midst of a noisy,
vulgar rush of people, most of them ugly, with whom I have
nothing to do, will perhaps hint to you why I am not altogether
in sympathy with your judgement on America. Not that I disagree
with your characterization of it; they say it has changed even in
these last ten years, but not essentially. I could perfectly recognize, though the genteel tradition may then have been stronger,
that America had "no interest for the life of the mind", was "without a head", and "alien". But why do you call this condition "lying fallow" and "deterioration"? Isn't the judgement of the American people rather the opposite, namely that its condition is constantly improving, and its labours splendidly fruitful? Not for the
"mind", which in our lips means, I suppose, the liberal or aristocratic life, the mind turned to pure reflection and pure expression and pure pleasure. But why need all the tribes of men sacrifice at our altar? I agree that it is barbarous and tragic to strain
after merely conventional ends, by attaining which nobody is
the happier, but everyone is sacrificed to some fetish. But isn't
America happy? The old genteel America was not happy; it was
eager to know the truth, and to be "cultured" and to love "art",

* From *The Letters of George Santayana*, ed. Daniel Cory (New York:
Charles Scribner's Sons, 1955).

and to miss nothing that made other nations interesting or distinguished; and it was terribly and constitutionally unhappy, because with its handicap and its meagreness of soul and its thinness of temper and its paucity of talent, it *could* not attain, nor even approach, any of those ideals. But is the new America unhappy? Does it feel that it is living in a desert, and thirsting for the gardens and the treasure-houses of the Arabian Nights? I think not: it wants simply the sort of life it has, only more of it. It wants comfort and speed and good cheer; it wants health and spirits, and a round of weddings, foot-ball games, campaigns, outings, and cheerful funerals; and it is getting them. In the midst of this, as a sort of joke (and you may make a business of joking) there is a patter of sophomoric art and lady-like religion—never mind what, if only it is new and funny. Why not? When I was at Harvard, from my Freshman days on, I "belonged" to the Lampoon: and that seems to me a sort of symbol or oracle: I belonged to the Lampoon just as much in the philosophical faculty, as I did in the Lampoon "sanctum". It was all a pleasant hardworking exuberance *by the way;* there was not, and could not be anything serious or substantial in it. But notice: *all* learning and all "mind" in America is not of this ineffectual sophomoric sort. There is your doctor at Baltimore who is a great expert, and *really knows how to do things:* and you will find that, in the service of material life, all the arts and sciences are prosperous in America. But it must be in the service of material life; because it is material life (of course with the hygiene, morality, and international good order that can minister to material life) that America has and wants to have and may perhaps bring to perfection. Think of that! If material life could be made perfect, as (in a very small way) it was perhaps for a moment among the Greeks, would not that of itself be a most admirable achievement, like the creation of a new and superior mammal, who would instinctively suck only the bottle? Imagine a race perfectly adapted to elevated railroads and aeroplanes and submarines, with a regular percentage of a neutral sex to serve as "school-marms", and not the least dissatisfaction with the extremes of the weather, the pains of childbirth or toothache (all pains being eliminated) or English as she is spoke by three hundred million Americans! I submit that such a race would be as well worth having and as precious in its own eyes (and any other criterion is irrelevant) as ever were the Chinese or the Egyptians or the Jews. And possibly on that basis of perfected material life, a new art and philosophy would grow unawares, not similar to what we call by those names, but having the same relation to the life beneath which art and philosophy amongst us ought to have had, but never have had actually. You see I am content to let the past bury its dead. It does not seem to me that we can impose on America the task of imitating Europe. The more different it can come to be, the better; and we must let it take its own course, going a long way round, perhaps, before it can shake off the last trammels of alien tradition, and learn to express itself simply, not apologetically, after its own heart. Of course, I don't mean that I feel confident that America will ever produce a true civilisation of a new sort; it may all come to nothing, as almost all experiments in nature do; but while the experiment is going on it seems only fair to give it a chance, and to watch it sympathetically . . .

Yours sincerely

❧ America's Young Radicals*

When I was a college professor, I sometimes wondered why there was no socialism among the sophomores. Now that I am not there to welcome it, the thing seems to have come.

I say *to welcome it*, because although I am a high Tory in my sympathies, I recognize that different hearts must be set on different things, and I like young people who have hearts, and who set them on something. It is a great pity if, for lack of self-knowledge or a congenial environment, they set them on the wrong thing, and miss their possible happiness, or miss even the noble martyrdom of knowing why they are unhappy. But they will not have set their hearts on the wrong thing simply because that thing may be indifferent or disagreeable to *me*. My personal feelings have nothing to do with the genuineness of their ideals, or with the worth of their happiness, if they are able to attain it. At most, my experience may make me suspect that these ideals may be unattainable, or that in choosing them these young men, in some cases, may have misunderstood their own nature, and may be pursuing something which, if they got it, would make them very sick. When that is so, a word of warning from an outsider may not be entirely useless.

The reason why it is easy to mistake the demands of one's own nature is that human instincts are very complex and confused, and that they mature at different times, or are suppressed or dis-

* Printed in *The Forum*, LXVII, May, 1922, 371-75.

guised altogether; whereas the fancy is peopled only by the shallow images of such things as we happen to have come upon in our experience. We cannot love, nor warmly imagine, what we have never seen; even when we hate things as we find them (as every fresh soul must in a great measure) our capacity to conceive better things is limited to such hints as actual things have vouchsafed us. We may therefore have no idea at all of what would really satisfy us; even if it were described to us in words, we should not recognize it as our ideal of happiness. It would seem cold, exotic, irrelevant, because nothing of that sort has as yet entered our experience, or lay in the path immediately open before us.

I was accordingly not at all surprised that the life of the ancients, although alone truly human and addressed to a possible happiness, should not appeal to young America. It is too remote, too simple; it presupposes the absence of this vast modern mechanical momentum, this rushing tide of instrumentalities on which young America is borne along so merrily. What surprised me a little was that everybody seemed content to go on swimming and swimming: for even when a man grumbled and worried about his difficulties or mishaps—athletic training, college clubs, family friction, dubious prospects, unrequited love—he yet seemed to be entirely at peace with the general plan of existence as he found it; not at all oppressed by the sense of any surrounding ugliness, vulgarity, vanity, servitude, or emptiness. Was there in these youths, I used to ask myself, so engaging often in their personal ardor, no human soul at all, but rather the soul of some working ant or unquestioning bee, eager to run on its predetermined errands, store its traditional honey, and build its geometrical cell, for the queen of the hive, the future Mrs. Ant or Mrs. Bee, to lay her eggs in? I am far from regarding romantic man as necessarily the best of animals, or a success at all, so far; and I am quite willing he should be superseded, if nature, in America or elsewhere, can evolve a superior species to take his place; but this sudden extinction of human passion seemed a little strange, and I doubted whether perfect happiness in mechanism was as yet possible even for the healthiest, busiest, most athletic, most domestic, and most conventional American. Might not the great American panacea for human wretchedness, Work, be not so much a cure as an anaesthetic?

And now, apparently, the awakening has come, at least to a few, and the sophomores (who are many of them out of college) have discovered the necessity of socialism. I call it socialism for short, although they are not all advocates of socialism in a technical sense, but style themselves liberals, radicals, or (modestly) the *Intelligentsia.* The point is that they all proclaim their disgust at the present state of things in America, they denounce the Constitution of the United States, the churches, the government, the colleges, the press, the theatres, and above all they denounce the spirit that vivifies and unifies all these things, the spirit of Business. Here is disaffection breaking out in what seemed the most unanimous, the most satisfied of nations: here are Americans impatient with America.

Is it simply impatience? Is it the measles, and by the time these sophomores are reverend seniors will it have passed away? Or is it a tragic atavism in individuals, such as must appear sporadically in all ages and nations, an inopportune sport of nature, hatching a bird of paradise in the arctic regions? Even in this case, pathetic as it is, nothing can be done except to wait for the unhappy creatures to come to a fluttering end, for lack of sunshine and appropriate worms. Untoward genius must die in a corner. I am ready to believe that these young radicals are geniuses and birds of paradise, as they evidently feel themselves to be; if so, their plaints ought to make a beautiful elegy; but it would still be a dying song. Or is it possible, on the contrary, that they are prophets of something attainable, boy-scouts with a real army behind them, and a definite future?

I have made a severe effort to discover, as well as I may from a distance, what these rebels want. I see what they are *against*— they are against everything—but what are they *for?* I have not been able to discover it. This may be due to my lack of understanding or to their incapacity to express themselves clearly, for their style is something appalling. But perhaps their scandalous failure in expression, when expression is what they yearn for and demand at all costs, may be a symptom of something deeper: of a radical mistake they have made in the direction of their efforts and aspirations. They think they need more freedom, more room, a chance to be more spontaneous: I suspect that they have had too much freedom, too much empty space, too much practice in being spontaneous when there was nothing in them to bubble out. Their style is a sign of this: it is not merely that they have no mastery of the English language as hitherto spoken, no clear sense of the value of words, and no simplicity; that they are without the vocabulary or the idiom of cultivated people.

That might all be healthy evolution, even if a little disconcerting to us old fogies, who can't keep up with the progress of slang. America has a right to a language of its own, and to the largest share in forming that pigeon-English which is to be the "world-language" of the future. But it is not comparatively only that the style of the young radicals is bad, nor in view of traditional standards: it is bad intrinsically; it is muddy, abstract, cumbrous, contorted, joyless, obscure. If their thoughts were cherished, if their principles and allegiances were firm, we should soon learn to read their language and feel it to be pure and limpid, however novel its forms. Dante wrote in a new dialect, provincial and popular; yet how all his words shine like dew on a sunny morning! But Dante had looked long and intently; he had loved silently; he knew what he felt and what he believed. No: it is not more freedom that young America needs in order to be happy: it needs more discipline.

Marginal Notes on Civilization in the United States*

The American conscience is not insincere; it is only belated, inapplicable. The sanctities are traditional; sentiment preserves and requires the habits and language of an elder age; it has all the sincerity of instinct. But it does not exactly fit the exigences of public life, which has been transformed and accelerated in a way which conscience can't keep up with, yet is dazzled by and has not the heart to condemn; for it has to keep house, as it were, with an obstreperous younger brother, the conscience of emancipated human nature, with its new set of illusions and its pride in its thundering, pushing life. The American intellect is shy and feminine; it paints nature in water-colours; whereas the sharp masculine eye sees the world as a moving-picture—rapid, dramatic, vulgar, to be glanced at and used merely as a sign of what is going to happen next. Mere man in America hardly has an articulate logic in which to express his practical convictions. . . .

M. Doumic, a French observer, has said that, while the English and Germans are races, the United States, like France, is a *milieu* —what American philosophy calls a "situation." Only in France the memory and discipline of past situations survives in the different classes and parties, in the church, army, government, and

* Printed in *The Dial*, LXXII, June, 1922, 553-68.

These marginalia were printed "in place of a formal review" of *Civilization in the United States*, ed. Harold Stearns (New York: Harcourt, Brace & World, 1922). I have selected about half of these "Notes" for inclusion here, and have somewhat altered their original order.—R. C. L.

literature; whereas in America, apart from a rather pale genteel tradition, only the present situation counts. It is the present task, the present state of business, and present fashion in pleasure that create the hearty unity and universal hum of America. . . . A proof that Americanism is the expression of a present material environment, is that the immigrants at once feel themselves and actually become typical Americans, more instinct with an aggressive Americanism than the natives of Cape Cod or the poor whites in the South. Another consequence is that the whole world is being Americanized by the telephone, the trolley car, the department store, and the advertising press. Americanism, apart from the genteel tradition, is simply modernism—purer in America than elsewhere because less impeded and qualified by survivals of the past, but just as pure in Spanish-Italian Buenos Aires as in Irish-Jewish New York. . . . A leading German whom I questioned on this subject (before the war) assured me that in New York he could not prevail on his children to speak German at home, nor to keep up any German traditions. The contagion and rush of the *milieu* are too strong.

The heartiness of American ways, the feminine gush and the masculine go, the girlishness and high jinks and perpetual joking and obligatory jollity may prove fatiguing sometimes; but children often overdo their sports, which does not prove that they are not spontaneous fundamentally. Social intercourse is essentially play, a kind of perpetual amiable comedy; the relish of it comes of liking our part and feeling we are doing it nicely, and that the others are playing up as they should. The atmosphere of sport, fashion, and wealth is agreeable and intoxicating; certainly it is frivolous, unless some passion is at work beneath, and even then it is all vanity; but in that sense, so is life itself, and a philosopher who is really a philosopher will not quarrel with it on that account. What else than vanity could life possibly be in the end? The point is that it should be spontaneous, innocent, and happily worked out, like a piece of music well-played. Isn't American life distinctly successful in expressing its own spirit?

I feel that there is a genuine spirit of humour abroad in America, and that it is one of the best things there. The constant sense

of the incongruous, even if artificially stimulated and found only
in trivial things, is an admission that existence is absurd; it is
therefore a liberation of the spirit over against this absurd world;
it is a laughing liberation, because the spirit is glad to be free;
and yet it is not a scornful nor bitter liberation, because a world
that lets us laugh at it and be free is after all a friendly world.
We have no need to bear that serious grudge against it which we
should be justified in bearing if it fooled us altogether. . . .

My own experience does not suggest that Americans are want-
ing in taste, knowledge, or aesthetic thinking; on the contrary, a
great preoccupation and anxiety about these things, a thirst for
culture and a desire not to miss or misunderstand anything, seem
to be a chief part of their spiritual misery. They are perpetually troubled lest they should not fully enjoy the morning sunshine and their delicious oatmeal and cream and cubist painting
and the poetry of Miss Amy Lowell; while their love for Botticelli
is a tender passion and their preference for Michael Angelo over
Raphael is a philosophic conviction. I hardly think that if the
aesthetics of Hegel and of Croce were taught in the high schools
the facial muscles of the nation would relax and they would burst
into passionate song, like Neapolitan minstrels. What I should
like somebody to explain is the American voice and language
and newspapers; where taste and sensibility are hardened to such
a pervasive ugliness (or else affectation) in these familiar things,
it is needless to look further for the difficulties which beset the
artist, in spite of his high ambitions and enlightenment. The artistic idiom is foreign to him; he cannot be simple, he cannot be
unconscious, he has no native, unquestioned, inevitable masters.
And it is not easy for native masters to spring up, the moral soil
is too thin and shifting, like sand in an hourglass, always on the
move; whatever traditions there are, practical men and reformers
insist on abandoning; every house is always being pulled down
for rebuilding; nothing can take root; nothing can be assumed as
a common affection, a common pleasure; no refinement of sense,
no pause, no passion, no candour, no enchantment. The thirty
authors of this book, for instance, give out that they are the salt
of the nation: "We have a vitality and nervous alertness," they
say, "which . . . might cut through the rocks of stupidity . . .

Our cup of life is full to the brim," and I have no reason to doubt
it. Yet none of them seems ever to have loved anything. . . .

In a thoroughly humanized society everything—clothes,
speech, manners, government—is a work of art, being so done as
to be a pleasure and a stimulus in itself. There seems to be an impression in America that art is fed on the history of art, and is
what is found in museums. But museums are mausoleums, only
dead art is there, and only ghosts of artists flit about them. The
priggish notion that an artist is a person undertaking to produce
immortal works suffices to show that art has become a foreign
thing, an *hors d'œuvre*, and that it is probably doomed to affectation and sterility.

Freedom—and young America furnishes a proof of this—does
not make for enlightenment; it makes for play. A free society
would create sports, feasts, religion, poetry, music; its enlightenment would be confined to a few scattered sages, as in antiquity.
What brings enlightenment is experience, in the sad sense of this
word—the pressure of hard facts and unintelligible troubles,
making a man rub his eyes in his waking dream, and put two and
two together. Enlightenment is cold water. Education is quite
another matter. "The purpose of this college," I heard the Master of Balliol say in 1887, "is to rear servants to the Queen." Education is the transmission of a moral and intellectual tradition,
with its religion, manners, sentiments, and loyalties. It is not the
instruction given in American schools and colleges that matters
much, or that constitutes an American education; what matters
is the tradition of alacrity, inquisitiveness, self-trust, spontaneous co-operation and club-spirit; all of which can ripen, in the
better minds, into openness to light and fidelity to duty. The test
of American education is not whether it produces enlightenment,
but whether it produces competence and public well-being. Mr.
Lovett does not seem to remember that mankind is a tribe of animals, living by habit and thinking in symbols, and that it can
never be anything else. If American education does not transmit
such a perfect human discipline as that of a Greek city or of the
British upper classes, that is not its fault; it works on a vaster
canvas with thinner pigments. But its defect lies in not being

thoroughly and deeply enough the very thing which Mr. Lovett condemns it for being—a transmitted life.

The undergraduate is not devoted to making money; he is not subject to women; he does, except when the pressure or fear of the outer world constrains him, only what he finds worth doing for its own sake. I wish reformers, instead of trying to make the colleges more useful and professional, would try to make the world more like the colleges. The things that the world might find worth doing for their own sake would perhaps be nobler than those that appeal to the undergraduate, though I am far from confident of that; but in any case, means would no longer be pursued as ends. The world would then shine with what is called honour, which is allegiance to what one knows one loves.

The prevalence of insanity, of "breaking down," and of "nervous depression" is one of the most significant things in America. It goes with overwork, with not having a religion or "getting religion" (which is an incident to not having one), with absence of pleasures, forced optimism, routine, essential solitude. An intense family life would prevent all these miseries, but it would take away personal liberty. The modern family is only the eggshell from which you are hatched; there you have your bed, clothes, meals, and relations; your life is what occupies you when you are out. But as you foregather only with chicks of your own age, who are as destitute as yourself, you remain without the moral necessaries. The test of a good school or college is its capacity to supply them. It is the only remaining spiritual home.

"Business is . . . blind . . . with extravagant reflex powers of accommodation and extension and almost no faculty of original imagination . . . It has brought about a marvellous economy of human effort. At the same time . . . it wastes the spirit . . . in the effort to create new and extravagant wants." Admirable summary; inventions and organization which ought to have increased leisure, by producing the necessaries with little labour, have only increased the population, degraded labour, and diffused luxury.

ᙖᕽ Americanism*

"The modern world is founded on two principles contrary to
nature: that money is prolific, and that the useful is the good.
This system multiplies without limit the needs and the servitude
of the people; destroys all leisure for the soul; withdraws from
regulation for human purposes those materials which the arts are
to transform; imposes on man the breathless rhythm of the machine and the acceleration proper to precipitated matter; applies
an inhuman measure to human action, and gives it a truly diabolical direction: because the end of all this delirium is to prevent man from remembering God."

These are the words of Jacques Maritain, a contemporary philosopher who exercises a marked influence in intellectual circles:
yet they must sound strange and archaic to most ears. Can anything existent be contrary to nature? And except perhaps for
some preacher rekindling the embers of emotion, what can be
the use of talking about "remembering God"? Nevertheless, for
the few who can lend to Maritain's words their intended definite
meanings, these words may seem to be full of concentrated wisdom. Modern civilization has an immense momentum, not only
physically irresistible but morally and socially dominant in the
press, politics, and literature of the liberal classes; yet the voice

* From *The Idler and His Works,* ed. Daniel Cory (New York: George
Braziller, Inc., 1957).

of a dispossessed and forlorn orthodoxy, prophesying evil, cannot be silenced, and what renders that voice the more disquieting is that it can no longer be understood. When the prophets or apologists of the modern world attempt to refute those vaticinations, they altogether miss fire, because of their incapacity to conceive what they attack; and even in the exposition of their own case they are terribly confused and divided. It is seldom indeed that their conscience or their thoughts have passed over entirely to the side of their action.

Let me attempt to formulate what our reply to Maritain might be, if we could do justice to his position and understand our own.

The ancients saw and imagined everything on the human scale. For them the terms of thought were obvious and unquestioned: either gross physical objects, with their observable habits, or else the categories and the passions of the human mind, as grammar or poetry might distinguish them. As for the unknown, they conceived it mythologically, by projecting into nature and enlarging to a divine scale these same human terms, and peopling the infinite with optical images, verbal powers, and invisible persons. What wonder if they felt at home, and thought they had discerned the true face of reality, by inspection in the foreground and by divination beyond? A man had but to open his eyes, and whet a little his natural understanding, and when once a few childish cobwebs or tears had been wiped away, the truth of things would luminously appear. If there was ever a conflict of dogmas under such circumstances, it could be only incidentally, when some confusion or diseased doubt had arisen by chance, or at the instigation of some wicked demon. That difficulty once solved, or that temptation vanquished, the philosopher could settle down again contentedly in the conscious possession of the truth.

Not that the classic sage needed to claim omniscience, or more than a relative and human rightness in his pictorial knowledge. But this qualified rightness was sufficient. Let God, he could say humbly, let the angels and demons watch over their several spheres. It is the part of man to cultivate his arts and purify his spirit. The arts proper to man were precisely those which, directly or indirectly, redounded to his spiritual benefit. Being on the human scale, these arts could be mastered and digested humanly, practiced openly, and piously transmitted and learned. Their products could shine with the infused beauty of labor and of love. The same impulses and powers that had given form to the work could afterwards contemplate it with joy and inward understanding. Everything reinforced and clarified humanity in man, and the non-human encircling mystery was masked as decently as possible in archaic symbols, expressing the various attitudes which human prudence must needs assume towards the inevitable or the unknown.

If Adam and Eve could have brought up their progeny in Eden, mankind would have needed no other system of philosophy than that of the ancients. But sorrow knows better; in the wilderness migration was pressing, war imminent, labor exasperated, and henceforth intellectual innocence and clearness were things not only difficult to attain but foolish to preserve. There were hints of horrible mysteries and perversities lurking beneath the surface of nature, in earthquakes, pests, and conflagrations, in deformed births, madness, death, and the mutual hatred and slaughter inseparable from life. Nature herself seemed secretly unnatural: her true order was alien and hidden, and not what the eye and heart of man had first supposed it to be. And to the world's unhomeliness a great division and unrest corresponded in the mind. Had mankind been now invited back to paradise, they would no longer have known what paradise to choose. How find happiness in peace, if we love danger? How be content with intellectual light, if we crave the darkness of power? Thus insoluble puzzles in things, and an infinite dissatisfaction in the soul joined in breaking down the classical harmony of the universe, innocently constructed on the human scale.

The first break, however, was not away from humanism. On the contrary, it led to a penitential contraction and concentration of the natural prospect, on lines more strictly moral and logical than ever. Almost at the same time all over the world, the Hebrew prophets, Socrates and Plato, the Indian and Chinese philosophers, transformed mythology and interpreted it in a new moral or spiritual sense. Its original office of dramatizing the round of nature, or magically assisting it, was suppressed, and the gods, or the forces of nature, were conceived as spiritual powers, guardians of personal or national virtue. What had been a garden became a fortress and a church. There was a desperate retrenchment of the spirit upon its home defenses, all else being declared essentially subordinate or relatively unreal. Another life or other lives for the soul were elaborately prophesied, so as to hearten and direct supernaturally the pilgrim spirit toiling through this world. Religion, as we know religion, became the center and the explanation of everything.

The course of religion, however, has never run smooth. To the innocent superficiality of thinking on the human scale, it adds the artifice of twisting the natural course of things into a moral fable. The wonder is that so many religions have been able to maintain or to recover something of their influence through so many ages. Founders or reformers of religion are necessarily exceptional men, men over whom moral faith and metaphysical imagination hold absolute sway. They very naturally impress and convince a few other exceptional souls; but if their teaching spreads widely over mankind, it must needs be greatly diluted and counteracted by all the instincts and insights of the old Adam. Religion for the majority can never be anything but a somnolent custom or an uncomfortable incubus. Practical disloyalty to it fills all the free moments of life; murmurs and jests against it are pervasive in society, even in the so-called ages of faith; and open rebellion is always smouldering in the sly intellect and the young heart.

An official door actually remained ajar even in human orthodoxy into inhuman regions. Astrology, alchemy, and magic might be questionable pursuits morally, but nobody questioned that physically a field existed which these arts might explore darkly. From the beginning mythology had scarcely disguised the monstrous or grotesque secrets of nature under dramatic masks; and the earliest philosophers had sketched naturalistic (and therefore inhuman) systems of the universe, still pictorial in their terms, but already infinite, impersonal, and aimless in their movement. Even Platonism and Christianity, in their demonology, recognized that under-working spirits might fill the air, and might be enticed or exorcised by appropriate rites.

Through this trap-door our modern experimental sciences have entered the stage; and it is important to notice their initial relation to the pictorial cosmology, naturalistic or religious, which previously filled the scene. It was never the possibility of magic sciences, or the truth of a kind attainable in them, that orthodoxy denied; but the pursuit of such knowledge was deprecated as morally dangerous, because such knowledge was tricky and insecure in itself, fed evil passions, and alienated the soul from her proper virtues, from her domestic affections, her eloquence, her religion. But the age in which the modern arts were launched upon their surprising career was not interested in those sanctified things; on the contrary, it had grown heartily sick of them, and hankered instead after strange knowledge, cheap riches, and troubled pleasures: it ached to pillage and to explore. It was the age of Doctor Faustus. Doctor Faustus was a learned man, but impatient, embittered, and lustful; full of contempt for that silly orthodox intellect, always thinking on the human scale. How much grander, if less edifying, were the real secrets of nature! He was not afraid of burning his fingers, nor of the devil; he was an intellectual busybody, mousing about among incipient impossible insights. He felt that there are profound unimaginable depths in nature, from which indefinite stores of energy might be drawn, if we could only hit on the right formulas and ceremonies. He did not hope for light: he was willing to potter about for ever, floundering among absurdities; but he hoped for power. He was the forerunner of Bacon and of the pragmatists.

The event has proved that Doctor Faustus, like Columbus, was not misled by his instinct for discovery. Nature truly has hidden depths, and if these depths are skilfully tapped, or if they shift of their own accord, all the surface may be transformed. Those grubbing alchemists and declaiming magicians were true prophets in principle: it was hardly their fault if they were still humanists and conceived the future triumphs of the arts in terms of a gorgeous and sensual omnipotence. They could not foresee that nature was pregnant with a metallic birth: had they foreseen it, we need not doubt that, after a moment of pained surprise, they would have heartily acquiesced. Romantic aspiration and impatience would be false to themselves if they did not readily accept the result of their own revolts. The fundamental motive is the thirst for change, and a belief that a happy change is possible. Experience must be transformed, enriched, freed from its present predicaments. If the next phase in the world's history turns out to be metallic, what of that? We have only to become a little more metallic ourselves, and indeed we are bound to do so. An age of mechanism will tend to alter the rate and quality of the passions in us, if not of the senses; ambition will turn in the direction in which it finds satisfaction possible, and the mechanic and the air-man will feel a happy thrill in living in a world made of taut wire. Even in the old days, most people were perfectly content not to be poets or saints, and to live by a current code of morals some-what different from the one preached to them in church. The mechanized democrat has merely learned to have the courage of his real convictions, and to laugh at all that retrospective snob-bery about being cultured and refined, a scholar and a gentleman. He is amply sustained by social contagion and approval, by ri-valry, by keenness to perform any chosen task, and if possible to break some record; also by a sense of technical mastery in con-trolling the unimaginable souls of his machines, even if it be in sport only and for no further purpose. Moreover, he escapes many of the old torments and vices of mankind: his animal pas-sions are muted by publicity and business, no less than his liberal thoughts. He cannot be cruel to his motors, as he might have been to his beasts of burden; and the instinct for success and co-operation renders him a friend to his associates, where personal pride, or even ideal enthusiasms, would have made him a mortal enemy in his heart to almost everybody. He claims, or ought to claim if he was consistent, no proprietary rights over his female companions, as if he were an old-fashioned husband or lover. He feels a certain comfort and dignity in his private self, isolated and undistinguished as he is in the million. If ever a sudden in-stinctive sympathy breaks through this isolation, he may even know a frank and complete friendship, natural to detached equals; a free bond which had been rendered impossible by the feudal entanglements of Christian society and religion. His romantic im-pulse is therefore not likely to die out, as if a mechanized exist-ence could have no zest. On the contrary, as the ethos of Chris-tendom fades more and more completely from the world, we may expect invention, competition, and organization, in labor and in sport, to grow always more keen, and to become more and more frankly their own excuse for being.

A special circumstance has made it easier for these principles to be accepted theoretically, at least in America, and to be turned into a national philosophy. Americans as a rule are tough in action, but tender in mind; their own secret philosophy might not have been popular among them, if it had been expressed in brutal materialistic terms. Even in Nietzsche, romantic materialism needed to be disguised by an idealistic vocabulary and a prophetic afflatus: you felt "uplift" as you were let down. This could happen, because the ambition of Doctor Faustus or of Francis Bacon, to transform human life by dominating matter, had never monopolized the public mind. A religious tradition and a metaphysical passion existed also. The worldliness of the Renaissance had been crossed by a wave of Puritan severity and mystical piety. Protestantism, by making private experience and private judgment the supreme court of appeal, had embarked upon a second reassertion of humanism: the newly discovered mechanical world might be as inhuman as it chose; it could never forfeit its moral function of being a trial and provocation for the human conscience; and the Stoic hygiene of the mind would suffice to disinfect that alien world, or to render its very horror inspiriting. Moreover, philosophical criticism of knowledge was ready to vindicate human ascendancy over the universe in a new and marvelous way, by reducing the universe not, indeed, to a human scale, but to a human locus. For according to idealistic or strictly empirical principles nothing open to a mind can possibly exist except within that mind, and by its consent or contrivance. Thus a second and truly invincible concentration and retrenchment of man's moral being reduced the spirit to a point, to the invisible ego or consciousness to which any world claiming recognition must appear. The ground was thereby admirably prepared for any philosopher trained in the Protestant tradition to become, if he liked, a worshipper of pure process. The old ark of salvation might be broken up without fear of the deluge, and the whole menagerie of more or less tamed human passions and the keeper, human reason, might be cheerfully committed to the waves; for you were assured that the flood itself was simply your spirit thinking, and unraveling its destiny according to your own secretly omnipotent will. Materialism in life or in science and a complete absorption in mechanical arts could thus prove per-

fectly congenial to the idealist: they were merely one phase in
the development of freedom. He finds these tasks before him because in the unconscious he has secretly chosen and loved them.
How simple and exhilarating the prospect before us, if there were
really no universe except this rambling experience itself, unfolding
its coils according to some free principle of absolute spontaneity,
and turning, as it goes, in whatever direction it chooses; never
condemned to remember the past, except as a point of departure,
nor to foresee the future, beyond the work in hand!

II

Such seems to be, when viewed from the inside, that amiable
philosophy of invention which Maritain finds diabolical. As proclaimed in America, where it is naturally most at home, it may be
said to rest on two principles: first, a romantic transcendentalism,
which views existence as a spontaneous moral adventure; and second, a pragmatic or instrumental conception of knowledge,
which declares that the conditions of success in this adventure can
be determined only by the very experiment which has transformed them. "There is a moving whole of interacting parts; a
center emerges wherever there is an effort to change them in a
particular direction." * Spontaneous impulses, blowing as they
list through a social world, thus provide at each moment the purposes and the standards requisite for progress. "Desires, affections, preferences, needs, and interests at least exist in human experiences; they are characteristic of it." We find ourselves inevitably, by virtue of that transcendental romanticism which is
our first principle, in an essentially moral, though perhaps unconscious, world: the enterprise of life, with all its cares, is the
substance of the universe. But in the exercise of our spontaneity
we have now discovered our other first principle, namely, that the
pictorial world of the ancients, drawn on the human scale, was all
moonshine; that knowledge is *knowledge* only in so far as it enables us to change things according to our desires; and that such
knowledge exists only in the mechanical arts. Without experimental verification or fitness ideas are not knowledge, but simply
ideas. They may arise, as dreams arise, out of the decoction of

* This quotation and the one which follows are from John Dewey's *The
Quest for Certainty* (New York: Minton, Balch and Co., 1929).—R.C.L.

past experiences; but they have no other than this vegetative quality and visionary status; they remain (in both senses of the word) immaterial. They are the dead leaves, not the tentacles of life. Even the tentacles (I mean the mechanical arts) are not similar to the controlling forces which they engage or appropriate: and the accompanying true knowledge is but a twist given to the original sensibility of the organism, when those forces are drawn into the vortex of human action and bent to the services of human interests. Such knowledge grafts the mind, through the applied sciences, upon the world of action; and at the same time it humanizes that world by filling it with artificial objects and improvements.

This philosophy combines idealism with practicality in a way obviously congenial to the American temper. Technically, however, the combination might seem to be effected paradoxically, in that the idealism or moralism concerns the *substance* or *ground* of events, according to the Faustian maxim that in the beginning was the Deed: while on the other hand the tests of rightness in thought and in action are thoroughly materialistic. Wouldn't it be more natural to put the material element at the bottom and at the origin of things, as in the systems of the early Greeks, and to leave the idealism for the ultimate harmonies, and the moral perspectives, which the mind might eventually find in that cosmos, or introduce into it? But no: spirit, and the whole moral life, would then be essentially idle, aristocratic, and contemplative—in a word, utterly un-American: and it is too late in the day for the spirit to be that. In the modern world spirit must work for its living or else, on Darwinian principles, it will be quietly eliminated. And what other position, save that of a primary energy, should a working spirit occupy, whose goal must be to master, transform, and enjoy a material world? And what shall the material world, in its turn, claim to be, except the chosen theme of the spirit that creates and transforms it? Even before the days of industrialism, wasn't this the burden of German idealism? We are still in the laboratory of Doctor Faustus. Cosmic brainstorms have settled down to the analysis of matter, and the manufacture of Homunculus, or the mechanical man.

Nevertheless, indications are not lacking that this superposition of material labors on spiritual freedom might be reversed, simply by tracing the implications of this very philosophy of enterprise; and we might be brought back to the classic conception of spiritual freedom superposed upon material labors. Experimental science and the arts which enshrine it, being instrumental, admittedly debouch on something else, which is ultimate; let us call it immediate experience. In this immediate experience the elements must be found that are to have a positive worth in themselves. Some satisfaction, confidence, and clearness will saturate daily life, and will constitute what (if carpers would allow) we might call a modicum of happiness. Happiness is not final in the temporal sense of having no sequel. On the contrary, the happy man is probably more energetic and better fitted to make his further action felt than is the invalid or the wretch. Yet happiness is ultimate *morally;* a sequence of efforts and achievements would evidently have no intrinsic value, and at best be only useful, unless it were pervaded in some measure by incidental pleasures and by a general reflective satisfaction in the life one is leading. It seems, therefore, to be simply a historical accident if at present the American philosopher finds his rewarding work chiefly or exclusively in experimental sciences and mechanical arts. These pursuits involve intrinsic values, in that he probably carries them on joyously and enthusiastically, unless he is too tired; and an eventual change in his interests might any day cause him to subordinate these particular activities to others, perhaps of a religious, political, or poetic sort. The transcendental spirit is nothing if not free: it may easily cease to be addressed exclusively to operations on matter, or to the abstract sciences that define the method of inventive arts.

If we renounced transcendental idealism and acknowledged the natural superposition of experience on nature, we should be merely awakening from the Satanic dream that we were creators and not creatures. Nature is the moving ground of experience and experience a play of moral counterpoint or conscious cross-lights upon the surface of nature. That we are creatures and not creators follows from the fact that we are born to die, are dependent on matter for our very existence, and are addressed in all our passions to our transitory fortunes in the material world. Such recognition of our animal status—no less obvious in our moral than in our physical being—would not compel us to abandon the transcendental point of view where this is in place, namely, in the survey of the world by any particular mind, with its special organs, from its special station, and in its special interests. We might still carry with us a relative, incidental, portable transcendentalism, like a field-glass slung on our backs, to focus our observations and guide our wanderings. But the region swept, no less than the interests subserved, would be frankly natural and variable; there would be no insolent claim to monopoly in giving direction to progress, no cheap—and how groundless!—airs of superiority to the past, no ignorant assumption that the tendency which we happen to obey at home, and for the moment, must be the central and victorious tendency in all mankind everywhere. Some respect might be shown for the living soul: each temperament and each philosophy might be suffered to speak for itself. For instance, the possibility of abolishing all this modern business of industrialism, mechanical arts, and experimental science would not be excluded. Some day, no doubt, these things will be abandoned, since they are luxuries, and require a compulsory devotion in mankind at large to rather inhuman pursuits. Yet if, for instance, India should now attempt to restore human life to its ancient simplicity, and to renounce industrialism, it might easily be overrun and subjugated by the iron hand of some neighbor less devoted to spiritual goods: or if they were left alone materially, they might subsist unregarded, as ancient life actually subsists today in the West in a few monasteries and sacred preserves surviving by insulation. We may safely assume, I think, that for the present civilization must continue to become increasingly mechanical.

III

Does this mean that Americanism must spread throughout the world? Yes and no: the equipment, the machinery, something of the manners developed in America will have to be adopted wherever a lively participation in the movement of affairs is desired. But this external participation in methods may only be accepted in self-defense, as they say the Japanese have accepted the Western arts. Something no doubt will be changed in the ancient soul by her new armor; but the explicit aim is to turn the modern arts into a defense for the ancient spirit. Quite in the same way, has not the City of the Vatican installed and set up two conspicuous poles for radio-telegraphy, almost as high as the cross of Saint Peter's?

Here I come at last to what seems to be the distinctive quality, the unshared essence, of Americanism as America breeds it. It consists in combining unity in work with liberty of spirit. There are plenty of sectarians in the United States, plenty of fanatics, propagandists, and dogmatists; but the American absorption in work—a work controlled and directed by the momentum and equilibrium of its total movement—causes all these theoretical passions to remain sporadic, private, harmless, and impotent. Their social effects cancel and disinfect one another; they count and modify the balance of action in so far as they are forms of business; in so far as they are definite ideas they evaporate in loud steam. If the Pope speaks through the radio, everybody listens and thinks that, after all, the old gentleman must be a good fellow; but nobody notices what he says. All that is not business is left free, because it is profoundly indifferent—a safety-valve and holiday folly for those who like it. In America, where all else is precision and hurry, the very speech of the people, when it is more than a business code for co-ordinating action, becomes languid and vacuous; it drawls, it becomes indirect, humorous, and playful, it renounces all responsibility, like whistling, and is not particularly interested in anything or even in itself. Why should this happen in a nation otherwise so lively, and so shrewd in practical perception? Because speech and thought, for the man of action, lag behind the automatic decision by which his action is determined; he sees, he aims, and he hits the mark. Why should he trouble, after that, to express the fact simply in words, to focus description on the truth, or to trouble about what anything is exactly? For him speech and thought are essentially superfluous, belated, pathetic: if he must talk or think, he will take to amiable banter, as if he were fooling with a child: and his work over, the wake of his thoughts will be like those soapy patterns left wavering in the sea-water by the impetuous churning of the screws.

Isn't this looseness in everything in so far as it may not be useful, this blankness of will in respect to ultimates, an evident application of the principles of liberalism dominant in the nineteenth century? No doubt this liberalism retained some part of the enthusiasm for liberty, for breaking chains, which had inspired Rousseau and Fichte; but these philosophers were no prophets of machinery, nor of any sort of material progress. They looked rather to a return to nature, or to patriarchal austerity; they expected mankind, once freed, to become ecstatic and heroic. In the liberalism of the industrial era this sense of being stifled under an alien incubus had largely disappeared. The object was less to snatch liberty by revolution than to profit by it in commerce and to concede it by legislation in all indifferent matters, so as to secure the largest possible co-operation of the public in the work of material progress. Religion in particular was to be made private and optional: so too, if liberalism had been consistent, would have been nationality, marriage, family life, higher education, and all other moral traditions. Property, on the contrary, was sacred, being a requisite stimulus and test for industrial proficiency. A common-school education, too, might need to be compulsory, in order to instil into the entire community capacity for initiative, love of work, optimism, and respect for success. Thus liberalism was tolerant of everything except indifference to material well-being, either in oneself or in others. It favored the accumulation of wealth; Big Business must be highly organized, and requires Big Brains at the top. On the other hand, wealth must not stagnate in a few hands, as if there were any public advantage in princely fortunes or princely ways. The millionaire must remain a man of business, an object of emulation, and an example of success in work. If nepotism or routine crept into the management of affairs, ruin would not be far off. The state must be addressed to Business, and Business must be managed by Brains. Wealth must circulate and be widely diffused; and if once the standard of material well-being is high enough, all else will be spontaneously added by the goddess of liberty.

What would be the state of morals and culture if these principles had been thoroughly applied? The question is speculative, because the revolution in England and America, and even the French one, only scotched the snake: powerful ecclesiastical, aristocratic, financial, and academic traditions survived, to indoctrinate the public mind, and keep up the standards of humanism. In America especially the English common law, English literature, and British philosophy remained an active ferment; yet in many ways these pervasive influences, while alien to industrialism and to experimental science, were not unsympathetic to Americanism. They, too, combined confidence in practice with anarchy in theory; they tended to foster co-operation in work with independence of spirit. Moral and intellectual anarchy did not, however, become at all alarming. There was not life or energy enough in radical minds to destroy the ruling conventions, maintained by inertia, by custom, and by that respectability without which no Business would be firmly established. And such heresy as there was, lest a killing vacuum should form around it, soon became a nucleus of orthodoxy in its own corner, warmed by the hot eloquence of a few enthusiasts.

Americanism allows that laissez-faire in moral life which it denies in commerce and industry. Not, of course, that it officially tolerates burglars, murderers, forgers, or adulterers. Legal morality still adheres to the general code of Christendom: but all religions, and therefore all theoretical codes of morals, were to be equally tolerated. The question at once arises, how long, if all moral codes are tolerated, those who hold those views can be restrained from putting them in practice. And what authority can the dominant morality retain? Evidently none: yet it is wonderful how long it has taken the liberal world to discover that it has deliberately abandoned mankind to moral anarchy. It has been only in recent years that the Russian revolution, Madame Caillaux, D. H. Lawrence, and André Gide have openly and conscientiously written down robbery, murder, adultery, and sodomy among the inalienable rights of man.

We are still in the liberal world, not at all alarmed by a moral chaos, if only a mechanical industrial order, firmly advancing beneath, renders that moral chaos harmless and entertaining. Or rather—since this vanity of the moral order renders it, for a puritan utilitarian mind, essentially immoral—no moral life is countenanced at all save the moral life involved in the very discipline and service of mechanism. Americanism might become a more definite and unified regimen than that which I have defined: the freedom of spirit in it might be surrendered to unity in work. Freedom would then subsist, or be recoverable, only in the orthodox manner, by a voluntary conformity with fate. Every impulse not involved in the common task would have to be killed off; and the so-called freedom that survived would be only that of whole-hearted service. The romantic indetermination of the course to be taken by events would allow us to imagine, somewhat ambiguously, that we personally initiated a part of that mighty movement by which we were irresistibly borne along. Americanism in this case would drop the ingredient, still discernible there, of somewhat lax English liberty, and would conform instead to the German ideal of always living in a thorough unison with the Zeitgeist. This ideal unites thorough social discipline with complete moral anarchy. Everyone is expected to obey, at each moment, the passing inspiration of the national Will: but since that Will has no natural ground and is itself the ground of everything else, its successive phases come as they happen to come. No revulsion of feeling can be perverse, no ambition illegitimate. Indeed, as Hegel says, all the phases of existence will be mad, reason being manifested meantime in the necessary instability of everything.

As yet, however, America is full of mitigations of Americanism. There are survivals; there are revolts; there is a certain hesitation in the main current itself, carrying the nation towards actions and sentiments not altogether congruous with experimental progress. For instance, intervention in the last war can only be very partially interpreted as an expression of Americanism. If freedom of spirit was more characteristic of the British and French than of the Germans, unity in work was more characteristic of the Germans than of the British or French. If we translate the Eternal Feminine of Goethe into experimental physical terms, and call it a tempting passivity in matter, obedient in all directions to an infinitely plastic will, we may actually identify the American trust in work and experiment with German romanticism. Both are equally hostile to any fixity in human morals, in institutions, or in ideas. The punctilio that would stick at violating an old treaty or at practicing on occasion a little surgical ruthlessness, seems from a cosmic point of view a ridiculous weakness. Yet it was precisely this weakness, this punctilio, together with a distaste for the Juggernaut car of coarse idealism, that was finally able to turn the American mechanism against the German, to the serious derangement of the latter. What remains doubtful is whether the two mechanisms, somewhat re-adjusted, will not survive and perhaps merge, while the weakness, the punctilio, and the distaste disappear. Will man throw the reins on the neck of his iron horse, or will he lead it by the halter to the domestic stable, there to be fed on judicious rations, and brought out for labor or sport only when natural human virtues, rooted independently in the soul, require such an instrument?

It is all a question of recognizing, obeying, and saving the human soul. Whenever the flux of matter is organized into an animal life, a relatively permanent and self-preserving soul comes into existence. This animal soul or psyche is a center of organization and moral direction for the body of that creature and for all his arts. Did he cease for a moment, under the contagion of ambient influences or of his own vicious habits, to defend his peculiar life, and to subjugate the surrounding world as far as possible to his own native rhythms and moral uses, he would be committing suicide— a sort of slow suicide by radiation, by the dissolution of his living unity and inner life. The test of rationality in his actions is that they should tend to liberate the native potentialities of *that* soul, and render *that* life more perfect after its own kind. Such perfection is compatible with growth, being the measure and the standard of it: and it is compatible with variety and true freedom in the realm of spirit. As human perfection is not identical physically in the two sexes, or at all ages, or in all races, so it will not be identical morally under all circumstances. The point is that in each of its forms life should remain vital, perfect, and appropriate. It should be *vital*, that is, fed by sap rising from its hereditary root, spontaneously, gladly, freely. A life should also be *perfect*, that is, harmonious with itself, and culminating in a distinct form or order in which all the parts are included without being distorted. Finally, life should be *appropriate;* that is, capable of maintaining itself and feeding on its surroundings, by adopting for its vitality a type of perfection which circumstances render possible at that particular time and place. If vitality were lacking, the soul would dissolve in its parts, perhaps with little souls of their own, and would miss that spiritual actuality which comes of synthesis. There would be intellectual and moral nullity, as in inorganic matter. If harmony were not attained, any synthesis attempted would remain painful and strained: there would be distraction and torment, and a worse fate than unconsciousness. And the same would happen, if, in spite of some inner unity, the soul found all her needs unprovided for and all her hopes vain, on account of the maladaptation of her structure to her circumstances. Yet this need of communion and adjustment outwards goes no farther than is requisite to preserve the two internal conditions of a good life, namely, harmony and vitality. The soul therefore always remains master in the moral sphere: obliged perhaps to bide her time and to lie low during some horrible deluge, but never receiving direction save from her own nature.

The relation of a soul to bodily life and to action in the world may be expressed in two ways: first, critically and materialistically, by saying that when an organism arises and exercises self-preserving functions a sensitive and perhaps intelligent soul is found to animate it; and second, dramatically or mythologically, by saying that when a soul of some specific sort descends into matter she organizes that portion of matter in a way consonant with her native powers. The two ways, for a moralist, terminate in the same fact: that for the human soul there is a spiritual life possible, but conditioned by the sort of commerce which the soul carries on with the body and with the world. That this spiritual life—meaning the entire conscious fruition of existence in perception, feeling, and thought—is the seat and judge of all values I take to be an axiom: every maxim, every institution, and the whole universe itself, must be tested morally by its effect on the spirit. The merits of Americanism, and the direction in which we should wish it to develop, therefore hang exclusively on the sort of spiritual life which it may foster. How does unity in work affect the spirit? And how does freedom of spirit affect it?

IV

American unity in work has a peculiar and perhaps temporary character, due to the great opportunities and rewards which work of the experimental industrial sort has found in the new world. The moral value of this kind of work is one question: the moral value of unity in work of any kind is another question, and more speculative. As to the first, what could appeal more to the virgin mind, or be more exciting, than to explore and pillage a virgin universe? And what could be more artful and slyly victorious than to enlist that universe, like a domesticated animal, in the service of human comfort? And what could be more stimulating to intelligence than this successful labor? But here a glance at the actual state of modern society (of which America exhibits the unalloyed essence) may well check the flow of our reasoning. Enterprising, busy, competent, certainly; happy in work, perhaps; enlightened intellectually by that competence and that science? Hardly. Fed and liberated in mind so that the other half of Americanism, freedom of spirit, may be nobly enjoyed? Certainly not.

I know that the distinctively American philosophy, pragmatism or instrumentalism, warms to the praise of experimental science, and even asserts that there is no other sort of valid knowledge. This opinion is itself symptomatic. The word "knowledge" (like the word "truth," sometimes used by pragmatists as if synonymous with "knowledge") is commonly a eulogistic word; and if all other intellectual possessions save strictly experimental science are denied the title of knowledge, we may suspect that, even if admitted as forms of feeling or of poetry, they will be rather despised. Yet before experimental science had made much progress, perception, familiarity, and insight, on the human scale and in pictorial and dramatic terms, had richly furnished the mind, and sufficed to guide it pertinently in all indispensable matters. All the mechanical arts which experiment has created are luxuries, luxuries in which the poor are now compelled to indulge, instead of in their ancient luxuries, such as religion, story-telling, piping, ribaldry, dancing, and fine holiday clothes. Doubtless those legends and sports kept them scientifically ignorant and unprogressive. Yet considered intellectually, or as furniture for the mind, the artificial abstractions which modern science substitutes for the natural symbols of the senses and fancy have no greater value. They are not truth substituted for illusion, but one language substituted for another. And what a language! Essentially vacant, thin, dark, and unintelligible, it has only one merit: it is a vehicle of power—of power, I mean, over matter. For the purposes of dealing with the flux of matter, far removed in its dynamic texture from the human scale, this experimental and mathematical science is alone relevant: the old arts were only customs, and treated natural things almost as if they were persons, and the sailor steered his ship as if he were driving a horse. When that rude acquaintance gave out, the prayers, oracles, and incantations of the classic mind were nothing to the purpose. The essential darkness of modern science goes naturally with its utility: how should matter not be dark to spirit? A pragmatic knowledge of it is knowledge enough. Such knowledge contains the most expeditious methods of doing business, with the greatest safety and the least possible expense of thought. After business is dispatched (or while it is carried on, if such doubleness does not involve too much distraction) the mind is free to enjoy the sensations, the vistas, the hopes which its contacts with nature are capable of arousing. If geography, history, letters, and worldly wisdom are no longer called "knowledge," they are not absolutely forbidden to survive: they remain a part of experience, idle in so far as not useful in material work, but admissible, perhaps, as by-play and recreation.

Here we may observe that unity in work, in the American as in all other systems, tends to impose unity of spirit. There is a lot of spirit in Americanism, so much that it threatens to overwhelm that liberty and looseness of mind which have hitherto been conjoined with it. If the simple and fearless American admires and trusts the vast momentum of modern business, he does so because his soul shares that momentum. The mechanized democrat is full of hope and assurance, and as far as his imagination can go, he is full of kindness: it is always in physical action that comradeship is most hearty: as you rise from action to thought—especially to original and emotional thought—sympathy becomes more nebulous: it requires the material force of eloquence or ritual words to rekindle it to flame. The whole strength of modern enthusiasm comes from its open or secret sympathy with matter. It cries against material poverty or suffering; it relies on the force of numbers; it foretells irresistible material revolutions: and it dreams of the euphoria of a universal material health. This matter is undoubtedly alive, and if the soul which animates this body prospers within, nothing could be more satisfactory. Nature would have realized here one form of perfection. Yet the human purpose and spiritual sanction must be kept paramount throughout and the question may be raised at any moment whether this mechanical adventure has not unhinged the human mind from its vital animal frame, and imposed on it a mad impersonal ambition. The greatest external success may easily involve an essential failure. The success, being physical, might go on indefinitely; but what if the moral failure should pervade the experiment?

The ancient association of man with nature was on the human

scale as in agriculture, architecture, ship-building, and sea-faring; it was filial, brotherly, poetic, even perhaps religious. The disasters involved might occasionally be terrible, but they were incidental. Peace could return; the young will could spontaneously begin its labors anew, as it would its wooing; and the domination of reason might soon be partially reasserted in the arts. But when the miner began to dig deep into the bowels of the earth, in order to feed some smoking furnace with fuel; or when the alchemist began really to transform matter, and the chemist to analyze it down to almost vanishing elements, then something unholy mingled with their zeal. They no longer followed the rhythm of the seasons in their labor, or even that of day and night. Avidity drove them on unrelentingly, until perhaps they dropped exhausted, their natural passions faded away, religion became unnecessary and foreign, speech telegraphic, humor trivial and thin, and the whole mind quick and dry, like a ticking clock. They acquired a kind of expert knowledge; but the effect of habitually thinking only in imageless technical terms was to reduce the mind to a set of signals: and perhaps he who increases knowledge of this sort only increases sorrow, by increasing the material commitments and burdens of life, without increasing its spiritual fruits. And this is not the worst. Mechanical art and abstract science avowedly terminate in objects and transformations on the human scale, open to direct experience. But these terminal objects and transformations, the actual experience which the thoroughly mechanized mind enjoys and morally possesses, become themselves poor and childish in the extreme. A man may be tired of being an instrument, but he is not trained to be anything else. In his leisure, any sort of sensual or emotional pabulum will do for him; he wants simply to relax into whatever pleasure is cheapest, silliest, and most good-natured. He reads the modern newspaper and goes to the cinema. It seems as if science which is merely useful and work which is thoroughly economic were bound to end in an experience which is wholly mean.

Union in work has been imposed before in hunting and fighting communities, at least in the intermittent phases of their more intense activities; but this was under the pressure of circumstances, making such union imperative; and a vague and despised freedom to muse as one liked might be allowed to fill up the idle intervals. Many of the notes of romantic poetry and philosophy seem echoes of that barbarous age. Union in work has also existed in more special circles, religious or military, as almost down to our own day in the English aristocracy. Union in such cases was expected to flow naturally from an underlying identity of taste, breeding and capacity. It was essentially an army of sporting leaders, winning its battles on the playing fields of Eton. Something of this kind, *mutatis mutandis*, might be found in the older genteel America, with its honorable hereditary merchants and capitalists, whose achievements culminated in public-spirited foundations and after-dinner speeches. But this society had no liberty of spirit at the top, among the efficient. Spiritual liberty—how incomplete and halting!—was relegated to the second-rate men who served the storm-troops of progress in the mild capacity of clergymen or teachers: their office was to study and to praise the spirit of their betters, and to transmit it to the next generation. Independence of mind, or moral initiative, appeared, if at all, only ineffectually, in the third-rate quasi-foreign ragtag of Bohemian poets and artists and stray intellectuals, whom the law tolerated but whom society surrounded by a freezing vacuum. In a word, where there is union in work, unless this union express a native identity of temper in everybody, liberty —meaning endless diversity—of spirit is dead or dying. At best there can be only that inner liberty which even a Jesuit may enjoy, if his heart can expand to the utmost limit under the accepted discipline. Unless an identical moral nature and set of possibilities are common to all the individuals concerned, unity in work can be nothing but slavery.

V

There is a sense in which man, in so far as he is not adapted to the matter which affects his well-being, must always be the slave of that matter. Indeed, if we defined matter functionally and morally, and called it *the butt of action*, or *the sum of all dynamic and possibly conflicting agencies in the world*, it would follow that union in work was always desirable on the plane of matter. This, I think, is the secret of American strength and American competence. But the plane of matter, while it is that on which survival must be determined, is not that on which the value of what survives can be judged. Moreover, any material equilibrium is always imperfect and precarious because, as Spinoza says, the force of the universe infinitely exceeds the force of any one part of it, such as man or a human society. Integrity can seldom be established in a single man, much less in a community; and the rebellious elements, each with a will of its own, never cease to sulk, to shift their ground, or to break away altogether and set up a rival order on their own account. Criminal these treasons and heresies will be called by the conscience of the dominant organism, as long as that conscience survives; and any lover of form, however impartial he may be, must regret that anarchy which allows incompatible movements to collide inopportunely, and to defeat every possible harmony. Yet inwardly considered, and in their vital origin, the marplots are innocent enough; they are perhaps wonderfully brave; a formative impulse of a new sort is active within them, and causes them to detest and seek to destroy the overruling force, physical or moral, which hopes to suppress them. The tears of the historian should never turn to wrath.

Americanism at first was itself revolutionary, and it still strives to throw off, as useless parasites and impediments, all the older traditions of mankind. But it has become itself a tradition: it has developed a soul that would impose itself on human nature, and remake all human souls in its own image. It is the function of any soul to gather up matter into a living body, with all the radiating arts, and all the spiritual lights which such arts and such a life may kindle. It would be a perfect abdication and idolatry for any soul to forget her own function and to yield instead to the deadly fascination which the general mechanism of the universe may sometimes exercise on the senses and on the automatic habits of the body. The general cataract of nature or of history is, for any soul, only a monstrous and all-devouring chaos. What irony there would be in having learned to control matter, if we thereby forgot the purposes of the soul in controlling it, and disowned the natural furniture of the mind, our senses, fancy, and pictorial knowledge! The greater part of human life, by a biological necessity, must always be carried on in terms of sense, passion, and language. The contribution of experimental science and industrial invention would be useful if it were incorporated in a life of reason adequate to the whole powers of the soul: it would be fatal if it succeeded in monopolizing reason, and substituted blind work for free imagination. We know the impulses that come to the surface in such a mechanized mind, and make up human experience. They are boyish impulses, a series of wagers, and acrobatic marvels, and playful whims. Nothing ulterior of any consequence results from the performance; when a trick in the game is won or lost, you are simply made ready for the next trick. Your soul is vulgarized; you become a clown when you are not a dullard; and the unofficial holiday sides of your nature, when they break through, break through without dignity, order, or formed habits of expression. It is from such a condition that mankind emerged when, in remote antiquity, it began to be civilized. The change came not by studying matter, but by so acting towards it that one no longer needed to study it. The arts had been established in such a way that the practice of them was intelligent and the fruits agreeable. Mankind has now acquired, as it were, new senses, or a new telescopic and microscopic range of attack upon matter: this is a new and better instrument with which to operate. But the purpose must remain the same. If Doctor Faustus, in view of the wonders of nature open to experiment, sold his soul to the devil, he is not forbidden, when the secret is out, to cheat the devil who had morally cheated him, and to repent. Perhaps America, more innocently misled than that old reprobate, may more quickly turn to repentance.

ಌ *From* Dominations and Powers*

Restricted Democracy

A thorough scientific psychology of the workings of universal suffrage in populous nations would be instructive. It is being attempted in the United States, not so much, apparently, for the sake of science as in the service of business organisation and of democracy itself, assumed to be a sacred principle. But between the lines of these statistical investigations, there looms the spectre of universal hygienic hypnotisation; for when the statistical psychologists find out what strings and wires move the human psyche, they will have all those strings and wires in their hands and, being legally commissioned to pull them, will have to do so. And then the truly political question will arise for them: *To what end* should the race be scientifically caused to act, to think, and to vote? Have they all a similar primal Will? Are they all capable of the same ultimate virtues?

The white population of the United States is composed entirely of races that in the Old World had possessed distinct and sometimes, as in the case of the Jews, very ancient, exclusive, and tenacious traditions. Had these races arrived in America simultaneously, in the proportions in which their blood now

---

* The excerpts included here are drawn from Book III of Santayana's *Dominations and Powers* (New York: Charles Scribner's Sons, 1951): "Restricted Democracy," Chapter 15, pp. 355-57; "The American 'Melting-Pot'," Chapter 16, pp. 359-60; "The United States as Leader," Chapter 42, pp. 457-61.

flows in the veins of United States citizens, perhaps the striking homogeneity of language, spirit, and manners that now appears in them all would not have arisen. But chronologically, during the seventeenth century, apart from a few Dutch, all the colonists were British, and it was not until the nineteenth century that floods of Irish, Germans, Jews, Italians, Scandinavians, and Poles added themselves to the British stream which still continued to flow in. Those late-comers were plunged into a social and political *milieu* already highly characteristic. It had institutions, manners, and ways of thinking, and often a religion altogether new to the immigrants, yet so self-complacent and insistent that it made it difficult for the strangers, unless received by groups of their own countrymen already separately settled and organised, to preserve their old ways. Especially in the larger cities the pressure of the American method of working and planning for quick returns imposed itself on every one who wished to keep his head above water. Nobody could afford to sulk or had time to think, except about business; and the trade-winds of prosperity, ruffling over small personal failures, were so impetuous, hearty, and kindly that the passion for sailing before them was irresistible.

This uniformity of American manners and sentiment is a product of contagion; it works from outside, from popular schools, sports, newspapers, films, and political cries: a daily round so continuous and monotonous as to become automatic and seem to those who undergo it the only thing. It might well be expected to cancel all racial and traditional diversity in the people, if the source of it were not external even in the old American stock and sustained even in them only by mechanical compulsion and social pressure. Everyone is caught in the same vortex and, in so far as the soul is vocal, in a vocal vortex also.

But the human psyche is not altogether vocal or mechanically moved. It has a seminal bent, a spontaneous inner proclivity, often an individual originality and turn for invention. This was clearly proclaimed by the New England sages of the age before the Civil War. But they were few and idealistic. They were overwhelmed by the major current, into which they themselves wished to pass; and they were increasingly subdued to the colour of what they worked in, and hailed as prophets of the brave new world that was taking shape in complete disregard of their private spirits.

The American "Melting-Pot"

The early history of government in the United States exhibits different types of democracy, both locally and morally commingled.

Natural democracy appears among independent pioneers, joining forces casually or in small emigrant groups. These casual comrades were not foreigners to one another: they were chiefly British, chiefly Protestants, all were enterprising, all bent on gaining great wealth while preserving a radical independence. Yet there was likely to be, from the beginning, a profound distrust of one another latent among them. In spite of belonging to the same rising flood of revolution in Christendom, they represented various currents within that flood, taking different turns and sliding into various pools of a relative tranquillity. Some emigrants represented factions in British political life that already demanded a revolutionary democracy; others felt themselves to be potential landlords, more absolute and on a larger scale than the Old World, already pre-empted and riddled with privileges and mortgages, allowed to its hereditary nobility. A few were actually cavaliers, younger sons of great families, bound to outdo, in El Dorado, the unfair advantages of their elder brothers at home.

We may say that in this democratic concourse of social atoms there lay types of oligarchy in the germ which would assert themselves when they got a chance. Even in public and political life, oligarchical instincts and intuitions reassert themselves when planning or where executive capacity is needed. The few whom education and private fortune had accustomed to understand and manage complex affairs put their heads together, took the lead in framing resolutions and proposing measures; and if they did so in conventional language, without any air of superiority, the vaguely puzzled and vaguely trustful crowd accepted their suggestions, so that a private minority actually dominated the popular majority that nominally dominated the active members.

The American passion for organisation is no doubt fostered by the competition in efficiency and commercial economy; but

I suspect that it is secretly stimulated also by thirst for distinction. For this passion appears where no material advantage is expected: in amateur sports, for instance, and in the innumerable Societies and Associations and Clubs and Greek Letter Fraternities that segregate their members, not because initially distinguished, but because they thirst to become in some way segregated and distinguishable. Sometimes—I think exceptionally—real affinities produce special clubs; but often a club is founded for no reason except the hope of creating special affinities. Two fraternities or two houses will be founded in a college instead of one only, so that emulation may supply an interest in belonging to them at all and a flattering belief in each that it is better than the other.

Such feeble echoes of tribal feuds and tribal taboos may seem ridiculous amidst the swarming, rumbling, and smoking flats of modern industry with their tragic revolutions and wars; and certainly those manifestations of homesickness seem impotent bubbles in the flood of democracy sweeping over the world. Yet in the midst of this deluge, in the family and social life of those most identified with the new order, there are more serious symptoms of a radical aversion from it, an aversion that may well survive the inundation, and reappear, like the submerged crests of the ancient mountains when the waters recede. . . .

The United States as Leader

. . . What Fitness have the United States . . . to become the secular arm of Reason in checking the unreason of the world?

I had not, in 1934, ventured to name the United States as one of the powers that might be entrusted with that universal political duty. The American people had refused to join the League of Nations, more by an instinct of general distrust than by an insight into the folly of expecting an assembly of sovereign powers to possess or to carry out a consistent policy. The prevalence of representative government and the habit of being docile to majorities, when no fundamental interests were at stake, made Americans slow to feel that danger. And it was under this domestic illusion that, in 1946, a replica of the rejected and extinct League of Nations, with the aggravating feature of right of veto for each of the great powers, was established under

American leadership on American soil. Except for that veto, which at once paralysed all decisive action, it would have been natural for the United States to have begun to offer its own forces, then very strong and fit, to carry out the decrees of the universal authority. This authority, indeed, would have been little but a chorus to approve, or at most to retard by some accidental scruple, the special foreign policy of the United States.

At the same moment, by the unprecedented election of a President for a third and fourth term of office, and by an immense extension and elaborate organisation of all the departments of State, the American Government was becoming an automatic power, far more intelligent and determined than any floating and temporary majority in Congress; so that a traditional great government, comparable to the Roman, might have arisen in the United States and might have legally, and by general consent, have established its universal jurisdiction.

Would such an American hegemony have operated justly and deserved to endure?

There are several respects in which it would seem eminently capable of doing so. In the first place, the American people are good; their mentality is settled and pervasive; they are devoted and ingenious in improving the instruments and methods of material economy: and it is precisely in this sphere that they would have been called upon to act for the welfare of all mankind. They would have done so honestly, diligently, guided by experts in every department; and while a cumbrous official system, with much pedantry and delay and some false and premature theories, might have intervened, there need not have been, in their government, that open, perhaps unconscious, selfishness which many imperial governments have shown in the past. And this not because Americans are superhumanly unselfish, but because in questions of universal peace and universal trade their self-interest coincides with that of all other nations, or would at least do so if it were clearly understood and strictly confined to material economy.

But would an American management of international affairs be really confined to the economic sphere? It is no doubt the desire to keep American enterprise alive and progressive, by establishing everywhere rational commercial relations advantageous to both sides, that fundamentally inspires what the Russians call American imperialism; but quickness and sagacity in the economic arts are human virtues, and in the human psyche which is the agent in politics, they cannot stand alone. By the obvious well-being which they bring, they breed self-satisfaction and complacency; and the technically just belief that rational trade is profitable even to the less enterprising party excites a pleasing passion for doing good. And there are so many other goods, like education and training, that help to secure prosperity and in turn are favoured by it! The authority that controlled universal economy, if it were in American hands, would irresistibly tend to control education and training also. It might set up, as was done in the American zone in occupied Germany, a cultural department, with ideological and political propaganda. The philanthropic passion for service would prompt social, if not legal, intervention in the traditional life of all other nations, not only by selling there innumerable American products, but by recommending, if not imposing, American ways of living and thinking.

Now, this is, perhaps unintentionally, to transgress the limits of rational control and to exercise an influence that may be justly resented. If you wish to practice a mechanical art, the expert mechanic can rationally teach you how to do it; but if you wish to think or to practice a liberal art, another man, because he is self-satisfied, must not run up unasked and tell you to do it otherwise than as your vital liberty directs. The restraints that circumstances and the nature of things impose on your Will may be kindly pointed out to you before you commit yourself to a hopeless course; but the choice of your way must be left to you, if the authority that controls society is rational and friendly.

If, for instance, some community preferred not to trade at all, seeing that it could live suitably on native products, the universal government ought to limit its action in regard to that community to preventing their interference with the peace and liberty of their neighbours. It is a government, not a religion with a militant mission, that is demanded. It comes to serve and to keep order, not to dominate where it has no moral roots.

. . . The fruits of monopolist adventure and of incessant mechanical invention have dangled in America before the eyes of ambitious youth and of capitalist old age; it was a world in progress and ulterior repercussions and settlements were not considered. The militancy of trade and of political reform seemed vital and almost normal, and undoubtedly it lent a speed and brilliancy to the growth of industry and of wealth in the nineteenth century which seemed to contemporaries an unmixed good, to be pursued and intensified for ever.

It is only now that the multiplication of mechanisms has become a nightmare, omnipresent advertisements a plague, the overgrown proletariat a quicksand beneath the feet of wealth, and the hierarchy of occupations a reversion to a sort of serfdom. In Europe this tragedy of commercialism is perceived; in America it seems to rumble still invisible below the horizon. And it may be a serious question whether a universal government in American hands would not attempt to revitalise the commercial optimism of the nineteenth century, by the aid of new inventions and better coordination of resources. Or would it face the inevitable limit to industrial expansion, and establish a stable economic order in a world where labour might again merge with self-rewarding arts, and imagination turn from devising machines to cultivating liberal arts and enlarging moral freedom?

IV

The American Imagination

ೇ҈ What Is a Philistine?*

. . . The ancient Philistines seem to have been less stubborn
than the modern. The jawbone of an ass was then an efficient
weapon against them, while now they can scarcely be mollified
by all the honey that flows from the mouth of our young lions.
It sufficed that a beautiful poet, a pastoral king, should defy their
armies for the Philistines of those days to perish by the thousands and the ten thousands. How different it is now! Imagine
the champion of our latter-day Philistia, Goliath become the
spirit of some great corporation, to come forth with taunts before
the army of the chosen people. And imagine some youthful saint,
fresh from the unpolluted hills, and confident in the power of
reason, to accept the challenge, and say, "Thou comest armed
with the weight of five thousand shekels of brass, with a weaver's
beam for a spear, pointed with six hundred shekels of iron, and
one bearing a volume of Political Economy goes before thee;
but I come to thee in the name of the Lord of Beauty, of the God
of true and inward Happiness, whom thou hast defied. This day
will the Lord deliver thee into my hand, and I will smite thee and
take the souls of men away from thee: and I will give the high
chimneys of the factories of the Philistines to the fowls of the
air, and their deep furnaces to the beasts of the earth, that all
the world may know that there is a God in Israel." Would our
intrepid David, after all this bold language, find any smooth

* Printed in *The Harvard Monthly*, XV, No. 3 (December, 1892), 89-97.

stones in the brook, or have any skill with the sling, to smite the forehead of that Goliath? I am afraid the assembly would have reason to laugh at him, and to remain convinced that, in our day at least, it is with the sword and the spear that the Lord saveth.

The Bible tells us no more about the Philistines. We need not wonder at it, for such a beautiful apparition as David was capable, if anything ever was, of making an end of them. And shamed, as it were, by his life and his song, Philistia disappeared from the earth for several thousand years, to reappear at last in modern Germany. For although the modern Philistine is not necessarily Teutonic, yet it was the German imagination and learning that first noted the similarity between certain elements of modern society and the ancient enemies of Samson and David. In those idyllic days when the Fatherland was happy with the empire of the air, the German student, tender, unpolitical stripling that he was, delighted to quaff his beer and ogle his lass under the trellises of a rural inn, or to sit all night in the vaulted *Rathskeller* of his university town, where his idealistic soul glowed with genial enthusiasm, and the ruddy image of Gambrinus, astride upon a barrel, leered at him from the painted wall. As his imagination kindled with the fumes of the malt mingled with the inspirations of genius, he saw in his expanding consciousness the fulfilment of the law and the prophets. And when he was awakened at last by the necessity, perhaps, of paying his bill, he spontaneously gave to his fleshly and unsympathetic host the name of *Philister*, as being his natural enemy, and the chief earthly obstacle to the infinite fulfilment of his dreams.

From the blameless inn-keeper, who doubtless understood nothing of the student's cant, the epithet was extended to all shop-keepers, towns-men and merchants, until we hear Heine dividing the population of Gottingen into students, professors, Philistines, and kine. These classes, he is careful to add, are not mutually exclusive; but even with this qualification his classification is now out of date. No one would think of drawing a distinction now-a-days between the Philistines and the professors of Germany. The ordinary German professor is, with the possible exception of the German parson, the most contented dweller in Philistia Felix. Full of reverence for the state of which he is the organ, and for the lexicons and monographs which he devours and brings forth with physiological regularity, he rejoices in the consciousness of being a normal and well-regulated cell in the organism of modern society and of modern science. If you asked him what he or any other cell gained thereby, he would look upon you with astonishment, and reply: My living! How should it be an expense of spirit in a waste of shame to write dull and unnecessary books, when these enlarge the "literature" of science and are placed upon the shelves of libraries? And as for the student, with his *Notizen* and his hourly odoriferous slice of sour *Butterbrod;* of what are his dreams but of a *Kneipe* or a degree, a low debauch or an *ordentliche Professur?* Both masters and pupils are excellent examples of that unquestioning subordination of mind to matter and of ends to means which is the essence of Philistinism.

If Heine could now revisit his native country the class that he would contrast with Philistines would be musicians. They alone, with a small retinue of painters and poets, and other lovers of decaying arts, constitute Bohemia, and inherit the spiritual freedom of the former student. Music is the most exclusively aesthetic and unutilitarian of the arts, and by a sort of sarcasm of fate, or by the tendency of a restless and disorganized society to run into extremes, is the one now most passionately and successfully pursued. The musician lives, if not by ideas, at least by emotions, and in his enthusiasm for beauty, in his capacity for rapture, in his unfettered life, he shows the blithe spirit of an angel, too often combined, alas! with the habits of a pig. For musical susceptibility is a thing by itself, easily separable from every other element of culture; and in this fact we have, perhaps, the true cause of the present pre-eminence of music, since the less beauty we are able to see in external things the more we fall back upon the pure beauty of sensation. But cultivation in general and cleanliness in particular were never necessary to spirituality; and in spite of his unpleasant neglect of the body, the musician is all over the world, and especially in Germany where he most abounds, the champion of the soul, who like his patron the Psalmist defies the hosts of the Philistines.

It is in England, however, and in this country, that we are wont to think the Philistine most at home. Everybody knows Mr. Matthew Arnold's division of the English into barbarians, Phi-

listines, and rabble, and also his subsequent remark that America
is the paradise of Philistinism. It is obvious from these sayings, as
well as from that of Heine already quoted, that the Philistines
must be many and heterogeneous. They are not to be easily described except by exclusion; the other classes contrasted with
them are all more definite and describable. For we all know
what a musician is, and students and professors we have always
with us. Kine and rabble are a distinct and well-known estate,
happily not yet numerous in this New World. They are that
species of animal which, although externally human, is without
family, arts, or religion. And the barbarians we also know, or
wish to, for they are the aristocracy. They are the country gentlemen and club men, who hunt, cruise, shoot, bathe, dress, and
go upon the grand tour; men who love their horses, their hounds,
their parks, and their dinner, and who regard a poet and a scholar,
like Mr. Arnold, as something intermediate between a peda-
gogue and a comedian,—a subtle person fed and clothed at the
expense of society for the delight and amusement of the lords of
the earth. And the men of culture—a class too insignificant in
numbers to be included in the general division—are such as Mr.
Arnold himself, and occupy in England the place held by the
musicians in Germany. The Englishman is of course immensely
superior in civilization, but he lives in a society grossly barbarian,
and catches some of the traits of the ruling caste; he washes and
he dines at eight o'clock, and he is not wholly without snobbery.

All these various classes of the non-Philistine are comparatively easy to recognize and to define roughly. But what charac-
teristics shall we say are distinctive of the vast remainder, which
by common consent we call the Philistines? Well, we may begin
by saying without much fear of contradiction that one essential trait of the Philistine is conventionality. We have all heard
that the English middle class is eminent for dullness and stupidity. The English Philistine is a man of narrow, wholly practical interests, rigid and verbal principles, stubborn contempt for
what is alien or new, and not less dogged attachment to what is
authoritative and home-spun. But this description does not apply
to the emancipated middle class: it does not at all apply to the
American, who is also a Philistine. The conventionality we
mean must be carefully distinguished from Toryism. To be a

Tory is at least to have affections and prejudices which in their very irrationality seem to have something un-Philistine about them. Toryism is an instinctive if not a reasoned avowal of the value of a social ideal; it is attachment to the hierarchy in church and state, and to the rural life of England. To get Philistinism pure and unalloyed we must turn to the prosperous shop-keepers and merchants who dwell in towns, compared with whom your country Tory is a figure of romance. For the prosperous business man, who is a radical, has prejudices without affections, and his thoughts are governed by insistence on a doctrine rather than by loyalty to an institution. His mind is empty without being free. And it is, I should say, of the essence of the Philistine mind to have rigidity without substance. However narrow a life may be, however ignorant of the wide world of nature and thought, if it is governed by some true perception, if it has hold upon some immediate and vital good, it escapes conventionality. For that reason neither a saint nor a voluptuary can be a Philistine; they know too well what they are living for, and its intrinsic worth. Nor was that woman a Philistine whom Sir Edwin Arnold makes to say:

> "My heart
> Is little, and a little rain will fill
> The lily's cup that hardly moists the field.
> It is enough for me to feel life's sun
> Shine in my Lord's grace and my baby's smile.
> Pleasant my days pass, filled with household cares
> From sunrise when I wake to praise the gods
> And set my housemaids to their tasks, till noon
> When my Lord lays his head upon my lap
> Lulled by soft songs and wavings of the fan.
> And so to supper time at quiet eve
> When by his side I stand and serve the cakes.
> But if death called Senani, I should mount
> The pile, and lay that dear head in my lap
> My daily way, rejoicing when the torch
> Lit the quick flame and rolled the choking smoke.
> For it is written if an Indian wife
> Die so, her love shall give her husband's soul

For every hair upon her head a crore
Of years in Swerga. Therefore fear I not."

Such a woman could hardly have been what we call a woman
of culture; she would not have enjoyed Wordsworth or Ruskin
even in a translation. But it is her quiet indifference to both trans-
lations and originals, her perception of the primary things in life,
and her repose in them, that makes her noble. No one who leads
the simple life of the senses and the affections can be called a
Philistine. To reach that condition there must supervene a certain sophistication, and the mind must lose its perception of
primitive facts in its attention to conventional maxims. Philistinism is life at second hand.

Nothing, for instance, is so Philistine as the habit of asking the
money value of everything, and of talking, as our newspapers do,
of a thousand-dollar diamond and a ten-thousand-dollar fire. A
man whose eye was single would tell you how much the one
sparkled and the other blazed. But the Philistine's senses are
muffled by his intellect and by his habit of abbreviated thinking. His mental process is all algebra, a reckoning that loses sight
of its original values and is over without reaching any concrete
result. Now the price of an object is an algebraic symbol; it is an
abstract term, invented to facilitate our operations, which remains arid and unmeaning if we stop with it and forget to translate it again at the end into its concrete equivalent. It is vulgar to
esteem things for their cost, but not vulgar to esteem them for
the qualities which make them costly. I believe the economists
count among the elements of the value of an object the rarity
of its material, the labor of its manufacture, and the distance of
the country from which it is brought. Now all these qualities,
if attended to in themselves, appeal greatly to the imagination.
We have a natural interest in what is rare and affects us with unusual sensations. What comes from a far country carries our
thoughts there, and gains by the wealth and picturesqueness of
its associations. And that on which human labor has been spent,
especially if it was a labor of love and is apparent in the product,
has one of the deepest possible claims to admiration. So that the
standard of cost, the most vulgar and Philistine of all standards,
is such only when it remains empty and abstract. Let the thoughts

wander back and consider the elements of value, and our appreciation, from being verbal and commercial, becomes real and poetic.

One characteristic of the Philistine mind, then, is its resting in the merely conventional. It is in a hurry and deals in abbreviations. Dexterity in the use of symbols and respect for the instruments of calculation make it forget the vision of the real world and the primitive source of all value in the senses and the affections. It used to be a doctrine of philosophers that the world was made for man and everything in it designed for his comfort and salvation. That belief is now impugned, and people think that the universe may have other purposes, if it has any purpose at all, than one which is so disproportionate to its extent and which it is so slow in accomplishing. But I know not whether it is on account of this new philosophy, or on account of ancient habits and practical impulses, that we have got into a way of living as if not only the aim of Nature, but also the aim of man and of society, lay beyond man himself. We have multiplied our instruments, and forgotten our purposes; and, what is still worse, we have made of ourselves instruments for the production of changes in Nature, and consented to regard our consciousness as a device for the better making and doing of things. We have forgotten that there is nothing valuable or worthy in the motion, however rapid, of masses, however great, nor in the organization of societies, however great and powerful, unless the inward happiness of men is thereby increased or their misery diminished. This idolatry, that subordinates the life of man, his thoughts and his actions, to the production of external effects in the world, is the religion of Philistia; and nothing so much arouses the inspired rage of the true prophet; witness the cry of Leopardi:

> Age in which I was born,
> Thou fool that, heaping treasure for the morrow,
> Unto each sad today but addest sorrow,
> I hold thy pride in scorn!

But if blindness to the elemental and immediate is one condition of Philistinism, indifference to the supreme and ultimate is another. Our Indian woman not only perceives the intrinsic sufficiency of simple joys, she also conceives of a highest duty and

consolation, she forms an idea of her place in the universe, and
has a religion. Now a Philistine may be very religious in his
gregarious way, his faith may be orthodox and his conduct irre-
proachable. But he would cease to be a Philistine if he had instinctive piety and an inward, imaginative appreciation of his
faith. For these things require a certain wealth of emotion and
scope of imagination; they involve what we call unworldliness.
To be unworldly is to look upon the judgment of society, its
prizes and its pleasures, with the serenity and sadness of one
whose treasure is elsewhere and whose eyes have beheld the
vision of better things. It is to live in the sight of the ideal,

> Ayant devant les yeux, sans cesse, nuit et jour,
> Ou quelque saint labeur ou quelque grand amour.

It matters not what the sacred passion or what the work of
love may be: the infinite surrounds us in every direction, and
all who at any time have caught a glimpse of it have something
in common. They have for a moment escaped convention and
felt the relativity and possible indifference of all earthly goods.
That is what the Philistine has never done. He has never shaken
off his vulgar passions nor felt the weight of original sin; his life,
like that of a beast of burden, has not been either a revel or a
sacrifice, but a stolid response to successive stimulations.

If this be the sad condition of the Philistine, we need hardly
ask why he has another quality, which many people may think
the most essential to him, namely, indifference to the beauties of
art. For art appeals to the vividness of sensation and to the sweep
of fancy; it charms by clearness of form and by infinity of suggestion. But we have seen how the Philistine can never repose in
sense, since every sensation is to him merely a sign and symbol,
a signal that something is to be done. And he is equally incapable
of attaining to imagination, for what he sees and hears suggests to
him facts, and facts in turn suggest to him nothing. So that if
you set a Philistine before a picture, he will be inevitably bored.
He can do nothing to the picture except buy it, and that is soon
accomplished. He is too active and industrious a man to stand
gaping at it, pretending he enjoys the harmony of its color, the
balance of its design, or the richness of its light and shade. And
he is too honest to say that the picture represents anything

more than a man's face, or a pretty view, or whatever else the subject may be. If the reproduction is accurate, as far as his perception goes, he will be pleased to notice the fact. But how the image of a face can represent anything besides, or the copy of a landscape be more beautiful than the original, he can never conceive. The comprehension of that depends on the awakening of many dim and profound suggestions, on the creation in the beholder's mind of some ideal of beauty or of happiness, on the quick passing of some infinitely tragic and lovely vision. And such things are not engendered in the Philistine brain. . . .

ᏞᎦ The Elements and
   Function of Poetry*

If a critic, in despair of giving a serious definition of poetry, should be satisfied with saying that poetry is metrical discourse, he would no doubt be giving an inadequate account of the matter, yet not one of which he need be ashamed or which he should regard as superficial. Although a poem be not made by counting of syllables upon the fingers, yet "numbers" is the most poetical synonym we have for verse, and "measure" the most significant equivalent for beauty, for goodness, and perhaps even for truth. Those early and profound philosophers, the followers of Pythagoras, saw the essence of all things in number, and it was by weight, measure, and number, as we read in the Bible, that the Creator first brought Nature out of the void. Every human architect must do likewise with his edifice; he must mould his bricks or hew his stones into symmetrical solids and lay them over one another in regular strata, like a poet's lines.

Measure is a condition of perfection, for perfection requires that order should be pervasive, that not only the whole before us should have a form, but that every part in turn should have a form of its own, and that those parts should be coördinated among themselves as the whole is coördinated with the other parts of some greater cosmos. Leibnitz lighted in his speculations upon a conception of organic nature which may be false

* Chapter X of *Interpretations of Poetry and Religion* (New York: Charles Scribner's Sons, 1900).

as a fact, but which is excellent as an ideal; he tells us that the difference between living and dead matter, between animals and machines, is that the former are composed of parts that are themselves organic, every portion of the body being itself a machine, and every portion of that machine still a machine, and so *ad infinitum;* whereas, in artificial bodies the organisation is not in this manner infinitely deep. Fine Art, in this as in all things, imitates the method of Nature and makes its most beautiful works out of materials that are themselves beautiful. So that even if the difference between verse and prose consisted only in measure, that difference would already be analogous to that between jewels and clay.

The stuff of language is words, and the sensuous material of words is sound; if language therefore is to be made perfect, its materials must be made beautiful by being themselves subjected to a measure, and endowed with a form. It is true that language is a symbol for intelligence rather than a stimulus to sense, and accordingly the beauties of discourse which commonly attract attention are merely the beauties of the objects and ideas signified; yet the symbols have a sensible reality of their own, a euphony which appeals to our senses if we keep them open. The tongue will choose those forms of utterance which have a natural grace as mere sound and sensation; the memory will retain these catches, and they will pass and repass through the mind until they become types of instinctive speech and standards of pleasing expression.

The highest form of such euphony is song; the singing voice gives to the sounds it utters the thrill of tonality,—a thrill itself dependent, as we know, on the numerical proportions of the vibrations that it includes. But this kind of euphony and sensuous beauty, the deepest that sounds can have, we have almost wholly surrendered in our speech. Our intelligence has become complex, and language, to express our thoughts, must commonly be more rapid, copious, and abstract than is compatible with singing. Music at the same time has become complex also, and when united with words, at one time disfigures them in the elaboration of its melody, and at another overpowers them in the volume of its sound. So that the art of singing is now in the same plight as that of sculpture,—an abstract and conventional thing surviving by force of tradition and of an innate but now impotent impulse, which under simpler conditions would work itself out into the proper forms of those arts. The truest kind of euphony is thus denied to our poetry. If any verses are still set to music, they are commonly the worst only, chosen for the purpose by musicians of specialised sensibility and inferior intelligence, who seem to be attracted only by tawdry effects of rhetoric and sentiment.

When song is given up, there still remains in speech a certain sensuous quality, due to the nature and order of the vowels and consonants that compose the sounds. This kind of euphony is not neglected by the more dulcet poets, and is now so studied in some quarters that I have heard it maintained by a critic of relative authority that the beauty of poetry consists entirely in the frequent utterance of the sound of "j" and "sh," and the consequent copious flow of saliva in the mouth. But even if saliva is not the whole essence of poetry, there is an unmistakable and fundamental diversity of effect in the various vocalisation of different poets, which becomes all the more evident when we compare those who use different languages. One man's speech, or one nation's, is compact, crowded with consonants, rugged, broken with emphatic beats; another man's, or nation's, is open, tripping, rapid, and even. So Byron, mingling in his boyish fashion burlesque with exquisite sentiment, contrasts English with Italian speech:—

> I love the language, that soft bastard Latin
> Which melts like kisses from a female mouth
> And sounds as if it should be writ on satin
> With syllables which breathe of the sweet South,
> And gentle liquids gliding all so pat in
> That not a single accent seems uncouth,
> Like our harsh Northern whistling, grunting guttural
> Which we're obliged to hiss and spit and sputter all.

And yet these contrasts, strong when we compare extreme cases, fade from our consciousness in the actual use of a mother-tongue. The function makes us unconscious of the instrument, all the more as it is an indispensable and almost invariable one. The sense of euphony accordingly attaches itself rather to another and more variable quality; the tune, or measure, or rhythm of speech. The elementary sounds are prescribed by the language we use, and the selection we may make among those sounds is limited; but the arrangement of words is still undetermined, and by casting our speech into the moulds of metre and rhyme we can give it a heightened power, apart from its significance. A tolerable definition of poetry, on its formal side, might be found in this: that poetry is speech in which the instrument counts as well as the meaning—poetry is speech for its own sake and for its own sweetness. As common windows are intended only to admit the light, but painted windows also to dye it, and to be an object of attention in themselves as well as a cause of visibility in other things, so, while the purest prose is a mere vehicle of thought, verse, like stained glass, arrests attention in its own intricacies, confuses it in its own glories, and is even at times allowed to darken and puzzle in the hope of casting over us a supernatural spell.

Long passages in Shelley's "Revolt of Islam" and Keats' "Endymion" are poetical in this sense; the reader gathers, probably, no definite meaning, but is conscious of a poetic medium, of speech euphonious and measured, and redolent of a kind of objectless passion which is little more than the sensation of the movement and sensuous richness of the lines. Such poetry is not great; it has, in fact, a tedious vacuity, and is unworthy of a mature mind; but it is poetical, and could be produced only by a legitimate child of the Muse. It belongs to an apprenticeship, but in this case the apprenticeship of genius. It bears that relation to great poems which scales and aimless warblings bear to great singing—they test the essential endowment and fineness of the organ which is to be employed in the art. Without this sensuous background and ingrained predisposition to beauty, no art can reach the deepest and most exquisite effects; and even without an intelligible superstructure these sensuous qualities suffice to give that thrill of exaltation, that suggestion of an ideal world, which we feel in the presence of any true beauty.

The sensuous beauty of words and their utterance in measure suffice, therefore, for poetry of one sort—where these are there is something unmistakably poetical, although the whole of poetry, or the best of poetry, be not yet there. Indeed, in such words as "The Revolt of Islam" or "Endymion" there is already more than mere metre and sound; there is the colour and choice of words, the fanciful, rich, or exquisite juxtaposition of phrases. The vocabulary and the texture of the style are precious; affected, perhaps, but at any rate refined.

This quality, which is that almost exclusively exploited by the Symbolist, we may call euphuism—the choice of coloured words and rare and elliptical phrases. If great poets are like architects and sculptors, the euphuists are like goldsmiths and jewellers; their work is filigree in precious metals, encrusted with glowing stones. Now euphuism contributes not a little to the poetic effect of the tirades of Keats and Shelley; if we wish to see the power of versification without euphuism we may turn to the tirades of Pope, where metre and euphony are displayed alone, and we have the outline or skeleton of poetry without the filling.

> In spite of pride, in erring reason's spite,
> One truth is clear, Whatever is, is right.

We should hesitate to say that such writing was truly poetical; so that some euphuism would seem to be necessary as well as metre, to the formal essence of poetry.

An example of this sort, however, takes us out of the merely verbal into the imaginative region; the reason that Pope is hardly poetical to us is not that he is inharmonious,—not to a defect of euphony,—but that he is too intellectual and has an excess of mentality. It is easier for words to be poetical without any thought, when they are felt merely as sensuous and musical, than for them to remain so when they convey an abstract notion, —especially if that notion be a tart and frigid sophism, like that of the couplet just quoted. The pyrotechnics of the intellect then take the place of the glow of sense, and the artifice of thought chills the pleasure we might have taken in the grace of expression.

If poetry in its higher reaches is more philosophical than history, because it presents the memorable types of men and things apart from unmeaning circumstances, so in its primary substance and texture poetry is more philosophical than prose because it is nearer to our immediate experience. Poetry breaks up the trite conceptions designated by current words into the sensuous qualities out of which those conceptions were originally put together. We name what we conceive and believe in, not what we see; things, not images; souls, not voices and silhouettes. This naming, with the whole education of the senses which it accompanies, subserves the uses of life; in order to thread our way through the labyrinth of objects which assault us, we must make a great selection in our sensuous experience; half of what we see and hear we must pass over as insignificant, while we piece out the other half with such an ideal complement as is necessary to turn it into a fixed and well-ordered world. This labour of perception and understanding, this spelling of the material meaning of experience is enshrined in our work-a-day language and ideas; ideas which are literally poetic in the sense that they are "made" (for every conception in an adult mind is a fiction), but which are at the same time prosaic because they are made economically, by abstraction, and for use.

When the child of poetic genius, who has learned this intellectual and utilitarian language in the cradle, goes afield and gathers for himself the aspects of Nature, he begins to encumber his mind with the many living impressions which the intellect rejected, and which the language of the intellect can hardly convey; he labours with his nameless burden of perception, and wastes himself in aimless impulses of emotion and reverie, until finally the method of some art offers a vent to his inspiration, or to such part of it as can survive the test of time and the discipline of expression.

The poet retains by nature the innocence of the eye, or recovers it easily; he disintegrates the fictions of common perception into their sensuous elements, gathers these together again into chance groups as the accidents of his environment or the affinities of his temperament may conjoin them; and this wealth of sensation and this freedom of fancy, which make an extraordinary ferment in his ignorant heart, presently bubble over into some kind of utterance.

The fulness and sensuousness of such effusions bring them nearer to our actual perceptions than common discourse could come; yet they may easily seem remote, overloaded, and obscure to those accustomed to think entirely in symbols, and never to be interrupted in the algebraic rapidity of their think-

ing by a moment's pause and examination of heart, nor ever
to plunge for a moment into that torrent of sensation and imagery over which the bridge of prosaic associations habitually
carries us safe and dry to some conventional act. How slight
that bridge commonly is, how much an affair of trestles and
wire, we can hardly conceive until we have trained ourselves to
an extreme sharpness of introspection. But psychologists have
discovered, what laymen generally will confess, that we hurry
by the procession of our mental images as we do by the traffic
of the street, intent on business, gladly forgetting the noise and
movement of the scene and looking only for the corner we
would turn or the door we would enter. Yet in our alertest
moment the depths of the soul are still dreaming; the real world
stands drawn in bare outline against a background of chaos and
unrest. Our logical thoughts dominate experience only as the
parallels and meridians make a checker-board of the sea. They
guide our voyage without controlling the waves, which toss for
ever in spite of our ability to ride over them to our chosen ends.
Sanity is a madness put to good uses; waking life is a dream
controlled.

Out of the neglected riches of this dream the poet fetches his
wares. He dips into the chaos that underlies the rational shell
of the world and brings up some superfluous image, some emotion dropped by the way, and reattaches it to the present object; he reinstates things unnecessary, he emphasises things ignored, he paints in again into the landscape the tints which
the intellect has allowed to fade from it. If he seems sometimes
to obscure a fact, it is only because he is restoring an experience.
We may observe this process in the simplest cases. When Ossian, mentioning the sun, says it is round as the shield of his
fathers, the expression is poetical. Why? Because he has added
to the word sun, in itself sufficient and unequivocal, other words,
unnecessary for practical clearness, but serving to restore the
individuality of his perception and its associations in his mind.
There is no square sun with which the sun he is speaking of
could be confused; to stop and call it round is a luxury, a halting in the sensation for the love of its form. And to go on to tell
us, what is wholly impertinent, that the shield of his fathers
was round also, is to invite us to follow the chance wanderings

of his fancy, to give us a little glimpse of the stuffing of his own brain, or, we might almost say, to turn over the patterns of his embroidery and show us the loose threads hanging out on the wrong side. Such an escapade disturbs and interrupts the true vision of the object, and a great poet, rising to a perfect conception of the sun and forgetting himself, would have disdained to make it; but it has a romantic and pathological interest, it restores an experience, and is in that measure poetical. We have been made to halt at the sensation, and to penetrate for a moment into its background of dream.

But it is not only thoughts or images that the poet draws in this way from the store of his experience, to clothe the bare form of conventional objects: he often adds to these objects a more subtle ornament, drawn from the same source. For the first element which the intellect rejects in forming its ideas of things is the emotion which accompanies the perception; and this emotion is the first thing the poet restores. He stops at the image, because he stops to enjoy. He wanders into the by-paths of association because the by-paths are delightful. The love of beauty which made him give measure and cadence to his words, the love of harmony which made him rhyme them, reappear in his imagination and make him select there also the material that is itself beautiful, or capable of assuming beautiful forms. The link that binds together the ideas, sometimes so wide apart, which his wit assimilates, is most often the link of emotion; they have in common some element of beauty or of horror.

The poet's art is to a great extent the art of intensifying emotions by assembling the scattered objects that naturally arouse them. He sees the affinities of things by seeing their common affinities with passion. As the guiding principle of practical thinking is some interest, so that only what is pertinent to that interest is selected by the attention; as the guiding principle of scientific thinking is some connection of things in time or space, or some identity of law; so in poetic thinking the guiding principle is often a mood or a quality of sentiment. By this union of disparate things having a common overtone of feeling, the feeling is itself evoked in all its strength; nay, it is often created for the first time, much as by a new mixture of old pigments Perugino could produce the unprecedented limpidity of his colour, or Titian the unprecedented glow of his. Poets can thus arouse sentiments finer than any which they have known, and in the act of composition become discoverers of new realms of delightfulness and grief. Expression is a misleading term which suggests that something previously known is rendered or imitated; whereas the expression is itself an original fact, the values of which are then referred to the thing expressed, much as the honours of a Chinese mandarin are attributed retroactively to his parents. So the charm which a poet, by his art of combining images and shades of emotion, casts over a scene or an action, is attached to the principal actor in it, who gets the benefit of the setting furnished him by a well-stocked mind.

The poet is himself subject to this illusion, and a great part of what is called poetry, although by no means the best part of it, consists in this sort of idealisation by proxy. We dye the world of our own colour; by a pathetic fallacy, by a false projection of sentiment, we soak Nature with our own feeling, and then celebrate her tender sympathy with our moral being. This aberration, as we see in the case of Wordsworth, is not inconsistent with a high development of both the faculties which it confuses,—I mean vision and feeling. On the contrary, vision and feeling, when most abundant and original, most easily present themselves in this undivided form. There would be need of a force of intellect which poets rarely possess to rationalise their inspiration without diminishing its volume: and if, as is commonly the case, the energy of the dream and the passion in them is greater than that of the reason, and they cannot attain true propriety and supreme beauty in their works, they can, nevertheless, fill them with lovely images and a fine moral spirit.

The pouring forth of both perceptive and emotional elements in their mixed and indiscriminate form gives to this kind of imagination the directness and truth which sensuous poetry possesses on a lower level. The outer world bathed in the hues of human feeling, the inner world expressed in the forms of things, —that is the primitive condition of both before intelligence and the prosaic classification of objects have abstracted them and assigned them to their respective spheres. Such identifications, on which a certain kind of metaphysics prides itself also, are not discoveries of profound genius; they are exactly like the ob-

servation of Ossian that the sun is round and that the shield of his
fathers was round too; they are disintegrations of conventional
objects, so that the original associates of our perceptions reappear; then the thing and the emotion which chanced to be simultaneous are said to be one, and we return, unless a better
principle of organisation is substituted for the principle abandoned, to the chaos of a passive animal consciousness, where all
is mixed together, projected together, and felt as an unutterable
whole.

The pathetic fallacy is a return to that early habit of thought
by which our ancestors peopled the world with benevolent and
malevolent spirits; what they felt in the presence of objects they
took to be a part of the objects themselves. In returning to this
natural confusion, poetry does us a service in that she recalls and
consecrates those phases of our experience which, as useless to
the understanding of material reality, we are in danger of forgetting altogether. Therein is her vitality, for she pierces to the
quick and shakes us out of our servile speech and imaginative
poverty; she reminds us of all we have felt, she invites us even to
dream a little, to nurse the wonderful spontaneous creations which
at every waking moment we are snuffing out in our brain. And
the indulgence is no mere momentary pleasure; much of its exuberance clings afterward to our ideas; we see the more and feel
the more for that exercise; we are capable of finding greater
entertainment in the common aspects of Nature and life. When
the veil of convention is once removed from our eyes by the poet,
we are better able to dominate any particular experience and, as
it were, to change its scale, now losing ourselves in its infinitesimal texture, now in its infinite ramifications.

If the function of poetry, however, did not go beyond this recovery of sensuous and imaginative freedom, at the expense
of disrupting our useful habits of thought, we might be grateful to it for occasionally relieving our numbness, but we should
have to admit that it was nothing but a relaxation; that spiritual
discipline was not to be gained from it in any degree, but must
be sought wholly in that intellectual system that builds the science of Nature with the categories of prose. So conceived, poetry
would deserve the judgment passed by Plato on all the arts of
flattery and entertainment; it might be crowned as delightful,

but must be either banished altogether as meretricious or at least confined to a few forms and occasions where it might do little harm. The judgment of Plato has been generally condemned by philosophers, although it is eminently rational, and justified by the simplest principles of morals. It has been adopted instead, although unwittingly, by the practical and secular part of mankind, who look upon artists and poets as inefficient and brainsick people under whose spell it would be a serious calamity to fall, although they may be called in on feast days as an ornament and luxury together with the cooks, hairdressers, and florists.

Several circumstances, however, might suggest to us the possibility that the greatest function of poetry may be still to find. Plato, while condemning Homer, was a kind of poet himself; his quarrel with the followers of the Muse was not a quarrel with the goddess; and the good people of Philistia, distrustful as they may be of profane art, pay undoubting honour to religion, which is a kind of poetry as much removed from their sphere as the midnight revels upon Mount Citheron, which, to be sure, were also religious in their inspiration. Why, we may ask, these apparent inconsistencies? Why do our practical men make room for religion in the background of their world? Why did Plato, after banishing the poets, poetise the universe in his prose? Because the abstraction by which the world of science and of practice is drawn out of our experience, is too violent to satisfy even the thoughtless and vulgar; the ideality of the machine we call Nature, the conventionality of the drama we call the world, are too glaring not to be somehow perceived by all. Each must sometimes fall back upon the soul; he must challenge this apparition with the thought of death; he must ask himself for the mainspring and value of his life. He will then remember his stifled loves; he will feel that only his illusions have ever given him a sense of reality, only his passions the hope and the vision of peace. He will read himself through and almost gather a meaning from his experience; at least he will half believe that all he has been dealing with was a dream and a symbol, and raise his eyes toward the truth beyond.

This plastic moment of the mind, when we become aware of the artificiality and inadequacy of what common sense perceives, is the true moment of poetic opportunity,—an opportunity, we may hasten to confess, which is generally missed. The strain of attention, the concentration and focussing of thought on the unfamiliar immediacy of things, usually brings about nothing but confusion. We are dazed, we are filled with a sense of unutterable things, luminous yet indistinguishable, many yet one. Instead of rising to imagination, we sink into mysticism.

To accomplish a mystical disintegration is not the function of any art; if any art seems to accomplish it, the effect is only incidental, being involved, perhaps, in the process of constructing the proper object of that art, as we might cut down trees and dig them up by the roots to lay the foundations of a temple. For every art looks to the building up of something. And just because the world built up by common sense and natural science is an inadequate world (a skeleton which needs the filling of sensation before it can live), therefore the moment when we realise its inadequacy is the moment when the higher arts find their opportunity. When the world is shattered to bits they can come and "build it nearer to the heart's desire."

The great function of poetry, which we have not yet directly mentioned, is precisely this: to repair to the material of experience, seizing hold of the reality of sensation and fancy beneath the surface of conventional ideas, and then out of that living but indefinite material to build new structures, richer, finer, fitter to the primary tendencies of our nature, truer to the ultimate possibilities of the soul. Our descent into the elements of our being is then justified by our subsequent freer ascent toward its goal; we revert to sense only to find food for reason; we destroy conventions only to construct ideals.

Such analysis for the sake of creation is the essence of all great poetry. Science and common sense are themselves in their way poets of no mean order, since they take the material of experience and make out of it a clear, symmetrical, and beautiful world; the very propriety of this art, however, has made it common. Its figures have become mere rhetoric and its metaphors prose. Yet, even as it is, a scientific and mathematical vision has a higher beauty than the irrational poetry of sensation and impulse, which merely tickles the brain, like liquor, and plays upon our random, imaginative lusts. The imagination of a great poet, on the contrary, is as orderly as that of an astronomer, and as large; he has the naturalist's patience, the naturalist's love of detail and eye trained to see fine gradations and essential lines; he knows no hurry; he has no pose, no sense of originality; he finds his effects in his subject, and his subject in his inevitable world. Resembling the naturalist in all this, he differs from him in the balance of his interests; the poet has the concreter mind; his visible world wears all its colours and retains its indwelling passion and life. Instead of studying in experience its calculable elements, he studies its moral values, its beauty, the openings it offers to the soul: and the cosmos he constructs is accordingly an ideal theatre for the spirit in which its noblest potential drama is enacted and its destiny resolved.

This supreme function of poetry is only the consummation of the method by which words and imagery are transformed into verse. As verse breaks up the prosaic order of syllables and subjects them to a recognisable and pleasing measure, so poetry breaks up the whole prosaic picture of experience to introduce into it a rhythm more congenial and intelligible to the mind. And in both these cases the operation is essentially the same as that by which, in an intermediate sphere, the images rejected by practical thought, and the emotions ignored by it, are so marshalled as to fill the mind with a truer and intenser consciousness of its memorable experience. The poetry of fancy, of observation, and of passion moves on this intermediate level; the poetry of mere sound and virtuosity is confined to the lower sphere; and the highest is reserved for the poetry of the creative reason. But one principle is present throughout,—the principle of Beauty,—the art of assimilating phenomena, whether words, images, emotions, or systems of ideas, to the deeper innate cravings of the mind.

Let us now dwell a little on this higher function of poetry and try to distinguish some of its phases.

The creation of characters is what many of us might at first be tempted to regard as the supreme triumph of the imagination. If we abstract, however, from our personal tastes and look at the matter in its human and logical relations, we shall see, I think, that the construction of characters is not the ultimate task of poetic fiction. A character can never be exhaustive of our materials: for it exists by its idiosyncrasy, by its contrast with other natures, by its development of one side, and one side only, of our native capacities. It is, therefore, not by characterisation as such that the ultimate message can be rendered. The poet can put only a part of himself into any of his heroes, but he must put the whole into his noblest work. A character is accordingly only a fragmentary unity; fragmentary in respect to its origin,—since it is conceived by enlargement, so to speak, of a part of our own being to the exclusion of the rest,—and fragmentary in respect to the object it presents, since a character must live in an environment and be appreciated by contrast and by the sense of derivation. Not the character, but its effects and causes, is the truly interesting thing. Thus in master poets, like Homer and Dante, the characters, although well drawn, are subordinate to the total movement and meaning of the scene. There is indeed something pitiful, something comic, in any comprehended soul; souls, like other things, are only definable by their limitations. We feel instinctively that it would be insulting to speak of any man to his face as we should speak of him in his absence, even if what we say is in the way of praise: for absent he is a character understood, but present he is a force respected.

In the construction of ideal characters, then, the imagination is busy with material,—particular actions and thoughts,—which suggest their unification in persons; but the characters thus conceived can hardly be adequate to the profusion of our observations, nor exhaustive, when all personalities are taken together, of the interest of our lives. Characters are initially imbedded in life, as the gods themselves are originally imbedded in Nature. Poetry must, therefore, to render all reality, render also the background of its figures, and the events that condition their acts. We must place them in that indispensable environment which the landscape furnishes to the eye and the social medium to the emotions.

The visible landscape is not a proper object for poetry. Its elements, and especially the emotional stimulation which it gives, may be suggested or expressed in verse; but landscape is not thereby represented in its proper form; it appears only as an element and associate of moral unities. Painting, architecture, and gardening, with the art of stage setting, have the vis-

ible landscape for their object, and to those arts we may leave it.
But there is a sort of landscape larger than the visible, which
escapes the synthesis of the eye; it is present to that topographical sense by which we always live in the consciousness that there
is a sea, that there are mountains, that the sky is above us, even
when we do not see it, and that the tribes of men, with their different degrees of blamelessness, are scattered over the broad-
backed earth. This cosmic landscape poetry alone can render,
and it is no small part of the art to awaken the sense of it at the
right moment, so that the object that occupies the centre of vision may be seen in its true lights, coloured by its wider associations, and dignified by its felt affinities to things permanent and
great. As the Italian masters were wont not to paint their groups
of saints about the Virgin without enlarging the canvas, so as to
render a broad piece of sky, some mountains and rivers, and
nearer, perhaps, some decorative pile; so the poet of larger mind
envelops his characters in the atmosphere of Nature and history,
and keeps us constantly aware of the world in which they move.

The distinction of a poet—the dignity and humanity of his
thought—can be measured by nothing, perhaps, so well as by
the diameter of the world in which he lives; if he is supreme,
his vision, like Dante's, always stretches to the stars. And Virgil, a supreme poet sometimes unjustly belittled, shows us the
same thing in another form; his landscape is the Roman universe, his theme the sacred springs of Roman greatness in piety,
constancy, and law. He has not written a line in forgetfulness
that he was a Roman; he loves country life and its labours because he sees in it the origin and bulwark of civic greatness; he
honours tradition because it gives perspective and momentum
to the history that ensues; he invokes the gods, because they are
symbols of the physical and moral forces by which Rome struggled to dominion.

Almost every classic poet has the topographical sense; he
swarms with proper names and allusions to history and fable;
if an epithet is to be thrown in anywhere to fill up the measure
of a line, he chooses instinctively an appellation of place or
family; his wine is not red, but Samian; his gorges are not deep,
but are the gorges of Hæmus; his songs are not sweet, but
Pierian. We may deride their practice as conventional, but they

could far more justly deride ours as insignificant. Conventions do not arise without some reason, and genius will know how to rise above them by a fresh appreciation of their rightness, and will feel no temptation to overturn them in favour of personal whimsies. The ancients found poetry not so much in sensible accidents as in essential forms and noble associations; and this fact marks very clearly their superior education. They dominated the world as we no longer dominate it, and lived, as we are too distracted to live, in the presence of the rational and the important.

A physical and historical background, however, is of little moment to the poet in comparison with that other environment of his characters,—the dramatic situations in which they are involved. The substance of poetry is, after all, emotion; and if the intellectual emotion of comprehension and the mimetic one of impersonation are massive, they are not so intense as the appetites and other transitive emotions of life; the passions are the chief basis of all interests, even the most ideal, and the passions are seldom brought into play except by the contact of man with man. The various forms of love and hate are only possible in society, and to imagine occasions in which these feelings may manifest all their inward vitality is the poet's function,—one in which he follows the fancy of every child, who puffs himself out in his day-dreams into an endless variety of heroes and lovers. The thrilling adventures which he craves demand an appropriate theatre; the glorious emotions with which he bubbles over must at all hazards find or feign their correlative objects.

But the passions are naturally blind, and the poverty of the imagination, when left alone, is absolute. The passions may ferment as they will, they never can breed an idea out of their own energy. This idea must be furnished by the senses, by outward experience, else the hunger of the soul will gnaw its own emptiness for ever. Where the seed of sensation has once fallen, however, the growth, variations, and exuberance of fancy may be unlimited. Only we still observe (as in the child, in dreams, and in the poetry of ignorant or mystical poets) that the intensity of inwardly generated visions does not involve any real increase in their scope or dignity. The inexperienced mind remains a thin mind, no matter how much its vapours may be heated and blown about by natural passion. It was a capital error in Fichte and Schopenhauer to assign essential fertility to the will in the creation of ideas. They mistook, as human nature will do, even when at times it professes pessimism, an ideal for a reality: and because they saw how much the will clings to its objects, how it selects and magnifies them, they imagined that it could breed them out of itself. A man who thinks clearly will see that such self-determination of a will is inconceivable, since what has no external relation and no diversity of structure cannot of itself acquire diversity of functions. Such inconceivability, of course, need not seem a great objection to a man of impassioned inspiration; he may even claim a certain consistency in positing, on the strength of his preference, the inconceivable to be a truth.

The alleged fertility of the will is, however, disproved by experience, from which metaphysics must in the end draw its analogies and plausibility. The passions discover, they do not create, their occasions; a fact which is patent when we observe how they seize upon what objects they find, and how reversible, contingent, and transferable the emotions are in respect to their objects. A doll will be loved instead of a child, a child instead of a lover, God instead of everything. The differentiation of the passions, as far as consciousness is concerned, depends on the variety of the objects of experience,—that is, on the differentiation of the senses and of the environment which stimulates them.

When the "infinite" spirit enters the human body, it is determined to certain limited forms of life by the organs which it wears; and its blank potentiality becomes actual in thought and deed, according to the fortunes and relations of its organism. The ripeness of the passions may thus precede the information of the mind and lead to groping in by-paths without issue; a phenomenon which appears not only in the obscure individual whose abnormalities the world ignores, but also in the starved, half-educated genius that pours the whole fire of his soul into trivial arts or grotesque superstitions. The hysterical forms of music and religion are the refuge of an idealism that has lost its way; the waste and failures of life flow largely in those channels. The carnal temptations of youth are incidents of the same maladaptation, when passions assert themselves before the conventional order of society can allow them physical satisfaction, and long before philosophy or religion can hope to transform them into fuel for its own sacrificial flames.

Hence flows the greatest opportunity of fiction. We have, in a sense, an infinite will; but we have a limited experience, an experience sadly inadequate to exercise that will either in its purity or its strength. To give form to our capacities nothing is required but the appropriate occasion; this the poet, studying the world, will construct for us out of the materials of his observations. He will involve us in scenes which lie beyond the narrow lane of our daily ploddings; he will place us in the presence of important events, that we may feel our spirit rise momentarily to the height of his great argument. The possibilities of love or glory, of intrigue and perplexity, will be opened up before us; if he gives us a good plot, we can readily furnish the characters, because each of them will be the realisation of some stunted potential self of our own. It is by the plot, then, that the characters will be vivified, because it is by the plot that our own character will be expanded into its latent possibilities.

The description of an alien character can serve this purpose only very imperfectly; but the presentation of the circumstances in which that character manifests itself will make description unnecessary, since our instinct will supply all that is requisite for the impersonation. Thus it seems that Aristotle was justified in making the plot the chief element in fiction: for it is by virtue of the plot that the characters live, or, rather, that we live in them, and by virtue of the plot accordingly that our soul rises to that imaginative activity by which we tend at once to escape from the personal life and to realise its ideal. This idealisation is, of course, partial and merely relative to the particular adventure in which we imagine ourselves engaged. But in some single direction our will finds self-expression, and understands itself; runs through the career which it ignorantly coveted, and gathers the fruits and the lesson of that enterprise.

This is the essence of tragedy: the sense of the finished life, of the will fulfilled and enlightened: that purging of the mind so much debated upon, which relieves us of pent-up energies, transfers our feelings to a greater object, and thus justifies and entertains our dumb passions, detaching them at the same time for a moment from their accidental occasions in our earthly life. An episode, however lurid, is not a tragedy in this nobler sense, because it does not work itself out to the end; it pleases without satisfying or shocks without enlightening. This enlightenment, I need hardly say, is not a matter of theory or of moral maxims; the enlightenment by which tragedy is made sublime is a glimpse into the ultimate destinies of our will. This discovery need not be an ethical gain—Macbeth and Othello attain it as much as Brutus and Hamlet—it may serve to accentuate despair, or cruelty, or indifference, or merely to fill the imagination for a moment without much affecting the permanent tone of the mind. But without such a glimpse of the goal of a passion the passion has not been adequately read, and the fiction has served to amuse us without really enlarging the frontiers of our ideal experience. Memory and emotion have been played upon, but imagination has not brought anything new to the light.

The dramatic situation, however, gives us the environment of a single passion, of life in one of its particular phases; and although a passion, like Romeo's love, may seem to devour the whole soul, and its fortunes may seem to be identical with those of the man, yet much of the man, and the best part of him, goes by the board in such a simplification. If Leonardo da Vinci, for example, had met in his youth with Romeo's fate, his end would have been no more ideally tragic than if he had died at eighteen of a fever; we should be touched rather by the pathos of what he had missed, than by the sublimity of what he had experienced. A passion like Romeo's compared with the ideal scope of human thought and emotion, is a thin dream, a pathological crisis.

Accordingly Aristophanes, remembering the original religious and political functions of tragedy, blushes to see upon the boards a woman in love. And we should readily agree with him, but for two reasons,—one, that we abstract too much, in our demands upon art, from nobility of mind, and from the thought of totality and proportion; the other, that we have learned to look for a symbolic meaning in detached episodes, and to accept the incidental emotions they cause, because of their violence and our absorption in them, as in some sense sacramental and representative of the whole. Thus the picture of an unmeaning passion, of a crime without an issue, does not appear to our romantic apprehension as the sorry farce it is, but rather as a true tragedy. Some have lost even the capacity to conceive of a true tragedy, because they have no idea of a cosmic order, of general laws of life, or of an impersonal religion. They measure the profundity of feeling by its intensity, not by its justifying relations; and in the radical disintegration of their spirit, the more they are devoured the more they fancy themselves fed. But the majority of us retain some sense of a meaning in our joys and sorrows, and even if we cannot pierce to their ultimate object, we feel that what absorbs us here and now has a merely borrowed or deputed power; that it is a symbol and foretaste of all reality speaking to the whole soul. At the same time our intelligence is too confused to give us any picture of that reality, and our will too feeble to marshal our disorganised loves into a religion consistent with itself and harmonious with the comprehended universe. A rational ideal eludes us, and we are the more inclined to plunge into mysticism.

Nevertheless, the function of poetry, like that of science, can only be fulfilled by the conception of harmonies that become clearer as they grow richer. As the chance note that comes to be supported by a melody becomes in that melody determinate and necessary, and as the melody, when woven into a harmony, is explicated in that harmony and fixed beyond recall; so the single emotion, the fortuitous dream, launched by the poet into the world of recognisable and immortal forms, looks in that world for its ideal supports and affinities. It must find them or else be blown back among the ghosts. The highest ideality is the comprehension of the real. Poetry is not at its best when it depicts a further possible experience, but when it initiates us, by feigning something which as an experience is impossible, into the meaning of the experience which we have actually had.

The highest example of this kind of poetry is religion; and although disfigured and misunderstood by the simplicity of men who believe in it without being capable of that imaginative interpretation of life in which its truth consists, yet this religion is even then often beneficent, because it colours life harmoniously with the ideal. Religion may falsely represent the ideal as a reality, but we must remember that the ideal, if not so represented, would be despised by the majority of men, who cannot understand that the value of things is moral, and who therefore attribute to what is moral a natural existence, thinking thus to vindicate its importance and value. But value lies in meaning, not in substance; in the ideal which things approach, not in the energy which they embody.

The highest poetry, then, is not that of the versifiers, but that of the prophets, or of such poets as interpret verbally the visions which the prophets have rendered in action and sentiment rather than in adequate words. That the intuitions of religion are poetical, and that in such intuitions poetry has its ultimate function, are truths of which both religion and poetry become more conscious the more they advance in refinement and profundity. A crude and superficial theology may confuse God with the thunder, the mountains, the heavenly bodies, or the whole universe; but when we pass from these easy identifications to a religion that has taken root in history and in the hearts of men, and has come to flower, we find its objects and its dogmas purely ideal, transparent expressions of moral experience and perfect counterparts of human needs. The evidence of history or of the senses is left far behind and never thought of; the evidence of the heart, the value of the idea, are alone regarded.

Take, for instance, the doctrine of transubstantiation. A metaphor here is the basis of a dogma, because the dogma rises to the same subtle region as the metaphor, and gathers its sap from the same soil of emotion. Religion has here rediscovered its affinity with poetry, and in insisting on the truth of its mystery it unconsciously vindicates the ideality of its truth. Under the accidents of bread and wine lies, says the dogma, the substance of Christ's body, blood, and divinity. What is that but to treat facts as an appearance, and their ideal import as a reality? And to do this is the very essence of poetry, for which everything visible is a sacrament—an outward sign of that inward grace for which the soul is thirsting.

In this same manner, where poetry rises from its elementary and detached expressions in rhythm, euphuism, characterisation, and story-telling, and comes to the consciousness of its highest function, that of portraying the ideals of experience and destiny, then the poet becomes aware that he is essentially a prophet, and either devotes himself, like Homer or Dante, to the loving expression of the religion that exists, or like Lucretius or Wordsworth, to the heralding of one which he believes to be possible. Such poets are aware of their highest mission; others, whatever the energy of their genius, have not conceived their ultimate function as poets. They have been willing to leave their world ugly as a whole, after stuffing it with a sufficient profusion of beauties. Their contemporaries, their fellow-countrymen for many generations, may not perceive this defect, because they are naturally even less able than the poet himself to understand the necessity of so large a harmony. If he is short-sighted, they are blind, and his poetic world may seem to them sublime in its significance, because it may suggest some partial lifting of their daily burdens and some partial idealisation of their incoherent thoughts.

Such insensibility to the highest poetry is no more extraordinary than the corresponding indifference to the highest religion; nobility and excellence, however, are not dependent on the suffrage of half-baked men, but on the original disposition of the clay and the potter; I mean on the conditions of the art and the ideal capacities of human nature. Just as a note is better than a noise because, its beats being regular, the ear and brain can react with pleasure on that regularity, so all the stages of harmony are better than the confusion out of which they come, because the soul that perceives that harmony welcomes it as the fulfilment of her natural ends. The Pythagoreans were therefore right when they made number the essence of the knowable world, and Plato was right when he said harmony was the first condition of the highest good. The good man is a poet whose syllables are deeds and make a harmony in Nature. The poet is a rebuilder of the imagination, to make a harmony in that. And he is not a complete poet if his whole imagination is not attuned and his whole experience composed into a single symphony.

For his complete equipment, then, it is necessary, in the first place, that he sing; that his voice be pure and well pitched, and that his numbers flow; then, at a higher stage, his images must fit with one another; he must be euphuistic, colouring his thoughts with many reflected lights of memory and suggestion, so that their harmony may be rich and profound; again, at a higher stage, he must be sensuous and free, that is, he must build up his world with the primary elements of experience, not with the conventions of common sense or intelligence; he must draw the whole soul into his harmonies, even if in doing so he disintegrates the partial systematisations of experience made by abstract science in the categories of prose. But finally, this disintegration must not leave the poet weltering in a chaos of sense and passion; it must be merely the ploughing of the ground before a new harvest, the kneading of the clay before the modelling of a more perfect form. The expression of emotion should be rationalised by derivation from character and by reference to the real objects that arouse it—to Nature, to history, and to the universe of truth; the experience imagined should be conceived as a destiny, governed by principles, and issuing in the discipline and enlightenment of the will. In this way alone can poetry become an interpretation of life and not merely an irrelevant excursion into the realm of fancy, multiplying our images without purpose, and distracting us from our business without spiritual gain.

If we may then define poetry, not in the formal sense of giving the minimum of what may be called by that name, but in the ideal sense of determining the goal which it approaches and the achievement in which all its principles would be fulfilled, we may say that poetry is metrical and euphuistic discourse, expressing thought which is both sensuous and ideal.

Such is poetry as a literary form; but if we drop the limitation to verbal expression, and think of poetry as that subtle fire and inward light which seems at times to shine through the world and to touch the images in our minds with ineffable beauty, then poetry is a momentary harmony in the soul amid stagnation or conflict,—a glimpse of the divine and an incitation to a religious life.

Religion is poetry become the guide of life, poetry substituted for science or supervening upon it as an approach to the highest reality. Poetry is religion allowed to drift, left without points of application in conduct and without an expression in worship and dogma; it is religion without practical efficacy and without metaphysical illusion. The ground of this abstractness of poetry, however, is usually only its narrow scope; a poet who plays with an idea for half an hour, or constructs a character to which he gives no profound moral significance, forgets his own thought, or remembers it only as a fiction of his leisure, because he has not dug his well deep enough to tap the subterraneous springs of his own life. But when the poet enlarges his theatre and puts into his rhapsodies the true visions of his people and of his soul, his poetry is the consecration of his deepest convictions, and contains the whole truth of his religion. What the religion of the vulgar adds to the poet's is simply the inertia of their limited apprehension, which takes literally what he meant ideally, and degrades into a false extension of this world on its own level what in his mind was a true interpretation of it upon a moral plane.

This higher plane is the sphere of significant imagination, of relevant fiction, of idealism become the interpretation of the reality it leaves behind. Poetry raised to its highest power is then identical with religion grasped in its inmost truth; at their point of union both reach their utmost purity and beneficence, for then poetry loses its frivolity and ceases to demoralise, while religion surrenders its illusions and ceases to deceive.

♋ Emerson*

Those who knew Emerson, or who stood so near to his time and to his circle that they caught some echo of his personal influence, did not judge him merely as a poet or philosopher, nor identify his efficacy with that of his writings. His friends and neighbours, the congregations he preached to in his younger days, the audiences that afterward listened to his lectures, all agreed in a veneration for his person which had nothing to do with their understanding or acceptance of his opinions. They flocked to him and listened to his word, not so much for the sake of its absolute meaning as for the atmosphere of candour, purity, and serenity that hung about it, as about a sort of sacred music. They felt themselves in the presence of a rare and beautiful spirit, who was in communion with a higher world. More than the truth his teaching might express, they valued the sense it gave them of a truth that was inexpressible. They became aware, if we may say so, of the ultra-violet rays of his spectrum, of the inaudible highest notes of his gamut, too pure and thin for common ears.

This effect was by no means due to the possession on the part of Emerson of the secret of the universe, or even of a definite conception of ultimate truth. He was not a prophet who had once for all climbed his Sinai or his Tabor, and having there beheld the transfigured reality, descended again to make authoritative report of it to the world. Far from it. At bottom he had no

* Chapter VIII of *Interpretations of Poetry and Religion.*

doctrine at all. The deeper he went and the more he tried to grapple with fundamental conceptions, the vaguer and more elusive they became in his hands. Did he know what he meant by Spirit or the "Over-Soul"? Could he say what he understood by the terms, so constantly on his lips, Nature, Law, God, Benefit, or Beauty? He could not, and the consciousness of that incapacity was so lively within him that he never attempted to give articulation to his philosophy. His finer instinct kept him from doing that violence to his inspiration.

The source of his power lay not in his doctrine, but in his temperament, and the rare quality of his wisdom was due less to his reason than to his imagination. Reality eluded him; he had neither diligence nor constancy enough to master and possess it; but his mind was open to all philosophic influences, from whatever quarter they might blow; the lessons of science and the hints of poetry worked themselves out in him to a free and personal religion. He differed from the plodding many, not in knowing things better, but in having more ways of knowing them. His grasp was not particularly firm, he was far from being, like a Plato or an Aristotle, past master in the art and the science of life. But his mind was endowed with unusual plasticity, with unusual spontaneity and liberty of movement—it was a fairyland of thoughts and fancies. He was like a young god making experiments in creation: he blotched the work, and always began again on a new and better plan. Every day he said, "Let there be light," and every day the light was new. His sun, like that of Heraclitus, was different every morning.

What seemed, then, to the more earnest and less critical of his hearers a revelation from above was in truth rather an insurrection from beneath, a shaking loose from convention, a disintegration of the normal categories of reason in favour of various imaginative principles, on which the world might have been built, if it had been built differently. This gift of revolutionary thinking allowed new aspects, hints of wider laws, premonitions of unthought-of fundamental unities to spring constantly into view. But such visions were necessarily fleeting, because the human mind had long before settled its grammar, and discovered, after much groping and many defeats, the general forms in which experience will allow itself to be stated. These general forms are

the principles of common sense and positive science, no less
imaginative in their origin than those notions which we now call
transcendental, but grown prosaic, like the metaphors of common speech, by dint of repetition.

Yet authority, even of this rational kind, sat lightly upon Emerson. To reject tradition and think as one might have thought if
no man had ever existed before was indeed the aspiration of the
Transcendentalists, and although Emerson hardly regarded himself as a member of that school, he largely shared its tendency
and passed for its spokesman. Without protesting against tradition, he smilingly eluded it in his thoughts, untamable in their
quiet irresponsibility. He fled to his woods or to his "pleachèd
garden," to be the creator of his own worlds in solitude and
freedom. No wonder that he brought thence to the tightly conventional minds of his contemporaries a breath as if from paradise. His simplicity in novelty, his profundity, his ingenuous
ardour must have seemed to them something heavenly, and they
may be excused if they thought they detected inspiration even
in his occasional thin paradoxes and guileless whims. They were
stifled with conscience and he brought them a breath of Nature;
they were surfeited with shallow controversies and he gave them
poetic truth.

Imagination, indeed, is his single theme. As a preacher might
under every text enforce the same lessons of the gospel, so
Emerson traces in every sphere the same spiritual laws of experience—compensation, continuity, the self-expression of the Soul
in the forms of Nature and of society, until she finally recognises
herself in her own work and sees its beneficence and beauty. His
constant refrain is the omnipotence of imaginative thought; its
power first to make the world, then to understand it, and finally
to rise above it. All Nature is an embodiment of our native fancy,
all history a drama in which the innate possibilities of the spirit
are enacted and realised. While the conflict of life and the shocks
of experience seem to bring us face to face with an alien and overwhelming power, reflection can humanise and rationalise that
power by conceiving its laws; and with this recognition of the
rationality of all things comes the sense of their beauty and order. The destruction which Nature seems to prepare for our
special hopes is thus seen to be the victory of our impersonal in-

terests. To awaken in us this spiritual insight, an elevation of
mind which is at once an act of comprehension and of worship,
to substitute it for lower passions and more servile forms of intelligence—that is Emerson's constant effort. All his resources of
illustration, observation, and rhetoric are used to deepen and
clarify this sort of wisdom.

Such thought is essentially the same that is found in the German romantic or idealistic philosophers, with whom Emerson's
affinity is remarkable, all the more as he seems to have borrowed
little or nothing from their works. The critics of human nature, in the eighteenth century, had shown how much men's
ideas depend on their predispositions, on the character of their
senses and the habits of their intelligence. Seizing upon this
thought and exaggerating it, the romantic philosophers attributed to the spirit of man the omnipotence which had belonged
to God, and felt that in this way they were reasserting the supremacy of mind over matter and establishing it upon a safe and
rational basis.

The Germans were great system-makers, and Emerson cannot
rival them in the sustained effort of thought by which they
sought to reinterpret every sphere of being according to their
chosen principles. But he surpassed them in an instinctive sense
of what he was doing. He never represented his poetry as science,
nor countenanced the formation of a new sect that should nurse
the sense of a private and mysterious illumination, and relight
the fagots of passion and prejudice. He never tried to seek out
and defend the universal implications of his ideas, and never
wrote the book he had once planned on the law of compensation,
foreseeing, we may well believe, the sophistries in which he
would have been directly involved. He fortunately preferred a
fresh statement on a fresh subject. A suggestion once given, the
spirit once aroused to speculation, a glimpse once gained of some
ideal harmony, he chose to descend again to common sense and
to touch the earth for a moment before another flight. The faculty of idealisation was itself what he valued. Philosophy for him
was rather a moral energy flowering into sprightliness of
thought than a body of serious and defensible doctrines. In practising transcendental speculation only in this poetic and sporadic
fashion, Emerson retained its true value and avoided its greatest

danger. He secured the freedom and fertility of his thought and did not allow one conception of law or one hint of harmony to sterilise the mind and prevent the subsequent birth within it of other ideas, no less just and imposing than their predecessors. For we are not dealing at all in such a philosophy with matters of fact or with such verifiable truths as exclude their opposites. We are dealing only with imagination, with the art of conception, and with the various forms in which reflection, like a poet, may compose and recompose human experience.

A certain disquiet mingled, however, in the minds of Emerson's contemporaries with the admiration they felt for his purity and genius. They saw that he had forsaken the doctrines of the Church; and they were not sure whether he held quite unequivocally any doctrine whatever. We may not all of us share the concern for orthodoxy which usually caused this puzzled alarm: we may understand that it was not Emerson's vocation to be definite and dogmatic in religion any more than in philosophy. Yet that disquiet will not, even for us, wholly disappear. It is produced by a defect which naturally accompanies imagination in all but the greatest minds. I mean disorganisation. Emerson not only conceived things in new ways, but he seemed to think the new ways might cancel and supersede the old. His imagination was to invalidate the understanding. That inspiration which should come to fulfil seemed too often to come to destroy. If he was able so constantly to stimulate us to fresh thoughts, was it not because he demolished the labour of long ages of reflection? Was not the startling effect of much of his writing due to its contradiction to tradition and to common sense?

So long as he is a poet and in the enjoyment of his poetic license, we can blame this play of mind only by a misunderstanding. It is possible to think otherwise than as common sense thinks; there are other categories beside those of science. When we employ them we enlarge our lives. We add to the world of fact any number of worlds of the imagination in which human nature and the eternal relations of ideas may be nobly expressed. So far our imaginative fertility is only a benefit: it surrounds us with the congenial and necessary radiation of art and religion. It manifests our moral vitality in the bosom of Nature.

But sometimes imagination invades the sphere of understanding and seems to discredit its indispensable work. Common sense, we are allowed to infer, is a shallow affair: true insight changes all that. When so applied, poetic activity is not an unmixed good. It loosens our hold on fact and confuses our intelligence, so that we forget that intelligence has itself every prerogative of imagination, and has besides the sanction of practical validity. We are made to believe that since the understanding is something human and conditioned, something which might have been different, as the senses might have been different, and which we may yet, so to speak, get behind—therefore the understanding ought to be abandoned. We long for higher faculties, neglecting those we have, we yearn for intuition, closing our eyes upon experience. We become mystical.

Mysticism, as we have said, is the surrender of a category of thought because we divine its relativity. As every new category, however, must share this reproach, the mystic is obliged in the end to give them all up, the poetic and moral categories no less than the physical, so that the end of his purification is the atrophy of his whole nature, the emptying of his whole heart and mind to make room, as he thinks, for God. By attacking the authority of the understanding as the organon of knowledge, by substituting itself for it as the herald of a deeper truth, the imagination thus prepares its own destruction. For if the understanding is rejected because it cannot grasp the absolute, the imagination and all its works—art, dogma, worship—must presently be rejected for the same reason. Common sense and poetry must both go by the board, and conscience must follow after: for all these are human and relative. Mysticism will be satisfied only with the absolute, and as the absolute, by its very definition, is not representable by any specific faculty, it must be approached through the abandonment of all. The lights of life must be extinguished that the light of the absolute may shine, and the possession of everything in general must be secured by the surrender of everything in particular.

The same diffidence, however, the same constant renewal of sincerity which kept Emerson's flights of imagination near to experience, kept his mysticism also within bounds. A certain mystical tendency is pervasive with him, but there are only one or two subjects on which he dwells with enough constancy and

energy of attention to make his mystical treatment of them pro-
nounced. One of these is the question of the unity of all minds
in the single soul of the universe, which is the same in all creatures; another is the question of evil and of its evaporation in
the universal harmony of things. Both these ideas suggest themselves at certain turns in every man's experience, and might receive a rational formulation. But they are intricate subjects, ob-
scured by many emotional prejudices, so that the labour, impartiality, and precision which would be needed to elucidate
them are to be looked for in scholastic rather than in inspired
thinkers, and in Emerson least of all. Before these problems he is
alternately ingenuous and rhapsodical, and in both moods equally
helpless. Individuals no doubt exist, he says to himself. But, ah!
Napoleon is in every schoolboy. In every squatter in the western
prairies we shall find an owner—

> Of Cæsar's hand and Plato's brain,
> Of Lord Christ's heart, and Shakespeare's strain.

But how? we may ask. Potentially? Is it because any mind, were
it given the right body and the right experience, were it made
over, in a word, into another mind, would resemble that other
mind to the point of identity? Or is it that our souls are already
so largely similar that we are subject to many kindred promptings and share many ideals unrealisable in our particular circumstances? But then we should simply be saying that if what makes
men different were removed, men would be indistinguishable, or
that, in so far as they are now alike, they can understand one
another by summoning up their respective experiences in the
fancy. There would be no mysticism in that, but at the same time,
alas, no eloquence, no paradox, and, if we must say the word, no
nonsense.

On the question of evil, Emerson's position is of the same kind.
There is evil, of course, he tells us. Experience is sad. There is a
crack in everything that God has made. But, ah! the laws of the
universe are sacred and beneficent. Without them nothing good
could arise. All things, then, are in their right places and the universe is perfect above our querulous tears. Perfect? we may
ask. But perfect from what point of view, in reference to what
ideal? To its own? To that of a man who renouncing himself and

all naturally dear to him, ignoring the injustice, suffering, and impotence in the world, allows his will and his conscience to be hypnotised by the spectacle of a necessary evolution, and lulled into cruelty by the pomp and music of a tragic show? In that case the evil is not explained, it is forgotten; it is not cured, but condoned. We have surrendered the category of the better and the worse, the deepest foundation of life and reason; we have become mystics on the one subject on which, above all others, we ought to be men.

Two forces may be said to have carried Emerson in this mystical direction; one, that freedom of his imagination which we have already noted, and which kept him from the fear of self-contradiction; the other the habit of worship inherited from his clerical ancestors and enforced by his religious education. The spirit of conformity, the unction, the loyalty even unto death inspired by the religion of Jehovah, were dispositions acquired by too long a discipline and rooted in too many forms of speech, of thought, and of worship for a man like Emerson, who had felt their full force, ever to be able to lose them. The evolutions of his abstract opinions left that habit unchanged. Unless we keep this circumstance in mind, we shall not be able to understand the kind of elation and sacred joy, so characteristic of his eloquence, with which he propounds laws of Nature and aspects of experience which, viewed in themselves, afford but an equivocal support to moral enthusiasm. An optimism so persistent and unclouded as his will seem at variance with the description he himself gives of human life, a description coloured by a poetic idealism, but hardly by an optimistic bias.

We must remember, therefore, that this optimism is a pious tradition, originally justified by the belief in a personal God and in a providential government of affairs for the ultimate and positive good of the elect, and that the habit of worship survived in Emerson as an instinct after those positive beliefs had faded into a recognition of "spiritual laws." We must remember that Calvinism had known how to combine an awe-struck devotion to the Supreme Being with no very roseate picture of the destinies of mankind, and for more than two hundred years had been breeding in the stock from which Emerson came a willingness to be, as the phrase is, "damned for the glory of God."

What wonder, then, that when, for the former inexorable dispensation of Providence, Emerson substituted his general spiritual and natural laws, he should not have felt the spirit of worship fail within him? On the contrary, his thought moved in the presence of moral harmonies which seemed to him truer, more beautiful, and more beneficent than those of the old theology. An independent philosopher would not have seen in those harmonies an object of worship or a sufficient basis for optimism. But he was not an independent philosopher, in spite of his belief in independence. He inherited the problems and the preoccupations of the theology from which he started, being in this respect like the German idealists, who, with all their pretence of absolute metaphysics, were in reality only giving elusive and abstract forms to traditional theology. Emerson, too, was not primarily a philosopher, but a Puritan mystic with a poetic fancy and a gift for observation and epigram, and he saw in the laws of Nature, idealised by his imagination, only a more intelligible form of the divinity he had always recognised and adored. His was not a philosophy passing into a religion, but a religion expressing itself as a philosophy and veiled, as at its setting it descended the heavens, in various tints of poetry and science.

If we ask ourselves what was Emerson's relation to the scientific and religious movements of his time, and what place he may claim in the history of opinion, we must answer that he belonged very little to the past, very little to the present, and almost wholly to that abstract sphere into which mystical or philosophic aspiration has carried a few men in all ages. The religious tradition in which he was reared was that of Puritanism, but of a Puritanism which, retaining its moral intensity and metaphysical abstraction, had minimised its doctrinal expression and become Unitarian. Emerson was indeed the Psyche of Puritanism, "the latest-born and fairest vision far" of all that "faded hierarchy." A Puritan whose religion was all poetry, a poet whose only pleasure was thought, he showed in his life and personality the meagreness, the constraint, the frigid and conscious consecration which belonged to his clerical ancestors, while his inmost impersonal spirit ranged abroad over the fields of history and Nature, gathering what ideas it might, and singing its little snatches of inspired song.

The traditional element was thus rather an external and unessential contribution to Emerson's mind; he had the professional tinge, the decorum, the distinction of an old-fashioned divine; he had also the habit of writing sermons, and he had the national pride and hope of a religious people that felt itself providentially chosen to establish a free and godly commonwealth in a new world. For the rest, he separated himself from the ancient creed of the community with a sense rather of relief than of regret. A literal belief in Christian doctrines repelled him as unspiritual, as manifesting no understanding of the meaning which, as allegories, those doctrines might have to a philosophic and poetical spirit. Although as a clergyman he was at first in the habit of referring to the Bible and its lessons as to a supreme authority, he had no instinctive sympathy with the inspiration of either the Old or the New Testament; in Hafiz or Plutarch, in Plato or Shakespeare, he found more congenial stuff.

While he thus preferred to withdraw, without rancour and without contempt, from the ancient fellowship of the church, he assumed an attitude hardly less cool and deprecatory toward the enthusiasms of the new era. The national ideal of democracy and freedom had his entire sympathy; he allowed himself to be drawn into the movement against slavery; he took a curious and smiling interest in the discoveries of natural science and in the material progress of the age. But he could go no farther. His contemplative nature, his religious training, his dispersed reading, made him stand aside from the life of the world, even while he studied it with benevolent attention. His heart was fixed on eternal things, and he was in no sense a prophet for his age or country. He belonged by nature to that mystical company of devout souls that recognise no particular home and are dispersed throughout history, although not without intercommunication. He felt his affinity to the Hindoos and the Persians, to the Platonists and the Stoics. Like them he remains "a friend and aider of those who would live in the spirit." If not a star of the first magnitude, he is certainly a fixed star in the firmament of philosophy. Alone as yet among Americans, he may be said to have won a place there, if not by the originality of his thought, at least by the originality and beauty of the expression he gave to thoughts that are old and imperishable.

ᔔ Emerson the Poet*

Ladies and gentlemen:

The theme that draws us together this evening is a delicate one, and I confess I approach it with some trepidation. There is something about the soul, even in its toughest embodiments, which makes us pierce to its seat and sources with a certain dread, with a certain sense of possible profanation. The hand instinctively recoils from quick life and fears to touch the roots even of a weed or a cactus. And the poems I am required to speak of on this occasion are more like little roots and tendrils than like garden flowers intended to be sniffed at and plucked. The life within them is so unprotected and thinly veiled, so intimate, and so recent, that we may well fear that any close examination into them might degenerate into vivisection.

A poet must remain his own interpreter. That is what his genius and music are for. If he has not succeeded in delivering his message a critic, necessarily lacking the poet's first-hand experience and inspiration, can ill pretend to convey that message through cold reflections. Emerson himself never tires of warning us not to attempt pedantic estimates and reconstructions, for

> The passing moment is an edifice
> Which the Omnipotent cannot rebuild,

* An address delivered on May 22, 1903, at Harvard University during Emerson Memorial Week. The address is printed here for the first time in its entirety, by permission of the Columbia University Libraries.

and,

> Life is too short to waste
> In critic peep and cynic bark . . .
> . . . Mind thine own aim and
> God speed the mark.

Nevertheless, as no Emersonian maxim should be taken absolutely or pressed too hard, we may permit ourselves on this memorial occasion a look or two backwards, especially as it was a consequence of Emerson's spontaneous and meteoric habit of mind, that his expressions, in spite of the wide diffusion of what may be called their philosophy, seem already somewhat archaic and unseizable: archaic and unseizable particularly in the verses, which are at once so slight and so pregnant, so easy to deride if measured by priggish standards, and so hard to immerse again into that haze of wayward Puritanism and romantic spirituality in the midst of which they took shape.

The New England on which Emerson opened his eyes was a singular country. It manifested in an acute form something not yet quite extinct in America—the phenomenon of an old soul in a new body. The New England mind was highly sophisticated, wholly derivative, and dependent for its religious and literary habits on earlier English life, and through that earlier English life, on all the confused forces that had made Christendom, the Renaissance, and the Reformation. The Bible, read as a textbook of Calvinistic theology, the conventional school classics, with the soberer parts of English literature, made the culture of the time: and these elements were far from being regarded, as we might regard them today, as materials on which to draw at will in solving actual problems or in building further works: on the contrary they figured as eternal and immutable moulds of reason, and whatever intellectual life or passion there might be in the people was busy in rehearsing and reenacting those antique dramas which had once filled with their clamors so different and remote a stage. For in New England the land, the state, the social conditions were absolutely novel: the Indian wilderness still seemed to lie at people's back doors, the American government was but twenty years old, the war of 1812 was soon to accentuate that estrangement from the living spirit of the Old

World, which made the retention of its dead spirit all the more possible. Such estrangement, which had been at first among the Puritans an effect of horror at the world's iniquities, now became a matter of republican pride. If isolation brought any disadvantage it brought also a blessed relief. What else had the Pilgrims' heroism consisted in but in a great sacrifice for the sake of godliness and liberty? And what was more natural or consonant with the Lord's dealings, than that such heroism should be fruitful in all manner of good things? The inevitable simplicity of the new life was a part of its virtue, and its accidental isolation seemed a symbol of divine election and the harbinger of a new era of righteousness.

But no such pleasing reflections could remove the anomaly of an old soul in a young body, an anomaly much too violent to last. The dogmas which Calvinism had chosen for interpretation were the most sombre and disquieting in the Christian system, those which marked most clearly a broken life and a faith rising out of profound despair. But what profound despair or what broken life could exist in young America to give meaning and truth to those spectral traditions? People who looked and thought for themselves, people who yearned for that deeper sincerity which comes from shaking off verbal habits and making belief a direct expression of instinct and perception, challenged at last their ancestral dream, threw off its incubus, rubbed their eyes, as it were, in the morning light, and sprang into the world of nature.

In no man was this awakening more complete than in Emerson. No one greeted it with greater joy or recognized more quickly his inward affinity to nature rather than to the artificial moral world in which he had been reared. The scales dropped of themselves from his eyes and left his vision as pure and clear as if no sophistications had ever existed in the world. The instinct which took him at one leap into the bosom of reality, and brought him face to face with unbiassed experience, is the greatest evidence of his genius, or perhaps we should say, of his simplicity: for he shed the incrustations of time not by a long and mighty effort of reflection, not by a laborious sympathetic progress through all human illusions, but rather by a native immunity and repulsion on his part. Other people's troubles could not adhere to him; he remained, like a grain of sand, clean and whole in any environment. This simplicity clarified and disinfected the world for him as only the ripest wisdom could disinfect or clarify it for other men. How singular his privilege was in this respect, our own time may easily convince us, when we still find almost everybody entangled in all sorts of reticences and fears, trying to cover up nature's face, to disallow her laws, to supplement her gifts with contraband goods, or to turn her bodily upside-down by some metaphysical artifice. Emerson had a plentiful mysticism of his own, but it was spontaneous, fanciful, ingenuous; when a spirit has wings it needs no acrobatic system of philosophy. Natural activities and natural sentiments may have found some checks in Emerson's character and training, but nature herself wore no veils to his mind. His emancipation from tradition, in so far as the march of things is concerned, was entire. He retained no weakness for a sacred geography which is not exactly geography, or a sacred history which is not quite history. His world was the world of scientific observation and practical life; Spinoza's universe could hardly be more natural, nor Shakespeare's more unfalsified, nor Goethe's more liberal and large. What such men achieved by intellectual power, or just imagination, or acquaintance with life, Emerson attained by his innate and happy simplicity. He had but to open his eyes, and although what happened to offer itself to his glance may have lacked richness and volume and although his observation itself may have been desultory, yet he was a born master at looking deep and at looking straight.

But it is time we should ask ourselves what these direct and searching glances were fixed upon. Sometimes they rested on human life but more often and far more lovingly on Nature: for even when human life was the theme it was generally conceived as one more effluence and illustration of universal laws, and seldom from the point of view of positive human interests. The love of nature was Emerson's strongest passion: no other influence swayed him so often, stirred him so deeply, or made him so truly a poet. If he regarded any moral or political problem with sympathetic or steady attention, he immediately stated it in terms of some natural analogy and escaped its importunity and finality by imagining what nature, in such a conflict, would pass to next. What seems mysticism in his moral philosophy and baffles the reader who is looking for a moral solution, is nothing but this rooted habit of inattention to what is not natural law, natural progression, natural metamorphosis. Interest and delight in that spectacle overmasters every other feeling, so lovingly and sympathetically has its detail been observed, so grandly have its wider harmonies been imagined.

All Emerson's compositions are woven of mixed threads, and resemble the universe of Anaxagoras where everything was bound to contain every kind of substance. But perhaps the purest gold to be gleaned from all these quarries is what, borrowing a title from one of the poems, we may call collectively *Woodnotes*, verses inspired by blithe, attentive, rapturous perception of all the shifts and postures of natural things—plants, birds, skies, waters—by sympathetic immersion in those processes, by refreshment drawn from such vicarious elemental living. These Woodnotes are full of tenderness, humor, a pleasing mythical fancy, perhaps a tendency to trace rather fantastic analogies and to proclaim identity in things tolerably remote from one another; but we are free for the time being from mystical negations and artificial enigmas. The dominant note of exultation is not the forced optimism of a doctrinaire: it is a natural joy in joy, in variety, in harmony, in the affinities and wide suggestions of things; the observation is observation of fact, of movement, of things describable and characteristic. Sometimes this sympathy with nature actually breaks through the film of New England prudery and we read that

> Good fellow Puck and goblins
> Know more than any book. . . .
> The South-winds are quick witted,
> The schools are sad and slow.
> The masters quite omitted
> The lore we care to know.

It is useless to describe what is itself description, and quotation would carry us too far if we were to repeat all these Woodnotes or echo every phase of nature which they celebrate. One remark, however, before leaving this most delightful part of our subject. Emerson's love of nature was honest and unreserved: it was founded on nature's irresistible charm, grace, power, in-

finity. It was sincere adoration, self-surrendering devotion; it
was not qualified or taken back by any subsumption of nature
under human categories, as if after all she were nothing but
her children's instrument, illusion, or toy. "Dearest nature," as
he calls her, remained for him always a mother, a fountain not
only of inspiration but of life. The spiritual principle he discovered in her was her own spirit, which man, being a bubble in her
stream, might well breathe in for a moment and joyfully share:
but it was she that was the more deeply inspired. She was the
mistress and sibyl, he the pupil, the trembling interpreter of her
oracles. Firmly, even arrogantly, as Emerson could assert his
spiritual freedom in the face of men and human tradition, in
nature's presence he felt himself a child. His deepest wisdom
then seemed infused into him through devout contemplation,
through unreserved self-abandonment to her beauties, her laws,
her immensity. In nature's presence he had no transcendental
conceit. For this reason his poetry about nature, though fanciful
as such poetry may well be, remains always receptive, always
studied from life and free from sentimental impertinence. When
he idealizes most, he is still striving only to comprehend. If we
compare, for instance, his way of feeling the landscape with
Wordsworth's way, we shall see that he is less inclined to fall into
the pathetic fallacy. Emerson's transcendentalism, had he borrowed it from scholastic systems, might have given him a technical right to treat nature as a figment put together by man's
ingenuity for man's convenience; but he respected her too
much to impute to her so much respect for man; he saw her as
she really is and loved her in her indomitable and inhuman perfection. Not the least of his joys was the self-effacing one of
being able to conceive, and therefore to share, a life which creates,
animates, and destroys the human. He was charmed and comforted, quite without technical apparatus, by universal beauty.
He yielded himself insensibly and placidly to that plastic stress
which in breeding new forms out of his substance would never
breed anything alien to those principles of harmony and rhythm
which stand like sentinels at the gates of being and challenge
the passage into existence of anything contradicting itself or incongruous with its natural conditions. His best lyric flights express this honest and noble acceptance of destiny, this imagina-

tive delight in innumerable beauties which he should never see,
but which would be the heirs of those he had loved and lost in
their passage. So in the lines entitled Pan.

> O what are heroes, prophets, men,
> But pipes through which the breath of Pan doth blow
> A momentary music. Being's tide
> Swells hitherward, and myriads of forms
> Live, robed with beauty, painted by the Sun:
> Their dust, pervaded by the nerves of God,
> Throbs with an overmastering energy,
> Knowing and doing. Ebbs the tide, they lie
> White hollow shells upon the desert shore.
> But not the less the eternal wave rolls on
> To animate new millions, and exhale
> Races and planets, its enchanted foam.

In another place he represents the poet, troubled by premonitions of his own weakness and mortality, who says:

> Is there warrant that the waves
> Of thought in their mysterious caves
> Will heap in me their highest tide,
> In me therewith beatified?
> Unsure the ebb and flood of thought.
> The moon comes back, the spirit not.

And the spirit's reply:

> Brother, no decrepitude
> Chills the limbs of Time.
> On nature's wheels there is no rust
> Nor less on man's enchanted dust
> Beauty and Force alight.

And again, in "Woodnotes" proper:

> When the forest shall mislead me,
> When the night and morning lie,
> When sea and land refuse to feed me,
> 'Twill be time enough to die.
> Then will yet my Mother yield

> A pillow in her greenest field
> Nor the June flowers scorn to cover
> The clay of their departed lover.

But however beautiful and miraculous the summer woods might seem, or however fascinating those circles, laws, surfaces, and compensations of which the cosmos was full, there must be other elements in a poet's inspiration. All men of letters in the nineteenth century have been inclined to love and describe nature; but this somewhat novel theme has entered an imagination filled already with other matters, preoccupied, perhaps, with political or religious revolutions. A moral and human sub-stratum, a national and personal idiosyncrasy, has existed in every case and has furnished a background for the new vision of nature: and it makes a great difference in a poet whether behind the naturalist in him there lies, for instance, a theologian, a statesman, or an artist. In Emerson what lay behind the naturalist was in a measure a political thinker, a moralist interested in institutions and manners, a democrat and a Puritan; but chiefly what lay there was a mystic, a moralist athirst for some superhuman and absolute good. The effect of this situation upon his poetry is what remains for us to consider.

Nothing in all Emerson's writings is more eloquent and popular than some bits of his patriotic verse. There are not only the Concord and Boston hymns, but sparks of the same fire shoot out in other places: for Emerson could not have written so well upon occasion, I may almost say to order, if he had not been full already of the enthusiasm which that occasion demanded. Art or a merely sympathetic imagination never dictated a line to this Puritan bard, who if he was perfectly bland was also absolutely unyielding and self-directed. No forces affected him, save those which made him up. Freedom, in its various expressions, was his profoundest ideal, and if there was anything which he valued more than the power to push on to what might lie before, it was the power to escape what lay behind. A sense of potentiality and a sense of riddance are, as he might have said, the two poles of liberty. In America both poles were highly magnetic, for here, more than elsewhere, old things had been thrown off and new things were to be expected. Potentiality, cosmic liberty, nature perpetually transforming and recovering her energy, formed his loftiest theme; but the sense of riddance in escaping kings, churches, cities, and eventually self and even humanity was the nearer and if possible the livelier emotion.

The verses which he devoted to memories of the Revolutionary War and to the agitation against slavery, though brief, are the most thrilling and profound which those themes have yet inspired. Everybody knows of the "embattled farmers" who "fired the shot heard round the world." Perhaps less present to the younger generation are his stirring lines in which he denounced slavery and dreamt of the negro's future.

> Pay ransom to the owner
> And fill the bag to the brim.
> Who is the owner? The slave is owner
> And ever was. Pay him.

And while the master was thus bitterly challenged, the slave was idealized:

> He has avenues to God
> Hid from men of Northern brain,
> Far beholding, without cloud,
> What these with slowest steps attain.
> If once the generous chief arrive
> To lead him, willing to be led,
> For freedom he will strike and strive
> And drain his heart till he be dead.

We need not ask whether verses like these have a place in literature: it is certain that they have a place in American history and put vividly before us the passions of a momentous hour.

But Emerson's love of freedom did not need crying abuses to kindle it to flame: it was a speculative love that attached him to whatever was simple, untrammeled, idyllic in any time or sphere. As he detested what he called the "fopperies of the town," so he detested the fopperies of history: Europe made him only a better American. In the verses entitled "The Park" we see how his "conscience masterful," his "sentiment divine against the being of a line" found those he calls "the prosperous and beautiful" somehow unnatural and distinctly ungodly, as if they were too much exempt from the universal purifying flux; and he prized his titmouse's "wiry chant/ O'er all that mass or minster vaunt." Jehovah too, he was sure, had of late become a leveller, for he said

> I am tired of kings.
> I suffer them no more. . . .
> I will have never a noble,
> No lineage counted great.
> Fishers and choppers and ploughmen
> Shall constitute a state.
> So cut down the trees in the forest
> And build me a wooden house.

Wooden houses, or better still log cabins, were indeed Emerson's sacred architecture; and when he wished to excuse himself for not loving very much even the Boston of his day he expressed his aversion by referring to it generically as "the marble town." A town, even if largely in wood, had not only the disadvantage of not being the country, but also that of being something arrested and immovable. Its potentiality seemed to be exhausted and the mind dwelling there was not free. Freedom was thus associated with space rather than with action. To one whose life flowed so predominantly from within to have room was already to have enough opportunity, and he was more afraid of hindrance than of starvation.

The same general temper appears in all he says about love and friendship. A too great refinement and dread of intrusion seems to attenuate these feelings, yet it is only excessive sensitiveness that produces this appearance of frigidity. "Hast thou," he says in "Forbearance"

> Hast thou loved so well a high behavior
> In man or maid that thou from speech refrainedst
> Nobility more nobly to repay?
> O be my friend and teach me to be thine!

And again:

> I have no brothers and no peers
> And the dearest interferes.

> When I would spend a lonely day
> Sun and moon are in the way.

We are here at the frontiers of that province in Emerson's kingdom into which it is hardest to penetrate—the forbidden Thibet, with its Grand Lama, behind his Himalayas. When our philosopher substituted nature for the theological cosmos, and nature's magic providence for God's, he did not in the least feel that he had surrendered anything of spiritual value, anything that altered his personal religion or even his Christianity. This may seem an irrational persistence of habitual sentiments after the objects that aroused them have disappeared. But religion is not so simple a matter. It is not at bottom an account of credible facts producing, when duly reported, saving emotions in the soul. It is rather an expression of the soul's native emotions in symbols mistaken for facts, or in facts chosen for symbols. At least this is what religion was for Emerson, as for everybody who envisages things in the transcendental manner and reduces everything to its fighting weight in his own mental arena. Hence if one set of symbols is substituted for another, nothing is changed in the thing signified, in the inner life of the soul, except the vehicle of expression. All the unction and sanctity of religion may then survive its dogmas; for the meaning they once had for life is now transferred to other ideas. All ideas, we presently perceive, are fluid; and we are on the point of venturing the assertion that it matters very little what things exist or how long they endure, since the only reality is the perpetual motion that creates, transforms and exchanges them. We have seen how this perpetual motion, observable in nature, fascinated Emerson; but while the poet could justify and communicate his delight by dwelling on the forms and beauties of things in transition, the metaphysician would fain sink deeper. In his desperate attempt to seize upon the real and permanent he would fain grasp and hold fast the disembodied principle of change itself. This idea, loaded with religious passion, is one Emerson often attempted to put in verse.

> I tire of shams, I rush to be.
> I pass with yonder comet free,
> Pass with the comet into space.

"The lords of life, the lords of life, I saw them pass" says new-born man, awed by his gigantic visions: and nature, "dearest nature, strong and kind," consoles him:

> Darling, never mind.
> Tomorrow they will wear another face.
> The founder thou. These are thy race.

Again, at the end of "Threnody":

> Revere thy Maker: fetch thine eye
> Up to his style and manners of the sky.
> Not of adamant and gold
> Built he heaven stark and cold.
> No, but a nest of bending reeds
> Flowering grass and scented weeds.
> Built of tears and sacred flames
> And virtue reaching to its aims;
> Built of furtherance and pursuing,
> Not of spent deeds but of doing.
> Silent rushes the swift Lord
> Through ruined systems still restored.
> . . . .
> House and tenant go to ground,
> Lost in God, in Godhead found.

And in the well-known "Brahma":

> If the red slayer thinks he slays
> Or if the slain think he is slain,
> They know not well the subtle ways
> I keep and pass and turn again.
>
> Far and forgot to me is near
> Shadow and sunlight are the same
> The vanished gods to me appear
> And one to me are shame and fame.

The images, in so far as images exist here, are not different from those of *Woodnotes:* all is still a description of the natural world and its revolutions. Only now our emotion is differently directed. There we dwelt on particular things: we heard that

> A woodland walk,
> A quest of river-grapes, a mocking thrush,
> A wild-rose or rock-loving columbine,
> Salve all my wounds.

Now, instead of these definite images, we are asked to

> melt matter into dreams,
> Panoramas which I saw,
> And whatever glows or seems,
> Into substance, into Law.

This is no place in which to discuss the question whether substance or law are anything, or are worth anything, apart from
the things they contain or connect; but this we may observe
without launching into metaphysics: that pure substance and
mere law are not digestible by the Muse. *Woodnotes* she can
mimic; she cannot sing metaphysical abstractions. So that in these
passages what attracts us is still that very pageantry from which
we are to be weaned away. The beauty of the lines turns devil's
advocate and works against their moral. The attempt to clothe
such reflections in verse is intelligible: for these ideas impassion
a mystic more than does nature herself, and religious tradition
sanctions the impulse to approach such themes with elaborate eloquence, with symbolism, with music. Compositions so
prompted are religious exercises; and if something baffling and
uncouth about them offends the merely literary critic, he should
remember that the psalmist is no poet by trade, and cannot be
concerned with imaginative demands or artistic effects. The
beauties found in his works, however great, are bound to be sporadic; they come by inspiration and cannot be counted upon. "I
am not wiser for my age," he says, "Nor skilful by my grief."
He is the voice of a spirit which, since it has eternity to speak in
and auditors for all time, is in no haste to finish and cares nothing
whether it is quite understood by a particular generation. We
must not look for an artist where none wishes to exist.

Indeed to understand the situation we have but to question
Emerson about art, which is much as if we questioned the Virgin
Mary about mathematics. The answer will be worth recording:
it will show a certain alien sagacity and irrelevant pithiness,

but hardly any real acquaintance with the subject. He will ask us in turn:

> Can rules or tutors educate
> The semi-god whom we await?

Or he will say:

> Nature, hating art and pains,
> Baulks and baffles plotting brains.
> Casualty and Surprise
> Are the apples of her eyes.

Or he will tell us how the sea praises the cliffs, saying:

> Was ever building like my terraces?
> Lo! here is Rome and Nineveh and Thebes
> Karnak and pyramid.

Or he will recite the "Maiden-speech of the Aeolian Harp."

> Soft and softlier hold me, friends:
> Thanks if your genial care
> Unbind and give me to the air.
> Keep your lips or finger-tips
> For flute or spinnets dancing chips:
> I await a tenderer touch.
> I ask more and not so much.
> Give me to the atmosphere.

This impulse to elude art is no accident, in that our philosopher has had no artistic experience: the aversion is constitutional. Art is essentially artful and has a learnable technique; it is a docile and cumulative instinct, and in Emerson there was nothing cumulative and nothing docile. To teach the mind to see and feel seemed to him as unnatural as to give singing-lessons to a bird. The spirit was immortal and incorrigibly young. Its life consisted in quitting old habitations for new ones, carrying from one to another not discipline, nor sad experience, but only its own winged self, spirit pure and simple, spirit as inexhaustible as it was oblivious. Ingenuity was to be spontaneous and irresponsible: for every life had, after all, infinite wisdom in reserve, and the attempt to carry experience over from a wise man to fools would be like

laboriously conveying water from the crests of waves to fill up
the sea-hollows. We must wait rather for the winds to pass, and
the impulse to rise from the depths. Otherwise our art could not
be inspiration but artifice. So that art, too, would have to say at
last:

> I tire of shams, I rush to be.
> I pass with yonder comet free,
> Pass with the comet into space.
> Give me to the atmosphere.

If now we try to bring to a focus this desultory survey, what
shall we see in Emerson's poetic achievement? Briefly this: his
verses put together in a more pungent and concentrated form his
guiding ideas. They are filled with high thought, enthusiasm,
terseness; they contain snatches of lyric beauty. Their total burden is not distinguishable from that of the author's essays. This
burden is repeated with many variations and transpositions, and
the secret of understanding it consists in seeing that its changing
expressions are complementary and not mutually exclusive.
What exists in nature infinitely deployed exists potentially at
every moment in each of her parts; so that these parts, finding
the whole latent in themselves and their own soul latent in every
other thing, are able to understand one another and the whole
world, in proportion as they advance in self-knowledge.

The poems render this philosophy, as is natural, in its most
picturable form. They proclaim the divinity of nature, her
kinship with man, and her immortal fecundity in all things which
the human spirit might recognize to be beautiful and good if
keyed to heroism and rapt in contemplation. Undoubtedly the
beauty they celebrate involves cruelty, and the optimism they
preach demands abnegation. We may even add that such a continual hymn to nature's fluid harmonies allows us to forget altogether that laborious progress, that architecture of reason and art,
which is after all nature's masterpiece and which alone enables us
to appreciate her other works. For that man must have a long
civilization behind him who has learned to love nature for her
own sake.

But when allowance is made for such partialities as no philosopher and no prophet was ever free from, what more sacred and

delightful fountain of truth can we find anywhere than that which bubbles in this spirit? In an age that is putting off its traditional faiths and assuming instead innumerable material burdens, who can be more welcome than a thinker to whom all the sanctions of faith are inseparable from reason and all the forms of matter instinct with beauty and mind? Such a guide points in the direction of hope, he leads in the way of ultimate benefit. For as we sprang from earth and yet found that we were spirits, so by a further conquest and dominion over matter, both in thought and in action, we may enlarge that grandeur to which our dust is allied. We need but to dominate our follies and make ourselves at home in our own house. And who will say that this is impossible?

> When *reason* whispers low, Thou must,
> The *heart* replies: I can.

❧ Walt Whitman: A Dialogue*

McStout: Coming?

Van Tender: What, is it time?

McStout: Fifteen minutes before the game begins. We might take a stroll. It is such splendid weather!

Van Tender: Yes, and this is the best place to enjoy it. The warm wind blows in over you, and you can almost fancy how the trees feel when they thaw, and the sap begins to run, and the buds throb till they burst, and every leaf breathes and trembles. The plants don't have to move from their places to feel that it's spring. Why should we? You know my motto:

> Better than to stand to sit, better than to sit to lie,
> Better than to dream to sleep, better than to sleep to die.

But you can't expect to attain the highest good at one bound from the depths of Philistia. You can't do better for the present than to come in and stretch your energetic self on the other half of the window seat. Isn't it delicious? What better apology for idlers? Here you can breathe the air and look at the fresh grass, while you read a poet and cut a lecture. He tells you how in another country, perhaps, he felt what you are feeling now, as he watched the spring of another year. That is the best part of the pleasure, to know that it's human, and that all men have had it in common, from Adam down.

* Printed in *The Harvard Monthly*, X, No. 3 (May, 1890), 85-92.

McStout: And who is your poet now? Swinburne?

Van Tender: Oh, no.

McStout: Keats?

Van Tender: No; it's Walt Whitman. There is a time for everything, you know.

McStout: If, like you, one does nothing. No wonder you like Walt Whitman now and then for a change. You must be so tired of poetry.

Van Tender: Isn't this poetry? What is poetry?

McStout: A matter of words—more of words than matter. But if Walt Whitman is poetry, it isn't on account of the words. You don't pretend he can write English?

Van Tender: Not according to the English department. But that is a local standard. Could Homer pass an examination in Goodwin's moods and tenses? And doesn't he say Σμινθεῦ, which is a ἅπαξ λεγόμενον?

McStout: I dare say Homer talked as it was the fashion to talk in his day. And when English becomes a dead language and nothing survives but the *Leaves of Grass*, Whitman's style will be above criticism. But now English has the misfortune of being in use. A man can't make it to suit his fancy, and if he won't trouble himself to write the language of his fellows he can't expect them to learn his. How can you endure a man who has neither the accent of Christians, nor the style of a Christian, pagan, nor man?

Van Tender: Precisely for that reason: he produces a new effect, he gives you a new sensation. If you will show me a well-written book that contains the same emotion, I agree to bind the leaves of grass into bundles and cast them into the furnace. If only a man could become an artist in his words, and yet retain the innocence of his feelings! But to learn a method of expression is to become insensible to all it can't express. The schools don't teach us to paint what we see, but to see what others have painted.

McStout: I've heard of an old master who used to say to his pupils, "Copy if you want to be copied." When people are fascinated by the extravagant they show they haven't experience and training enough to appreciate what is sane and solid. Would you make no distinction between the normal and human and the eccentric and perverse? You toss sense and grammar to the Philistines, who ought to be correct since they can't be original. But your geniuses, you think, mustn't submit to standards; they create standards. If they didn't seem ridiculous to the vulgar, would they be truly sublime? You may say that if you like, but if originality is genius there are more great men at Somerville than at Cambridge. You can't get over the difference between sense and nonsense, between beauty and caprice. Any one can produce a new effect when fools are impressed by his blunders. You may like to hear Whitman's "barbaric yawp over the roofs of the world," but you must confess it is a whim of yours, and that a yawp is one thing and a poem another.

Van Tender: Certainly, I admit that a barbarism is an annoyance. When I come upon one it gives me a little shock, and I wish for the moment that it wasn't there. But there are models of English enough. I don't read Whitman for his verbal graces, although he has them, after his own fashion. If you wrote me a letter it might not be a model of style either, yet I should read it with interest if it told me what I wanted to hear. And Whitman does that. He hasn't the merits of Keats or of Shakspere, but he has merits of his own. His verses bring a message theirs couldn't bring, so I read theirs for their style and his for his inspiration. It is the voice of nature crying in the wilderness of convention.

McStout: I wish you could tell me what you mean by that. The only novelty I can see in him is that he mentions all sorts of things and says nothing about them. If you like pantheism and indecency, why aren't you satisfied with French novels and German philosophy? These are the same things in their genuine form.

Van Tender: It's not a theory or a description of things I get from Whitman. It's an attitude, a faculty of appreciation. You may laugh at his catalogues of objects, at his enumeration of places. But the hurrying of these images through the mind gives me a sense of space, of a multiplicity of things spread endlessly around me. I become aware of the life of millions of men, of great stretches of marsh, desert, and ocean. Have you never thought of the poetry of the planet? Fancy this little ball spinning along so fast, and yet so little in a hurry. Imagine the film of blue-gray water and the flat patches of land, now green, now brown, and dim clouds creeping over all. And near the ocean, here and there, conceive the troops of men and animals darkening the earth like so many ants. And think how little the murmur of one thousand jargons ruffles the air, and how the praises of each god are drowned in the vaults of his temple!

McStout: But all that is very different from Walt Whitman. Astronomy may have its impressive side, and even geography, when you connect it with the fortunes of mankind. Science is interesting, and if you can manage to make poetry out of it we shall have the first poetry in the world not resting on illusion. It seems to me that the illusion is what is poetic, and the fact is so only when in fancy we assimilate it to the fiction. The migrations of men from one land to another, for instance, are important events, and you may cast the glamour of poetry over them for a moment by dramatizing them. You may call the Strait of Magellan a Hellespont and himself a Jason. You may say the whole world is a Troad and the history of civilization a war of heroes. But if you mention the heroes, and their real qualities, where is the poetry? And if you reverse the process and try to explain the fables as history symbolized, or what not, you degrade the ideal and distort the facts. The reason why Walt Whitman is ridiculous is that he talks of real objects as if they could enter into poetry at all. It isn't art to point to objects, nor poetry to turn out "chants of Ohio, Indiana, Illinois, Wisconsin, Iowa, and Minnesota." Poetry deals with sensuous attractions, found nowhere on the map. To see them you must have a passport into fairy land.

Van Tender: Ah, you are caught at last! You have defined poetry. Now I wouldn't for a moment defend metaphysical confusions. The trouble with the German sort of criticism is that it isn't satisfied with the fact, but goes in search of a theory, as if a theory could be anything real and ultimate, or more than the flight of the soul from perception to perception, from emotion to emotion, on which alone she can alight to find rest and truth.

> Grau, theurer Freund, ist alle Theorie,
> Und grun des Lebens goldner Baum.

But what makes you think the essence poetry distils can't be extracted from every object? Why should one thing leave its type in the world of ideas, and not another! Trust me, beauty is everywhere, if we only had the genius to see it. If a man has the ability to make us feel the fitness, the necessity, the beauty of common things, he is a poet of the highest type. If some objects seem to you poetic rather than others, if Venice can be apostrophised and Oshkosh is unmentionable, it's because habit makes it easier to idealize them. This beauty has been pointed out so often that we know it by heart. But what merit is it to repeat the old tricks, and hum the old tunes? You add nothing to the beauty of the world. You see no new vision. You are the author of nothing, but merely an apprentice in the poetic guild, a little poet sucking the honey with which great poets have sweetened words. You are inspired by tradition and judged by convention. Yet this very convention must have been inspiration at first. The real objects about a man must have impressed him and he must have found words fit to communicate his impression. These words in that way became poetic, and afterwards any man who used them was an artist.

McStout: And you think literary tradition wholly arbitrary? You think it a mere accident that all hearts were touched by one man's words, and that all generations adopted his words and imitated his methods? Why was one poet's inspiration turned into a convention rather than another's? Evidently because he discovered and selected the truly interesting aspects of life, and dwelt upon those things which of themselves are beautiful. Don't you know how every age fancies it has a poet of original genius, that afterwards turns out to have been nothing but a fashionable mountebank? He had some trick that appealed to a particular mood or passion of the time, and his success in drawing attention for the moment is mistaken for a sign of greatness. That happens to Walt Whitman. The times are favorable to his vague pantheism, his formlessness, his confusion of values, his substitution of emotion for thought, his trust in impulse rather than in experience. Because we are too ignorant or too wilful to see the distinctions of things and of persons, we decree that there are no distinctions, and proceed to remodel literature and society upon that principle.

Van Tender: If the distinctions are real, there is no danger of their being destroyed. Things have different values, as one star differs from another star in brightness. All I insist on is that in all you can see light, if your eyes are open. Whitman would teach you, if you would only read him, to see in things their intrinsic nature and life, rather than the utility they may have for one another. That is his great merit, his sublime justice. It is a kind of profound piety that recognizes the life of everything in nature, and spares it, and worships its intrinsic worth. There is something brutal and fatuous in the habit we commonly have of passing the parts of nature in review and pronouncing them good or bad according to the effect they have on our lives. Aren't they as real as ourselves? In practical life we have to override them, for if we waited for justice and the ultimate good to direct what we should do, we should die before we had done anything. But it's the privilege of contemplation to be just. Listen to what Whitman says here:

I do not call the tortoise unworthy because she is not something
    else,
And the jay in the woods never studied the gamut, yet trills pretty
    well to me,
And the look of the bay mare shames silliness out of me.

McStout: This justice of yours may be sublime, but isn't it a trifle dangerous? By admiring the beasts so much we may come to resemble them,—or perhaps the resemblance is the cause of the admiration. You may say it is brutal to make ourselves a standard for other creatures; yet a human standard is better than none at all, and can we have any other? But Walt Whitman, I understand, would think it a great improvement if men imitated the animals more than they do.

Van Tender: Undoubtedly, in some respects. Here he explains it perfectly:

I think I could turn and live with animals, they are so placid and
    self-contained,
I stand and look at them long and long.
They do not sweat and whine about their condition,
They do not lie awake in the dark and weep for their sins,
They do not make me sick discussing their duty to God,
Not one is dissatisfied, not one is demented with the mania of
    owning things,
Not one is respectable or unhappy over the whole earth.

McStout: And not one writes bad prose or worse poetry, not one is untrue to his instincts as all this talk is untrue to the better instincts of man.

Van Tender: I knew it would come at last: Walt Whitman is immoral!

McStout: It isn't immoral to call a spade a spade, but it is immoral to treat life as a masquerade, as a magic pantomime in which acts have no consequences and happiness and misery don't exist.

Van Tender: Ah, but Whitman is nothing if not a spectator, a cosmic poet to whom the whole world is a play. And good and evil, although not equally pleasant to experience, are equally interesting to look at. Is it wrong to enjoy our misery when its distance from us makes contemplation of it possible? How else can the gods have been happy? To refuse us this pleasure is to deprive us of a consolation without preventing our suffering. Or do you think the knowledge of what life is would make us unfit to live? Should we be really more wicked if the sun were not a Puritan and dared to look on the world through the twenty-four hours?

McStout: Perhaps not, but the trouble with your contemplation and impartiality is that it unnerves a man and makes him incapable of indignation or enthusiasm. He goes into raptures over everything, and accomplishes nothing. The world is so heavenly to him that he finds nothing to do in it.

Van Tender: Except play his harp and wear his crown. Is it nothing to perceive the beauty of the world, and help other men to perceive it? I don't mean simply the pleasure of art itself. I mean the widening of your sympathies, your reconciliation with nature. What better thing is there for a man than to remember now and then that the stars are laughing at him, to renounce his allegiance to his own preferences and passions and by understanding to enter into those of other men? We can't play at life without getting some knocks and bruises, and without running some chance of defeat. But our best moments are the breathing spells when we survey the field and see what a glorious game it all is.

McStout: I'm glad we may do that, especially as the other game is over.

Van Tender: What! is it possible we have been talking so long?

McStout: There are the men coming back. We've won, though. You can tell by their faces.

Van Tender: So you see we weren't really needed. For all our philosophy, the world wags on.

❧ The Poetry of Barbarism II: Walt Whitman*

The works of Walt Whitman offer an extreme illustration of this phase of genius,† both by their form and by their substance. It was the singularity of his literary form—the challenge it threw to the conventions of verse and of language—that first gave Whitman notoriety: but this notoriety has become fame, because those incapacities and solecisms which glare at us from his pages are only the obverse of a profound inspiration and of a genuine courage. Even the idiosyncrasies of his style have a side which is not mere perversity or affectation; the order of his words, the procession of his images, reproduce the method of a rich, spontaneous, absolutely lazy fancy. In most poets such a natural order is modified by various governing motives—the thought, the metrical form, the echo of other poems in the memory. By Walt Whitman these conventional influences are resolutely banished. We find the swarms of men and objects rendered as they might strike the retina in a sort of waking dream. It is the most sincere possible confession of the lowest—I mean the most primitive—type of perception. All ancient poets are sophisticated in comparison and give proof of longer intellectual and moral training. Walt Whitman has gone back to the innocent style of Adam, when

---

* From Chapter VII of *Interpretations of Poetry and Religion.*
† Santayana had characterized the genius of "barbarism" as that of impassioned youth, rebellious to tradition and all convention, and in its exuberance careless of life's purposes or form.—R. C. L.

the animals filed before him one by one and he called each of them by its name.

In fact, the influences to which Walt Whitman was subject were as favourable as possible to the imaginary experiment of beginning the world over again. Liberalism and transcendentalism both harboured some illusions on that score; and they were in the air which our poet breathed. Moreover he breathed this air in America, where the newness of the material environment made it easier to ignore the fatal antiquity of human nature. When he afterward became aware that there was or had been a world with a history, he studied that world with curiosity and spoke of it not without a certain shrewdness. But he still regarded it as a foreign world and imagined, as not a few Americans have done, that his own world was a fresh creation, not amenable to the same laws as the old. The difference in the conditions blinded him, in his merely sensuous apprehension, to the identity of the principles.

His parents were farmers in central Long Island and his early years were spent in that district. The family seems to have been not too prosperous and somewhat nomadic; Whitman himself drifted through boyhood without much guidance. We find him now at school, now helping the labourers at the farms, now wandering along the beaches of Long Island, finally at Brooklyn working in an apparently desultory way as a printer and sometimes as a writer for a local newspaper. He must have read or heard something, at this early period, of the English classics; his style often betrays the deep effect made upon him by the grandiloquence of the Bible, of Shakespeare, and of Milton. But his chief interest, if we may trust his account, was already in his own sensations. The aspects of Nature, the forms and habits of animals, the sights of cities, the movement and talk of common people, were his constant delight. His mind was flooded with these images, keenly felt and afterward to be vividly rendered with bold strokes of realism and imagination.

Many poets have had this faculty to seize the elementary aspects of things, but none has had it so exclusively; with Whitman the surface is absolutely all and the underlying structure is without interest and almost without existence. He had had no education and his natural delight in imbibing sensations had not been trained to the uses of practical or theoretical intelligence. He basked in the sunshine of perception and wallowed in the stream of his own sensibility, as later at Camden in the shallows of his favourite brook. Even during the civil war, when he heard the drum-taps so clearly, he could only gaze at the picturesque and terrible aspects of the struggle, and linger among the wounded day after day with a canine devotion; he could not be aroused either to clear thought or to positive action. So also in his poems; a multiplicity of images pass before him and he yields himself to each in turn with absolute passivity. The world has no inside; it is a phantasmagoria of continuous visions, vivid, impressive, but monotonous and hard to distinguish in memory, like the waves of the sea or the decorations of some barbarous temple, sublime only by the infinite aggregation of parts.

This abundance of detail without organisation, this wealth of perception without intelligence and of imagination without taste, makes the singularity of Whitman's genius. Full of sympathy and receptivity, with a wonderful gift of graphic characterisation and an occasional rare grandeur of diction, he fills us with a sense of the individuality and the universality of what he describes—it is a drop in itself yet a drop in the ocean. The absence of any principle of selection or of a sustained style enables him to render aspects of things and of emotion which would have eluded a trained writer. He is, therefore, interesting even where he is grotesque or perverse. He has accomplished, by the sacrifice of almost every other good quality, something never so well done before. He has approached common life without bringing in his mind any higher standard by which to criticise it; he has seen it, not in contrast with an ideal, but as the expression of forces more indeterminate and elementary than itself; and the vulgar, in this cosmic setting, has appeared to him sublime.

There is clearly some analogy between a mass of images without structure and the notion of an absolute democracy. Whitman, inclined by his genius and habits to see life without relief or organisation, believed that his inclination in this respect corresponded with the spirit of his age and country, and that Nature and society, at least in the United States, were constituted after the fashion of his own mind. Being the poet of the average man, he wished all men to be specimens of that average, and being the poet of a fluid Nature, he believed that Nature was or should be a formless flux. This personal bias of Whitman's was further encouraged by the actual absence of distinction in his immediate environment. Surrounded by ugly things and common people, he felt himself happy, ecstatic, overflowing with a kind of patriarchal love. He accordingly came to think that there was a spirit of the New World which he embodied, and which was in complete opposition to that of the Old, and that a literature upon novel principles was needed to express and strengthen this American spirit.

Democracy was not to be merely a constitutional device for the better government of given nations, not merely a movement for the material improvement of the lot of the poorer classes. It was to be a social and a moral democracy and to involve an actual equality among all men. Whatever kept them apart and made it impossible for them to be messmates together was to be discarded. The literature of democracy was to ignore all extraordinary gifts of genius or virtue, all distinction drawn even from great passions or romantic adventures. In Whitman's works, in which this new literature is foreshadowed, there is accordingly not a single character nor a single story. His only hero is Myself, the "single separate person," endowed with the primary impulses, with health, and with sensitiveness to the elementary aspects of Nature. The perfect man of the future, the prolific begetter of other perfect men, is to work with his hands, chanting the poems of some future Walt, some ideally democratic bard. Women are to have as nearly as possible the same character as men: the emphasis is to pass from family life and local ties to the friendship of comrades and the general brotherhood of man. Men are to be vigorous, comfortable, sentimental, and irresponsible.

This dream is, of course, unrealised and unrealisable, in America as elsewhere. Undeniably there are in America many suggestions of such a society and such a national character. But the growing complexity and fixity of institutions necessarily tends to obscure these traits of a primitive and crude democracy. What Whitman seized upon as the promise of the future was in reality the survival of the past. He sings the song of pioneers, but it is in the nature of the pioneer that the greater his success the quicker must be his transformation into something different.

When Whitman made the initial and amorphous phase of society his ideal, he became the prophet of a lost cause. That cause was lost, not merely when wealth and intelligence began to take shape in the American Commonwealth, but it was lost at the very foundation of the world, when those laws of evolution were established which Whitman, like Rousseau, failed to understand. If we may trust Mr. Herbert Spencer, these laws involve a passage from the homogeneous to the heterogeneous, and a constant progress at once in differentiation and in organisation—all, in a word, that Whitman systematically deprecated or ignored. He is surely not the spokesman of the tendencies of his country, although he describes some aspects of its past and present condition: nor does he appeal to those whom he describes, but rather to the *dilettanti* he despises. He is regarded as representative chiefly by foreigners, who look for some grotesque expression of the genius of so young and prodigious a people.

Whitman, it is true, loved and comprehended men; but this love and comprehension had the same limits as his love and comprehension of Nature. He observed truly and responded to his observation with genuine and pervasive emotion. A great gregariousness, an innocent tolerance of moral weakness, a genuine admiration for bodily health and strength, made him bubble over with affection for the generic human creature. Incapable of an ideal passion, he was full of the milk of human kindness. Yet, for all his acquaintance with the ways and thoughts of the common man of his choice, he did not truly understand him. For to understand people is to go much deeper than they go themselves; to penetrate to their characters and disentangle their inmost ideals. Whitman's insight into man did not go beyond a sensuous sympathy; it consisted in a vicarious satisfaction in their pleasures, and an instinctive love of their persons. It never approached a scientific or imaginative knowledge of their hearts.

Therefore Whitman failed radically in his dearest ambition: he can never be a poet of the people. For the people, like the early races whose poetry was ideal, are natural believers in perfection. They have no doubts about the absolute desirability of wealth and learning and power, none about the worth of pure goodness and pure love. Their chosen poets, if they have any, will be always those who have known how to paint these ideals in lively even if in gaudy colours. Nothing is farther from the common people than the corrupt desire to be primitive. They instinctively look toward a more exalted life, which they imagine to be full of distinction and pleasure, and the idea of that brighter existence fills them with hope or with envy or with humble admiration.

If the people are ever won over to hostility to such ideals, it is only because they are cheated by demagogues who tell them that if all the flowers of civilisation were destroyed its fruits would become more abundant. A greater share of happiness, people think, would fall to their lot could they destroy everything beyond their own possible possessions. But they are made thus envious and ignoble only by a deception: what they really desire is an ideal good for themselves which they are told they may secure by depriving others of their preëminence. Their hope is always to enjoy perfect satisfaction themselves; and therefore a poet who loves the picturesque aspects of labour and vagrancy will hardly be the poet of the poor. He may have described their figure and occupation, in neither of which they are much interested; he will not have read their souls. They will prefer to him any sentimental story-teller, any sensational dramatist, any moralising poet; for they are hero-worshippers by temperament, and are too wise or too unfortunate to be much enamoured of themselves or of the conditions of their existence.

Fortunately, the political theory that makes Whitman's principle of literary prophecy and criticism does not always inspire his chants, nor is it presented, even in his prose works, quite bare and unadorned. In "Democratic Vistas" we find it clothed with something of the same poetic passion and lighted up with the same flashes of intuition which we admire in the poems. Even there the temperament is finer than the ideas and the poet wiser than the thinker. His ultimate appeal is really to something more primitive and general than any social aspirations, to something more elementary than an ideal of any kind. He speaks to those minds and to those moods in which sensuality is touched with mysticism. When the intellect is in abeyance, when we would "turn and live with the animals, they are so placid and self-contained," when we are weary of conscience and of ambition, and would yield ourselves for a while to the dream of sense, Walt Whitman is a welcome companion. The images he arouses in us,

fresh, full of light and health and of a kind of frankness and
beauty, are prized all the more at such a time because they are
not choice, but drawn perhaps from a hideous and sordid environment. For this circumstance makes them a better means of escape
from convention and from that fatigue and despair which lurk
not far beneath the surface of conventional life. In casting off
with self-assurance and a sense of fresh vitality the distinctions
of tradition and reason a man may feel, as he sinks back com-
fortably to a lower level of sense and instinct, that he is returning to Nature or escaping into the infinite. Mysticism makes us
proud and happy to renounce the work of intelligence, both in
thought and in life, and persuades us that we become divine by
remaining imperfectly human. Walt Whitman gives a new expression to this ancient and multiform tendency. He feels his own
cosmic justification and he would lend the sanction of his inspiration to all loafers and holiday-makers. He would be the congenial patron of farmers and factory hands in their crude pleasures and pieties, as Pan was the patron of the shepherds of Ar-
cadia: for he is sure that in spite of his hairiness and animality,
the gods will acknowledge him as one of themselves and smile
upon him from the serenity of Olympus.

ဲ Genteel American Poetry*

Poetry in America before the Civil War was an honest and adequate phenomenon. It spoke without affectation in a language and style which it could take for granted. It was candid in its tastes, even in that frank and gentle romanticism which attached it to Evangelines and Maud Mullers. It modulated in obvious ways the honorable conventions of the society in which it arose. It was a simple, sweet, humane, Protestant literature, grandmotherly in that sedate spectacled wonder with which it gazed at this terrible world and said how beautiful and how interesting it all was.

The accent of these poets was necessarily provincial, their outlook and reflectiveness were universal enough. Their poetry was indeed without sensuous beauty, splendor, passion, or volume, but so was the life it expressed. To be a really great poet an American at that time would have had to be a rebel.

It would have been an interesting thing if a thunderclap had suddenly broken that cloudless new-world haying-weather, and if a cry of exasperation had escaped some strong soul, surfeited by the emptiness and blandness of that prim little moral circle that thought it had overcome everything when in fact it had touched nothing. But to the genteel mind of America, before Walt Whitman and the Civil War, there was no self-respecting opposition. Of course, in that boundless field of convention,

* Printed in *The New Republic*, III, No. 30 (May 29, 1915), 94-95.

prosperity and mediocrity, a wild poppy might struggle up weedily here and there amid the serried corn. But the irregular genius had no chance. He felt sincerely ashamed of himself. He hid his independence, fled to the back woods or to Europe, and his sad case was hushed up as if it had been insanity (for insanity was hushed up too) and buried with a whisper under the vaguely terrible epitaph DISSIPATED. He probably died young; at any rate he never "did" anything. Whoever was unharnessed was lost.

In England at about the same time or earlier there was a marked division between the poets who were national, conventional and edifying and those who were disaffected. Wordsworth and Tennyson were more than matched by Byron, Shelley, and Swinburne. What occasioned this division in England was the very distinct and intolerant character of the national mind. You either identified yourself with it and expressed it sympathetically, or you broke away from it altogether, denounced it as narrow, stupid, and oppressive, and removed yourself offendedly to Greece or to Italy, to sing of lovely sensuality or celestial justice. A circumstance that made such romantic truancy all the easier for poets was the classical cast of their education. History, religion, and literary tradition, united with the ease of travel, carried the mind of every educated man continually beyond the limits of his country and its present ways. When one's moral possessions are so largely of foreign extraction, it requires no break with one's education, but merely a certain deepening and arrest in it, for things not national to seem the right environment for the soul. Exile accordingly did not sterilize the British poets: on the contrary, it seemed to liberate their genius and carry them back, across the Reformation, to an England as poetical if not so vigorous as that of Shakespeare.

Why did not disaffected Americans figure among these poets of the foreign, or rather of the human, ideal? The provocation to secede was certainly not less than in England; for if the country was not dominated by any church or aristocracy, it was dominated no less rigidly by democracy and commercialism. The land was indeed broader, and those who felt spiritually restive could without any great scandal make for the Wild West. This was certainly a resource for adventurous temperaments; but those whose impatience was moral, whose need was not so much for room as for something to fill it, could hardly be satisfied there; for morally all America even to-day is far more monotonous and uniform than England ever was. It was perhaps this very pressure of sameness which might have justified a poetic protest, that prevented it from arising.

The insurrection that actually took place was that of Walt Whitman, with the magnificent intention of being wholly direct, utterly sincere, and bothering about nothing that was not an experience of the soul and of the sense here in the motley foreground of life. It is notable that this powerful insurrection in favor of what is modern and national has made so little difference. Of course, nothing can compel people to read or to like an author that displeases them. Perhaps Walt Whitman made the mistake of supposing that what was vital in America was only what was absolutely modern and native, to the exclusion of anything that might have been transplanted to this country ready-made, like the Christian religion or the English language. He wished to be wholly impressionistic, wholly personal, wholly American, and the result was perhaps that he was simply mystical, missing the articulation of the great world, as well as the constructive mind of his own age and country. After all, the future often belongs to what has a past. Walt Whitman renounced old forms without achieving a new one, and in his thought also there was more detritus than invention.

At any rate, the genteel manner having become obsolete, and the manner of the great mystical tramp not having taken root, the poetic mind of America suffered a certain dispersion. It was solicited in turn by the seductive aesthetic school, by the influence of Browning, with his historico-dramatic obsessions, by symbolism, by the desperate determination to be expressive even with nothing to express, and by the resolve to write poetry which is not verse, so as to be sure of not writing verse which is not poetry. The spontaneous me has certainly been beaten in the first round by the artistic ego. Meantime the average human genteel person, with a heart, a morality, and a religion, who is after all in the majority, is left for the moment without any poetry to give him pleasure or to do him honor.

ໃ& A Marginal Note*

"*The chronic state of our literature is that of a youthful promise which is never redeemed.*" The fate of the Harvard poets in my time—Sanborn, McCulloch, Stickney, Lodge, Savage, Moody—was a tragic instance of this. If death had not cut them all off prematurely, would they have fulfilled their promise? I think that Moody, who actually accomplished most, would have succeeded notably, in that as a dramatist or as a poet with a mission, he would have secured general attention and respect; but even so, it might have been at the expense of his early poetic colour and disinterested passion for beauty. Stickney, who was the one I knew best, could never, I am sure, have prospered in the American air. Although he was a Harvard man, he had been well taught privately first, and afterwards for many years studied in Paris. When he returned to Harvard to teach Greek, he was heroically determined to take the thing seriously, and to share enthusiastically the life of his country; but the instrument was far too delicate and sensitive for the work; his imaginative (yet exact) learning, his spiritual ardour, his remote allegiances (as for instance to Indian philosophy) could not have survived the terrible inertia and the more terrible momentum of his new environment. Not that America does not afford material opportunities and even stimulus for the intellectual life, provided it is not

* Taken from "Marginal Notes on Civilization in the United States," *op. cit.*

merely retrospective or poetical; a man like William James, whose plough could cut into rough new ground, left an indelible furrow; but he had a doctor's healthy attitude towards human ills, his Pragmatism was a sort of diagnosis of America, and even he would have found it uphill work to cultivate beauty of form, to maintain ultimate insights, or to live in familiar friendship with the Greeks and the Indians. I managed it after a fashion myself, because I was conscious of being a foreigner with my essential breathing tubes to other regions; nor did I really belong to the irritable genus; I had perhaps more natural stamina, less fineness, more unconcern, and the spirit of mockery, in the last resort, to protect me.

ࢼ Letters*

To Van Wyck Brooks

Rome, May 22, 1927

Dear Mr. Brooks

. . . Why do the American poets and other geniuses die young or peter out, unless they go and hibernate in Europe? What you say about Bournet (whom again I haven't read) and in your last chapter suggests to me that it all comes of *applied culture*. Instead of being interested in what they are and what they do and see, they are interested in what they think they would like to be and see and do: it is a misguided ambition, and moreover, if realized, fatal, because it wears out all their energies in trying to bear fruits which are not of their species. A certain degree of sympathy and assimilation with ultra-modern ways in Europe or even Asia may be possible, because young America is simply modernism undiluted: but what Lewis Mumford calls "the pillage of the past" (of which he thinks I am guilty too) is worse than useless. I therefore think that art, etc. has a better soil in the ferocious 100% America than in the Intelligentsia of New York. It is veneer, rouge, aestheticism, art museums, new theatres, etc. that make America impotent. The good things are football, kindness, and jazz bands.

Yours sincerely,

* From *The Letters of George Santayana*.
† Randolph Bourne.

To William Lyon Phelps

Hotel Bristol, Rome
March 16, 1936

Dear Billy

. . . An important element in the tragedy of Oliver (not in his personality, for he was no poet) is drawn from the fate of a whole string of Harvard poets in the 1880's and 1890's—Sanborn, Philip Savage, Hugh McCulloch, Trumbull Stickney, and Cabot Lodge: also Moody, although he lived a little longer and made some impression, I believe, as a playwright. Now all those friends of mine, Stickney especially, of whom I was very fond, were visibly killed by the lack of air to breathe. People individually were kind and appreciative to them, as they were to me; but the system was deadly, and they hadn't any alternative tradition (as I had) to fall back upon: and of course, as I believe I said of Oliver in my letter, they hadn't the strength of a great intellectual hero who can stand alone.

I have been trying to think whether I have ever known any "good" people such as are not to be found in my novel. You will say "There's me and Anabel: why didn't you put *us* into your book, to brighten it up a little?" Ah, you are not novelesque enough: and I can't remember anybody so terribly good in Dickens except the Cheerybell Brothers, and really, if I had put anyone like that in they would have said I was "vicious", as they say I am in depicting Mrs. Alden. But Irma was what I think good: she wasn't sillier than we all are, except that we keep our silliness quiet. And Oliver was very good: I don't think you like *good* people really, only *sweet* people—like Anabel and you!

To William Lyon Phelps

Hotel Bristol, Rome
February 16, 1936

Dear Billy

. . . You say I don't love life and that faith is necessary. Very true: I don't love life unconditionally; but I enjoy the "mere living" (as Browning has it) when I am in good health, which is most of the time: and I enjoy the episodes, unless I am rudely prevented from doing so. If you have my *Dialogues in Limbo*,

and will look at pp. 156-161, you will find Socrates and me defining the matter exactly. It was Oliver, not I, who didn't love life,
because he hadn't the animal Epicurean faculty of enjoying it in
its arbitrariness and transiency. He was a spiritual man, incapaci-
tated to be anything else, like Christ, who couldn't be a soldier
or athlete or lover of women or father of a family (or, even,
though I don't say so in the book, a good believing Christian).
Now that is a tragic vocation, like the vocation of the poet; it demands sacrifice and devotion to a divine allegiance: but poor
Oliver, ready for every sacrifice, had nothing to pin his allegiance
to. He was what the rich young man in the Gospel would have
been if he had been ready to sell his goods and give to the poor,
but then had found no cross to take up and no Jesus to follow.
Faith, as you say, is needed; but faith is an assurance inwardly
prompted, springing from the irrepressible impulse to do, to
fight, to triumph. Here is where the third sloppy wash in the
family tea-pot is insufficient. And without robustness an imposed
intellectual faith wouldn't do: it would only make a conventional
person. You say you can't understand how I seem to hold my
own in the world without faith, and almost without the world. It
is quite simple. I have the Epicurean contentment, which was not
far removed from asceticism; and besides I have a spiritual allegiance of my own that hardly requires faith, that is, only a humourous animal faith in nature and history, and no religious faith:
and this common sense world suffices for *intellectual satisfaction*, partly in observing and understanding it, partly in dismiss-
ing it as, from the point of view of spirit, a transitory and local
accident. Oliver hadn't this intellectual satisfaction, and he hadn't
that Epicurean contentment. Hence the vacancy he faced when
he had "overcome the world". Basta. Thank you a thousand
times for your friendship.

To Mrs. George Sturgis

Hotel Bristol, Rome.
Feb. 5. 1936

Dear Rosamond

   . . . The negation in Oliver was double: he not only was austere to the natural man, but he was austere to all the conven-

tions: to his mother, the Harvard philosophers, and even the Vicar's religion. And the dynamite was actually applied to him by Jim and Mario, and he failed to become human. Why was that? Just because he was tied up? But he wasn't tied up, intellectually: he was absolutely without deliberate prejudices. The real reason—and I am afraid I have failed to make this plain in the novel—was that he was a mystic, touched with a divine consecration, and *couldn't* give way to the world, the flesh, or the devil. He ought to have been a saint. But here comes the deepest tragedy in his lot: that he lived in a spiritual vacuum. American breeding can be perfect in form, but it is woefully thin in substance; so that if a man is born a poet or a mystic in America he simply starves, because what social life offers and presses upon him is offensive to him, and there is nothing else. He evaporates, he peters out.—That is my intention, or rather preception, in Oliver. The trouble wasn't that he wouldn't be commonplace: there are plenty of people to be commonplace: the trouble was that *he couldn't be exceptional, and yet be positive.* There was no tradition worthy of him for him to join on to.